C0-AMY-888

Divorce

THE MAN'S COMPLETE GUIDE TO WINNING

Lauren O. Vail

SOVEREIGN BOOKS
New York

Published by Sovereign Books
A Simon & Schuster Division of
Gulf & Western Corporation
Simon & Schuster Building
1230 Avenue of the Americas
New York, New York 10020
Designed by Irving Perkins
Manufactured in the United States of America
10 9 8 7 6 5 4 3 2 1

LIBRARY OF CONGRESS CATALOGING IN PUBLICATION DATA

Vail, Lauren O
Divorce.
Bibliography: p.
Includes index.
1. Divorce—United States. 2. Divorce suits—United States. I. Title.
KF535.V33 346'.73'0166 78-10355
ISBN 0-671-18382-6

Contents

Preface vii

1. *Introduction and First Preparations* 1
2. *Preliminary Dos and Don'ts* 8
3. *What to Expect from the Legal System* 16
4. *The Law of Divorce* 33
5. *How to Get Your Divorce—Grounds and Proofs* 70
6. *Custody* 90
7. *Find a Good Lawyer* 123
8. *Support, Property, and Custody Agreements* 136
9. *Trial Preparation—Evidence* 170
10. *Trial Preparation—Assembling the Case* 203
11. *Psychological Preparation* 213
12. *Beyond Divorce* 228

APPENDICES

A. *How to Do Your Own Legal Research* 234
B. *Helpful Readings* 246
C. *Men's Rights Organizations* 252
D. *Glossary* 258

Chapter Notes 267

Index 273

Preface

THIS BOOK is distinctly pro men in its viewpoint. It is not, however, against women. If the book is against anything, it is against the legal system of domestic relations law that prevails in the United States. Under this law both men and women are treated in an adverse and discriminatory manner.

This book represents one approach toward alleviation of the difficulties that men encounter when faced with problems of divorce or custody. The approach is simple. It requires, first, that the man involved in divorce proceedings learn what he can and cannot do legally. Second, it requires he do everything possible to further his cause. There is usually a lot that can be done, often because lawyers fail to do their job. However, the single greatest reason that men fail to do what they should is their ignorance of the law. This book is designed to reduce that ignorance.

The psychology of the American male is his second greatest point of vulnerability. His psychology frequently prevents him from doing what he could to protect himself. We hope, at least, to expose the nature of this problem to the reader so that he will be able to marshal his forces more effectively.

That the legal system regarding divorce and custody needs sweeping and serious reform cannot be denied. Preaching reform is not the purpose of this book, but the topic is seductive and we have admitted some discussion of it here and there.

The author of this book is a male who was aided in his research and experience by a female and another male. All have gone through divorce. All are reasonably educated. All have participated in the research necessary for the compilation of this book. None of the authors is a lawyer.

We anticipate that some readers may wish to ask us for information regarding their own situations. Regrettably, to answer such questions would be to engage in the unauthorized practice of law, an illegal activity. This fact represents just one example of the means by which the legal system denies the American people—male and female alike—needed information.

1

Introduction and First Preparations

DIVORCE, ALIMONY, and custody today affect many lives. There are about 455 divorces for every 1,000 new marriages, and the divorce rate continues its upward trend. You, as an American male—if you are married, if you have children, and especially if you are not wealthy—can be badly damaged if your marriage breaks up.

The truth is that the American male fares badly before the divorce courts. If a divorce is possible, likely, or in process, it therefore becomes important to advance your knowledge quickly in order to avoid the many problems and pitfalls that may lie ahead.

The American male divorcing today stands to lose far more than the wife he no longer loves. He may lose most or all of his assets, much of his income, and, most important, the children he loves so dearly.

Such was not always the case. In earlier times, the legal rights of men were extraordinary. Men virtually owned their wives, their children, and all assets. By the middle of the last century, this situation had changed, both in America and in England, which is where America obtained the legal foundation of the "common law." In America today, from the sense of legal theory, men and women are treated equally by the courts. In actuality, the law doesn't work that way.

To illustrate the way the law works, the disadvantages the American male can suffer under the law, and the dangerous risks he incurs because he does not understand the law, we present the case of a couple we will call Sue and Larry Smith.[1]

By the time the Smiths sought a divorce, Sue had a documented history of heavy drug use, alcoholism, and suicidal attempts. She frequently brought up the topic of divorce but Larry was loath to consider it. She had neglected their two young children, frequently leaving them in the hands of babysitters although she did not work. In an alcoholic stupor she served them still frozen food and unmixed instant potatoes for dinner. Marriage and other counseling had not helped. Finally, even Larry realized that the marriage was over.

At this point, Larry had good grounds for divorce and a good case for custody of the children and for keeping the house. But he lost it all. How? (1) Through politeness, he allowed Sue to file for the divorce and to obtain a "mental cruelty" divorce against him. While this is a frequently applied "uncontested" approach to divorce, Larry did not understand the strategic losses he would face when he attempted to ask for custody of his children. (2) Through ignorance of the law, he drove Sue to the airport with the children to see her safely off to stay with her parents during the pendency of litigation. Little did he suspect that the court would declare this to be "a verbal agreement between them that the wife should have custody of the children."

In comparing the way Larry handled the children with the way Sue handled them, Larry was obviously the better custodian. Despite this, Larry lost his children. He never understood the propensity of judges to award children to their mothers, regardless of the mother's qualifications. He never understood the risks and difficulties of fighting a custody battle across the boundaries of two different legal jurisdictions. He never realized that in each of his actions he was responding to the legal system instead of taking an *initiative* with which Sue would have to contend. Only at the end did he understand his losses, which included 48 percent of his before-taxes gross income, his children, $25,000 in legal fees, and his home, which had to be sold to satisfy his legal and related expenses.

Larry's is an extreme case. It contained excellent potential for success, nonetheless he lost. If properly developed, Larry's case should have resulted in his keeping the children and the house. He should have been divorced from his drunken wife. He should have not been required to pay any form of support. He should have experienced legal fees in the neighborhood of $8,000, not $25,000, despite the fact that he had to fight the case over two jurisdictions. As it is, not only did Larry lose, but the children, now ages two and four, face a future of being raised by the wrong parent. They are already showing signs of psychological and developmental damage.

Larry lost for three underlying reasons. First, he did not understand the law well enough to fully exercise his legal rights. Second, he was inactive, reacting passively to new situations and failing to take initiatives of his own. Third, he was male, subject to the way the courts deal with males and to his own good-guy male psychology, which led him to avoid pressing what advantages he had.

It is to these three problem areas that this book is addressed: ignorance of the law as it is applied, ill-considered actions as well as failure to act, and the disabling psychology of the American male. The intricacies of these problems are discussed in later chapters.

Fortunately, not every American male experiences a divorce (only about half of them do). And, most divorces, according to statistics, are settled amicably, with few if any of the difficulties that Larry experienced. According to one source, 85 percent of all divorces are uncontested. We are circumspect about this figure, since there is a lack of systematic method for gathering such data. We are doubly circumspect because the contest in practically all "contested" divorces does not occur in the courtroom. The actual contest occurs between the time the case is filed and the time it is brought to court. Despite such concerns, it is likely that more than 50 percent of all divorces are processed easily, smoothly, amicably, and inexpensively.

Our own research indicates that most men who have experienced extraordinary legal struggles did not suspect, at the outset, that theirs was going to be anything but a common, ordinary, simple, inexpensive divorce. If you have the slightest reason to believe that a legal contest is in the making, the following sections will be of importance to you.

Assess Your Position

Undertake an accurate assessment of your particular problems, and do so immediately. Be as objective as you possibly can. Drive all emotionalism from your brain, and think. Portions of the assessment must be accomplished in privacy. In such circumstances, have a pencil and paper to take notes on issues that come to mind. Assess the seriousness of your marital problem and the extent to which your particular situation has progressed. In making these assessments, dismiss all preconceptions, avoid all assumptions, and inspect all things anew.

Seriousness of the Marital Problem

Whether a divorce is likely and, if likely, whether it will be contested, depends on the seriousness of the marital problem. The following questions will help you judge how seriously your marriage is threatened.

Do you and your wife argue frequently? Do you argue violently? Has your sex life with your wife broken down? Has the word "divorce" been used seriously in your discussions? Has either of you seen a lawyer regarding divorce? Are you living separately? If so, was it you who moved out? Does she have the children? Do the two of you have difficulty in settling (agreeing upon) the division of property, assets, and income? Do you and your wife disagree on custody? Has a separation agreement been drafted? Have you signed it? Has divorce been filed?

If you have answered "Yes" to most of the above questions, there is a good probability that you will become involved in a divorce action. Next, assess the likelihood of serious contest. Such contests are characterized by numerous hearings before the court, frequent drafting and redrafting of various agreements, arguments between husband and wife regarding disposition of assets, income, debts, and children, heavy involvement of lawyers, and a pervasive acrimonious atmosphere. The contest almost always hinges upon one or both of two factors—money and children. If you and your wife are diametrically opposed on major financial issues (disposition of assets and incomes), and if both of you are unyielding in your positions, the stage is being set for a contest. If children are at issue, if you intend to have custody and if your wife wants them as well, a contest is certainly in the making.

The deeper you have gone into the proceedings of divorce, the greater the chance that you have already made errors that may need rectification to restore the strength of your original position.

How Far Progressed Is Your Case?

We can identify ten stages of progression into the divorce process. Many cases will not involve some of these stages, and some cases will encounter a particular stage in a different order than that presented below. The financial and emotional damage incurred at any particular stage can vary dramatically from one case to another.

STAGE 1: AMICABLE MARRIED SINGLES. Husband and wife live together but have developed separate activities not involving each other. Home is a place where meals are taken and where people sleep. Husband and wife may each feel lonely. Emotional interdependence between them is low.

STAGE 2: OPEN CONFLICT IN MARRIAGE. Characterized by frequent quarrels and abuses of one or both spouses by the other. Frequent negative thoughts about the spouse, perhaps coupled with intentional hostile and aggressive behaviors toward the spouse, ranging from nagging to violence. Sex life within the marriage is poor or dead.

STAGE 3: HOME AVOIDANCE. Husband finds excuses for not going home, perhaps by working long hours, volunteering for lengthy business trips, or spending time in bars after work. He may also fill evenings and weekends with outside activities in order to avoid having to be home. Similarly, wife may deliberately involve herself with activities outside the home whenever husband is around in order to avoid him. Love life may be dead within the marriage.

STAGE 4: INFIDELITY. One (or both) turns to others for emotional support and sex.

STAGE 5: TALK OF DIVORCE. One (or both) begins to recognize the marriage is on the rocks, constraining, inhibiting, failing to provide emotional support; may also think of doing better with a new partner. The topic of divorce has been brought up in discussions or arguments.

STAGE 6: INVOLVEMENT OF LAWYERS. One (or both) has seen a lawyer regarding divorce. A divorce may have been filed.

STAGE 7: PROPOSED SEPARATION AGREEMENT. An attempt has been made to settle issues of who gets what. Perhaps approached through discussions, perhaps through preliminary drafts of agreements.

STAGE 8: COMPLETED SEPARATION AGREEMENT. A formal separation agreement has been developed and signed by both husband and wife, acting on advice of their lawyers. The agreement settles such matters as alimony, child support, distribution of assets, custody, visitation rights.

STAGE 9: INTERIM HEARINGS. Special hearings have been held to provide for temporary alimony, child support, custody, or related matters until the court can hear the entire case at the divorce trial.

STAGE 10: TRIAL. Date has been set for trial, trial may be in the near future, perhaps within a month.

During the first three stages, husband and wife are still living together, but there are signs of weakness within the marriage. These stages represent early warning signs which, if detected by the husband, enable him to begin the careful development of his side of a divorce case.

Stage 4 is a clear indication that the marriage is in serious trouble. Unless something unusual occurs, a divorce will ensue. If the husband has been sleeping around, or if he finds his wife has been doing so, the necessity for preparing for a divorce is obvious. Stage 5 presents the important step of *recognition* that the marriage is in trouble. Recognition may not have been present in earlier stages. When either husband or wife recognizes that a divorce is needed, a divorce action is a near certainty.

Stage 6 represents the first involvement of the legal system. By Stage 7, a divorce will have been filed. Unless husband and wife reconcile their differences, there will be a divorce. The husband and wife will now experience increasing inability to reconcile either their marital differences or their differences regarding alimony, child support, custody, etc. At this point, the husband will discover that he is fighting not merely his wife, but her lawyer and an adverse legal system as well. If the husband has not earlier begun the preparation of his side of the divorce, his response must now be immediate and thorough. If the case is headed for contest, the unresponsive husband is, at this point, on the defensive.

If Stage 8 occurs soon after filing for divorce, and if things are amicable between husband and wife, the probability of a contested divorce is markedly reduced, other things being equal. Alternatively, if there are difficulties in obtaining a complete and satisfactory separation agreement, and if Stage 9 is reached, the chances of a full-blown contest are markedly increased. If the husband has not earlier involved himself in his case there is little chance that he will be able to overcome his inferior position. With extraordinary effort, he may be able to prevent inordinate losses.

By Stage 10 there is little opportunity for a husband who has not actively been developing his case; there simply is not enough time for him to do all that needs to be done. Alternatively, if the husband has been active, at least since Stage 6, he will find himself furiously active during Stage 10, and may effectively control the outcome of the trial. If the divorce has been processed without contest up to this point, the trial is almost certain to be a simple, brief, formal hearing without contest; it is possible that the husband's efforts to protect his position will have been a waste of time and energy.

It is important for the husband to understand that the outcome of the trial will depend strongly on the way in which he lives his life, and upon the degree to which he involved himself, throughout Stages 1 through 6, in actions to protect his future legal position. There is usually no way to predict whether the divorce will become contested, but if it does, the outcome will depend upon the way the husband acted during early stages. If the husband recognizes his marriage is moving from Stage 1 to some later stage, he should act to strengthen his position against all eventualities.

2

Preliminary Dos and Don'ts

For those entering or already involved in a divorce action it is important to get on top of things at the outset—to be in control of the situation rather than to be controlled by it. This is true regardless of the difficulty or ease of the contemplated divorce.

The suggestions which follow are intended to provide guidelines for action and behavior. Which of the "do's and don'ts" are applicable will depend on the particular case. If one is assured of a simple, uncontested divorce, a cursory reading may provide assurance that all is well. Alternatively, if the divorce is complicated or showing signs of contest, the following suggestions may be helpful indeed.

Sensitization to Activities

The first rule of survival is *renew your sensitivity to what is going on around you.* The routine of day-to-day living, the separated activities of husband and wife, and the growing indifference of each spouse to the other in a declining marriage cause one's perceptions to become dulled. Step back from the scene and view it anew. All things must be mentally questioned and nothing accepted on assumption or faith. It must not be assumed that people lie, nor that they tell the truth.

The purpose of the investigation is to determine whether there are, or have been, activities that are harmful to the husband's welfare or to the welfare of the children. If this is the case, the search continues with the additional purpose of documenting those activities.

Generally, harmful activities are not carried on openly. The offending partner engages in duplicity, offering innocent explanations for unacceptable behaviors. A wife will be alert to suspicions in others and will take additional measures to conceal what she is doing if she thinks she is being found out. Thus, while making this inquiry, it is important that all should seem normal.

Your search will necessarily involve invasions of your partner's privacy and a degree of covert activity on your own part. Presumably, you will not take up this course of action without good reason. In seeking the truth, you will focus on the inexplicable, the anomalous, the odd, the unusual, the illogical. Such indicators are more numerous than you might expect.

- Telephone or other conversations that suddenly stop or shift topic when one enters a room may be significant.
- Incoming mail can be checked for sender's return address as well as for postmarked date and city of origin.
- Letters that seem to disappear from the stack of incoming mail may be significant.
- Sudden reappearance of old boyfriends may be significant.
- Time needed for expressed activities may be compared with time actually expended.
- Any radical change in behavior may be significant. Examples include the initiation of lengthy vacations away from the home, the introduction of evenings out with friends, the rapid acquisition of a new and attractive wardrobe, the wife's freshened interest in her appearance before she leaves the house, a change in expense patterns, etc.
- Telephone bills may display telephone numbers called by the wife during the husband's absence.
- The wife's address/telephone number book may contain significant information, especially if she tends to carry it with her.
- Credit card receipts may show places visited and purchases made. Missing receipts may be suggestive.
- Increasing payments in cash rather than by check may reflect a reluctance to document expenses.

- The pattern of payments to babysitters may suggest a corresponding pattern of wife's absences from the home.
- Discarded letters, receipts, etc., can be recovered when emptying trash. Letters torn to bits may be significant.
- Little things may be significant—a matchbook cover from a strange place, smeared lipstick when the wife returns home, a cigarette butt of an unusual brand, a strange hair on clothing.
- Cancelled checks written by the wife indicate expenditures and may be checked; comparison of payee on the check with that indicated in the check stub or register may indicate anomalies.
- Automobile odometer mileage can be monitored. Check for unexplained mileage.

Hiding places for concealed items generally are places where the husband is not expected to go—the wife's jewelry box, lingerie drawer, sewing basket, laundry room. They may also include domains of the husband (for example, letters concealed beneath his winter clothing during the summertime). Papers may be taped on the backs or bottoms of drawers. Items may be left in the luggage or clothing that a wife took with her on a trip.

If written or printed evidences are found, the next step is to make photocopies of these items. Anything that can't be copied should be recorded in a notebook. If you are careful, you can carry out this search and documentation in such a way that nothing appears to have been touched. Nothing should be done in the presence of children, nor should children be questioned regarding the mother's activities; it is quite likely that they would relate such questioning to her.

Controlling Information

The second rule of survival is *control the flow of all information regarding your activities.* A wife may be very interested in monitoring her husband's activities, and she may be actively engaged in doing so. If the husband's behavior is not exemplary, the discovery and documentation of his activities can be damaging to his case. Suggestions include the following:

- Keep all sensitive materials out of the home and out of the office—they can be too easily discovered in such places.
- Do not allow sensitive mail to be sent to home or office. Use a post office box for the purpose.
- Do not allow sensitive telephone calls to be made to you at your home or office. Even if not directly overheard, the line may be tapped.
- Keep sensitive materials out of your pockets where they might be found while you sleep.
- Avoid activities which, if discovered and documented, could strengthen your wife's divorce case against you.
- Allow no one to have sensitive information except those people who must necessarily be informed.
- Consider "sensitive" anything remotely connected with the divorce (and that includes this book).

Protection of Assets and Income

The third rule of survival is *protect assets and income.* If a divorce becomes contested, the husband's assets and income may be severely threatened by the expense of contesting the divorce and by the award of property, assets, and income to the wife. Some suggestions for protecting your financial position are as follows:

- Don't move out of the house unless ordered by the court; let your wife move out instead. Keep the children with you if you think you will later want custody of them.
- Decrease your level of earnings. If you work more than one job, quit all but one which makes the most money. Stop working overtime.
- If your wife works, see that her earnings are combined in the family pool and expended on the family; discourage the use of her income solely according to her own wishes.
- Foster your wife's employment potential, through the provision of training, if necessary.
- Encourage your wife to increase the hours she works, to seek better-paying jobs, to become motivated toward making more money.
- If purchasing assets or property, purchase them in your name

alone or in her name alone to avoid disputes over jointly held assets.

- Winnow down the contents of savings accounts and checking accounts to prevent your wife from seizing the contents.
- Open a checking account in your name alone.
- Act to close all charge accounts. If your wife refuses to yield credit cards in your name or in both names, "lose" your wallet and notify the creditors of the loss. Have new cards sent to you at your post office box.
- Deposit pay in checking accounts after the day the bank reports the account balance, in order to keep the reported balance as low as possible.
- Set aside as much cash for your own use as possible. Don't keep the cash in a bank where records will be made of it.
- Gradually allow your personal and business-related expenses to rise by such things as improving your wardrobe, parking in a more expensive parking lot, eating lunch in restaurants, buying more or better tools or equipment or publications.
- Gradually acquire control and possession of all records of finances and of as many financial activities as possible.

The basic principles underlying the above suggestions are: (1) to get and hold physical possession of assets; (2) to increase your wife's income or income potential in relation to your own; (3) to reduce your wife's capability to act to your disadvantage; and (4) to reduce your wife's control of incomes and expenses.

Guidance of Affairs

The fourth rule of survival is *take vigorous guidance of your own affairs.* Reduce your dependence upon others for advice and decision-making. In particular, employ a healthy skepticism toward information provided by your wife or her lawyer. Throughout the divorce process, the power of the husband to say no to offerings, instructions, and commands of the other side is fairly strong. You should avoid all agreements, verbal or written, until you are sure of the long- and short-range implications, and until you are satisfied that a more favorable agreement cannot be obtained. Check problems out with a lawyer (not your wife's) before entering into an agreement or following advice or instructions from the other side. In one case, a husband and his mistress took his small son and moved into another state away from his wife. The wife contacted a lawyer who, in turn, contacted the mistress, threatening to file kidnapping charges against her unless the child was immediately returned. The terrified couple returned the child to the mother without first consulting a lawyer of their own. In their ignorance, they did not realize that the wife's lawyer was merely bluffing. It would have been impossible for the lawyer to bring any kind of charges against them.

Guidance of one's affairs implies some knowledge of the laws pertaining to divorce and custody. If pressed for a decision, before the implications are clear, you can respond by saying "I'll consider it," or "No." This book and the recommended readings[1] are appropriate guides for improving your knowledge.

Active guidance implies careful selection of a lawyer. (We provide a chapter on the topic.) It also implies keeping decision-making power rather than delegating it to the lawyer. The proper role of the lawyer is that of an advisor and technician in legal procedure. The proper role of the client is to make the decisions that affect his own life.

Active guidance also implies physical activity—doing those things that should be done. If the situation seems to require it, the husband should be willing to write letters, read books, make telephone calls, visit people, conduct investigations, or to do whatever else may be warranted, and he should undertake these activities with a vigorous, positive attitude. Things can happen quickly in a divorce. Allowing a backlog to build up may cost the husband any initiative he may have, and may seriously interfere with the proper development of his case.

Personal Conduct

The fifth rule of survival is *be a gentleman*. Maintain a good working relationship with your wife, at least as good as conditions permit, throughout the divorce process. To fail to do so is to invite contest.

Effort is required to retain such a relationship because the adversary system of divorce tends to force contests into being. The emotional trauma of divorce is serious, no matter what the cause of the breakup. Tempers flare easily, mistrust develops quickly, and dirty tricks are tempting. A husband should be understanding of his wife's emotional condition, and should not harass her. Even if the wife is an alcoholic or a drug addict, and if these are grounds for divorce, the husband should refrain from aggravating the situation unnecessarily. He should be kind, gentle, and absolutely nice. He should avoid arguments and use discussion instead. If for no other reason, the husband must show civility in order to calm his wife's temper and reduce her will to fight.

Being a gentleman does not mean bowing and scraping; neither does it mean taking verbal or physical abuse. The husband always has the option of walking out on a fight. Being a gentleman implies retaining a sense of self-worth and pride. If the wife is forcing the husband to live with humiliation, embarrassment, or the threat of blackmail, the husband may appear to acquiesce to her demands while telling himself that he will win out in the end. He may quietly document her statements and her blackmail for later presentation at court. The courts take a dim view of blackmail, even where the husband deserves it. The husband's sense of self-worth is important. If he loses it, he will also lose much of his capability to fight.

Being a gentleman implies that the husband watches his language carefully. He never uses foul, abusive, or threatening language to his wife (especially where others may hear him), or to his wife's lawyer (under any circumstances). Threatening remarks can be construed as assault. While the husband is careful to express the nature and depth of his feelings to his own lawyer, he is careful to avoid doing so to the other side. A show of anger or frustration can lead the other side to believe that they are performing successfully. The husband understands that he can say "No" calmly and confidently, even while he is sick with fear.

Being a gentleman means that the husband's behavior is seen to be proper by outsiders. This reduces the chances that they may be witnesses against him. Proper behavior includes doing all those things that can be done to prevent a contested divorce (unless the husband wants the divorce to be contested). Being a gentleman most definitely does not mean rolling over and playing dead.

Never Underestimate the Power of a Woman

The sixth rule of survival is *do not underestimate the power of your wife*. Underestimating the skills, power, and capacity for action of the wife is a frequent and serious error. All too often, husbands in divorce see their wives as incompetent, while the truth is that they are smart, tough, and resilient. Even an incompetent wife, when represented by a competent lawyer, can be an incredibly tough opponent, totally committed to combat. More than one husband has been surprised in court when his wife pulled out a complete portfolio documenting his affairs with other women in the most minute and embarrassing detail, when he believed her to be in complete ignorance of his illicit activities.

On the other hand, the wife's capacity to play fair and to behave honorably should not be underestimated, either. We know of wives who have flatly denied their lawyers' suggestions to strip the husband of his assets, even in conditions where many would feel justified in doing so.

The husband should view his wife as a competent person having the capability for either good or evil. His own good conduct should encourage her to behave accordingly. Many divorces are amicable solutions to what has become a lonely and difficult situation. In such circumstances, the wife can be an active partner who materially aids the husband throughout the divorce process by speeding the development of necessary arrangements, and cooperatively pressing the case forward. This is a desirable arrangement and everything possible should be done to attain it.

3

What to Expect from the Legal System

In the framework of law, divorce and custody are matters of civil law, not criminal law. Court procedures, standards of proof, and facts considered important vary widely between the two kinds of law. In the eyes of the law, extreme mental cruelty might be an offense so serious that your wife can get a divorce on that basis, but it is not the kind of offense for which you can be tried, convicted, and sentenced to prison. This distinction is an important one to keep in mind. It is also important to keep in mind that the same act may sometimes have both civil and criminal implications. For example, in the state of New Jersey, the act of adultery is a civil matter, and if you are convicted of it your wife can obtain a divorce from you. In New Jersey, the act of adultery is also a criminal offense, and if you are charged and convicted of it you can be sentenced to a year in prison.

The distinctions between civil and criminal law are extensive. Interstate flight to avoid prosecution for murder, a criminal act, is a Federal crime and can involve the Federal Bureau of Investigation and various states in a cooperative action to bring the offender to justice. Interstate flight to avoid prosecution for extreme mental cruelty is not a crime, not a misdemeanor, and, in fact, the law has never heard of such a thing. The implications of the difference between civil and criminal law are important, but at this point we wish merely to state that divorce, or the "grounds" upon which divorces are granted, is not a matter of concern to the police, the FBI, the CIA, or society at large. It concerns, generally, only yourself, your wife, and the body of civil law.

Despite the "civil" nature of divorce actions, in most states they are imbued with a sense of wrongdoing, or "fault." In most states, in order for a divorce to be granted, either the husband or the wife must be shown to have committed a terrible wrong to the other party. In some states, there must be *only one* wrongdoer: one party must be the good guy and the other the bad guy. In such states, if both the husband and wife are wrongdoers the court will not grant a divorce. The "fault" nature of divorce in most states underlies the legal approach known as the "adversary system."

The adversary system works like this: either the husband or the wife sues the other party for divorce, claiming that the other party committed a "fault" of sufficient severity to warrant a divorce. The party making such a charge is called the *plaintiff* or the *claimant*. The other party, the supposed wrongdoer, has the legal right to defend against these serious charges and is therefore known as the *defendant*. The plaintiff-defendant arrangement pits the husband against the wife and the wife against the husband, each charging that the other has committed a wrong so great that the marriage should be ended by divorce. Husband and wife are therefore adversaries; hence, "adversary system." Notwithstanding that the divorce is usually based on the "fault" of either the husband or the wife (or both), that the trial has a plaintiff and a defendant, that the courtroom seems filled by lawyers and judges, and that the atmosphere is one of great wrongdoing on somebody's part—still, the issue of divorce is not a criminal matter.

Some states, including California and Colorado, have a different approach to divorce, which does not involve the adversary system. The divorce process is referred to not as "divorce" but as "the dissolution of marriage." And while most states refer to divorce cases in an adversarial way ("the case of *Jones versus Jones*"), the California system refers to the case as "in relation to the marriage of Jones and Jones." Such nonadversarial states are in the distinct minority, however, and in property settlements, alimony concerns, and custody matters, adversarial practices creep into the nonadversarial systems. Even "no-fault" divorce states, while assuring a divorce, still rely on the adversarial system.

The machinery of the legal system begins to turn when either you or your wife goes to a lawyer and says, "I want a divorce."

What the system does from that point on depends in part on the nature of the problem you have brought to the system, and in part on the nature of the system itself. Generally, the more you ask the system to do for you the more it will do, the longer it will take, and the higher the price you will pay for its "services."

In all states, the legal system believes it has a say in whether you can have a divorce or whether you must stay married. It believes it has the right to say yes or no. In fact, *the state has the legal view that it is the third party to your marriage!* Believe it or not, when you and your wife said "I do," you picked up a silent partner without knowing it. Now, if you want a divorce, you can't tear up the contract without the consent of your silent partner.

As we have already indicated, generally the state will allow the marriage to be broken only when there are "grounds" for the divorce, that is, when a serious fault has been committed. More realistically, however, nearly anyone can get a divorce. In fact, there are only five complications that can interfere with getting a divorce if you want one. Not to be taken lightly, any of these complications can be severe enough to prevent a divorce. The complications are: (1) unfavorable law in your state or unfavorable court practice in your region; (2) inability of husband and wife to agree that a divorce is needed; (3) inability to agree on matters of custody; (4) inability to agree on matters of support or distribution of property; and (5) an insistence by either husband or wife that he or she has a right to a day in court. It is noteworthy that four of the five complications have to do with the husband and wife. Only the first is associated with the legal system *per se*. In any particular divorce, any or all of these complications may be present and in varying degree. Nonetheless, these are the *only* stumbling blocks to getting a divorce.

Most divorces are "uncontested."[1] An uncontested divorce is one in which none of the five complications is present in any significant degree. In most states, the law either permits uncontested divorces or else the law looks the other way. Uncontested divorces tend to go through, provided, of course, that the husband and wife have done their share of accommodation. When he and she have agreed that a divorce is the needed solution to the marital problems; when they have agreed upon a "settlement"—who gets the china, the house, the cars, the cats, the rugs, and Aunt Emma's old brass statue of Chloe; when they have agreed upon how much, if anything, he will pay her for alimony, and for how long, and what will be paid if he gets sick or dies; when they have agreed upon whether she or he gets the kids, or whether he takes the boys and she takes the girls; when neither of them feels sufficiently "wronged" by the other to demand that a court hearing be held so that the other party can be declared a "bad guy" —then they are all set for a neat "uncontested" divorce.

Under such conditions the system generally will be nice to them. After all, they will pay the system handsomely for very little work. They will meet all the necessary conditions, they will pay their money, and they will get their divorce.

Such divorces often "go by default," that is, they are granted by the judge as a result of a "default judgment." What actually happens is that one party (usually the wife in collaboration with the husband) trumps up charges against the other. The aggrieved party (wife) files for divorce, claiming that the other party (husband) has committed a marital fault (frequently "mental cruelty"). All the necessary agreements are formalized, and eventually the case comes to trial. During the trial the plaintiff (wife) is asked questions by her lawyer, and her answers (which she has memorized) will tend to prove that the other party is at fault. The husband (defendant) doesn't even go to the trial. Since the defendant is not personally present, he cannot defend himself against the charges brought by his wife. In consequence, *everything she says is considered to be absolutely true and she wins her divorce.*

There are dangers for the defendant in a default suit. For example, men who have let the divorce go by default sometimes have been surprised when that agreed-upon divorce was later used to prevent them from seeing their children.

Uncontested divorces require minimal legal talent. If you are headed for an uncontested divorce nearly any lawyer will do. Shop for a good price, $300 or less. In some states the going minimum (originally set by the State Bar Association) will be higher; in others, lower.[2]

"Contested divorces" refer to the dramatic courtroom battles you have read about or seen in the movies or on television. The courtroom, however, is seldom where the real contest takes place. This occurs between the time the divorce is initiated and the beginning of the trial. How serious the contest is depends on how many of the five complicating factors are present and how intense each complication is.

When the only complication is an unfavorable jurisdiction (that is, when the state or the local courts don't like to grant divorces), there seem to be only three options: first, to gather so much evidence of serious fault that the court will have no option but to grant the divorce; second, to dummy up such evidence; or third, to move into a jurisdiction that is more amenable to divorce. The third option has given rise to "migratory" divorce, in which one or both parties migrate into a favorable jurisdiction (Reno, Nevada, is popular), stay there long enough to establish residence, and then get the divorce.

If the local jurisdiction is not favorably disposed toward divorce, the basic problem will be to get the case to court with sufficient evidence of the proper type to allow the divorce to be granted. Historically, New York and New Jersey have been difficult jurisdictions for divorce. Until recently New York allowed only adultery as a fault of sufficient severity to warrant divorce. As a result, lawyers had connections with organizations that would furnish a girl, a hotel room, and a photographer. The husband, the girl, and the bed would get together, a picture would be taken, and grounds for divorce were established, with photographic evidence of the husband's "adultery."

If either the husband or wife insists on a trial to prove his or her blamelessness, or if the two cannot come to the necessary agreements, then they are moving into the realm of contested divorce. The inability to overcome these human difficulties will delay the divorce process and run costs into the thousands of dollars.

Frequently lawyers will apply pressure to bring about the necessary agreements and will discourage the "day in court." If they succeed, the case will probably be "settled" before it can go to trial. Court battles don't usually occur unless the lawyers feel that agreement can be reached no other way. At that point the case will go to court and the judge will decide the issues by mandating the necessary agreements.[3] Most contested cases are settled before trial, sometimes at the last minute. It is not unusual that, on the scheduled trial day, the lawyers, the parties, and the judge are all present, arguing in chambers, forcing an out-of-court agreement. This may take the entire day; then, nearly at closing time, the court opens for the first time and the trial is held, taking all of ten minutes to effect the divorce.

Notice that the nature of the contest is the removal of complications. When the complications have been cleared away, the divorce is no longer contested and the rest of the process goes smoothly. If the complications cannot be removed before the trial, then the case is contested in court, generally taking a day or two to be completed.

It should be pointed out that some lawyers do not always do their jobs, and that the adversary system is not conducive to obtaining the necessary agreements. It is all too easy for lawyers to disrupt the fragile communications between husband and wife, sometimes deliberately, effectively preventing the divorce from being settled. This enhances the probability that the case will be litigated, that the lawyers will be more heavily involved in writing agreements, arbitrating issues,[4] and dealing with legal side issues, with the result that their fees will be commensurately higher.

The law in the courtroom is stacked against the male; consequently, his best advantage lies in attaining favorable agreements before the case is tried. If such agreements cannot be obtained, then he must weigh the probable outcome of trial against the best he can do by bargaining. In some cases, the wife's demands are so excessive, and the bargaining position of the husband so weak, that the male has nothing to lose by going to trial. When that happens, he *should* go to trial—armed to the teeth with the best evidence and the most sound legal arguments he can muster.

This book is oriented to the needs of the American male as regards complicated divorce. While we have made the effort to incorporate information necessary for uncontested divorces, the primary thrust of our effort is toward the contested situation, in which one or more of the five complications is present. We remarked earlier that the way in which the system deals with a divorce depends on the problem the parties bring to it. While the legal system is reasonably nice about uncontested divorces, the anti-male bias of the system becomes more apparent as the contested nature of the divorce becomes more pronounced. You will meet this bias repeatedly—in statute law and case law, in the views of lawyers and judges, and even in opinions of psychologists, psychiatrists, social workers, medical doctors, and other persons who may become involved in your case. How these biases are brought to bear against the American male will be documented in the course of this book. For now, content yourself with the knowledge that they really do exist.

The legal system is much larger than you may have supposed. It consists partly of the American people, whose beliefs, hangups, and desires shape that elusive concept called "public policy" through the exercise of the vote. The state legislatures also are part of the legal system. Legislatures are the places where the laws are written, generally in response to public or political pressure. The two remaining components of the legal system are the lawyers and the judges. As far as your particular divorce is concerned, only the last two—lawyers and judges—are of immediate significance.

It is important to note that the entire legal system is, indeed, a system. Modifications of any single group will bring about modifications in all the others; two or three groups can interact to strongly affect the remainder. For the American male involved in a contested divorce it would be highly desirable to bring about changes in the attitudes of the American people, and to produce fairer laws in our legislatures. Unfortunately, such changes tend to occur very slowly, over great periods of time; they are too little and they come too late. Accordingly, we will concentrate our attention on the remainder of the system—lawyers and judges. You will need an understanding of each of these two groups as well as an appreciation of how they interact within the system.

What Can You Expect from Lawyers?

You should not expect your lawyer to be particularly interested in you as an individual, nor should you expect him to be particularly concerned with your welfare. Just like you, your lawyer is concerned mostly with himself and the money he makes at work. His being a lawyer does not free him from the hangups of the male stereotype; he considers his breadwinning activities to be his primary responsibility, as do you. As a doctor develops a bedside manner, so also does the lawyer who wishes to make money and develop a clientele. When you first meet a lawyer on a professional matter, you can expect he will exude intelligence, shrewdness, and concern for you and your problem. He would be foolish to do otherwise. He sees you as a potential source of income and he expects to be very well paid for his services—fees typically run between $35 and $150 per hour. If you believe that he sees you as other than a source of income, you are setting yourself up for a very unpleasant surprise.

The lawyer's second responsibility is to get along with judges and other lawyers; these people are his professional peers and associates and it is simply good business to retain favorable relations with them. The national, state, and local bar associations consist of lawyers and they serve to maintain friendly relations within the fraternity. Being friendly means, among other things, that lawyers occasionally refer clients to each other. Being friendly with judges is another matter. Judges are *very powerful people.* Offending a judge could mean that the lawyer would never win another case under that judge. Being friendly with judges sometimes means that lawyers can get tips from judges on how they are going to rule on legal issues. Because judges are so powerful and can affect the lives of lawyers so seriously, lawyers accord judges profound deference and respect. If you think a typical lawyer will risk offending either a fellow lawyer or a judge in order to fight for your cause, you will be badly mistaken. No lawyer in his right mind intends to put himself out of business on a lousy $2,000 divorce.

The lawyer's third responsibility is to his clients. You must bear in mind, however, that you are not the lawyer's only client. At any one time he will be working on the problems of a number of clients, and many of these clients represent a lot more money than you do. Expect favored treatment to be given clients who represent greater income and less work for the money. Understand, too, that divorce and custody problems are considered to be one of the less desirable fields of law. Moreover, the money in divorce cases isn't as good as it is in other areas, and after you've gone through a hundred or so cases they tend to get pretty boring. Do not expect the typical lawyer to do a Perry Mason job on your case.

You can expect your lawyer to be bright. In terms of intelligence, lawyers rank toward the top of the list, together with accountants, psychiatrists, and embezzlers. Intelligence, under current definitions, is mostly a measure of verbal ability. There is no difficulty in crediting lawyers with verbal ability. They are, as a group, possibly the most articulate in America. They like words and they like the things they can do with them.

Such being the case, you can generally expect that your lawyer will be smarter than you are, and that he will have a strong capability of speaking persuasively. He can tell you that black is white in such a way that you will have difficulty doubting him. You may find yourself trying to explain to a friend what your lawyer said, only to end up lamely saying, "but it sounded right—when he said it."

You can expect both the court and the lawyers to try to shape your case into a mold, to make it fit a neatly packaged series of circumstances that will allow the decision to be rendered with a minimum of hassle. The tradition of the legal system, in fact, requires a lawyer to "guide" his client to accept a "proper" conclusion to his case. This is sheer manipulation of the client. To the extent such manipulation is successful, the client will yield his position, bit by bit, until he fits the mold and the case can be dispensed with. The easy disposition of cases is desirable because more cases can be tried in less time (hence everyone makes more money), and because neither the judges nor the lawyers have to work as hard in coming to the decision. It takes work to really put together a divorce case, but if the client can be forced to take the traditional "proper" view much less needs to be done.

It is especially dangerous for the American male to accept the "proper" conclusion, since what is considered proper is based on the anti-male legal view of propriety. On the other hand, the wife can readily accept the "proper" view since she generally benefits under existing law and procedure. Paradoxically, when a husband recognizes the trap of a "proper" recommendation and refuses to go along with it, he sometimes finds himself being considered unreasonable by all and sundry—the wife, the lawyers, and the judge.

You should not expect anything but routine treatment from the typical lawyer. In most divorce cases there is no legal research done whatsoever. The reason is simple. After trying a couple of hundred divorce cases, a lawyer gets a pretty good feel for what the laws are, and a grasp of the most important cases, those that have set the "ground rules" for how the laws will be interpreted and applied. Consequently, he feels he can handle your case without doing any research at all. This would be fine if the individual client had nothing unusual about his case, but our feeling is that most clients have a number of unusual facets to their cases and that these will never be dealt with under the blanket approach unless the clients are unusually insistent.

You should not expect any particular assistance or guidance in preparing your case for trial. Throughout the divorce process you can expect to be chronically worried about what is happening, about what you should be doing or not doing, about how the case is going to be put together, about when things should happen, about why the case isn't moving more quickly, about what your lawyer is really doing for you. You will probably find this book of far greater assistance than your lawyer in answering such questions.

Do not expect your lawyer to know the law exhaustively. Our experience is that the typical lawyer's knowledge of matrimonial law is relatively shallow. One possible reason for this is that law, unlike most professions, does not tend toward specialization. There are perhaps 150 or so different kinds of medical doctors, each practicing a specialty; in law, however, there is no certification for special practice.

While you may find a lawyer who mostly deals with problems of divorce, who may even belong to an association of matrimonial lawyers, these facts do not necessarily mean that he is good. To be sure, a lawyer who spends most of his time trying divorces is apt to be better than one who spends most of his time writing wills, but most lawyers work as generalists, not as specialists. As such, they keep themselves spread over the great body of law with little expertise in any particular area.

You can expect your lawyer to be cynical. Thomas L. Shaffer expressed this cynicism well in his first principle of the common law, "People are no damned good."[5] The work of lawyers brings them into contact with people at their worst, and frequently, lawyers find their own principles in conflict with what the profession says should be done. The ethics of the profession require the lawyer to represent his client's interests in law—and to represent *only* the interests of his client. Sometimes the lawyer may have good reason to believe that this is exactly the wrong thing to do.

Consider an example. A mother is involved in a custody fight. She currently has custody, the father has filed for a custody hearing. The state, let's suppose, is one that observes the tender-years doctrine, which advises keeping young children with the mother. All the children are preschoolers. The father works full time. The lawyer's job is to retain custody for the mother. Nothing would be simpler. She is set to receive every benefit the law will afford her. With even a modicum of defense, the lawyer will manage to win the mother's case.

But suppose her lawyer has access to private information by which he knows that the mother is a drug addict, that she brutalizes the children in ways that leave no marks, that she feeds her drug habit by prostitution, that she cares for the children poorly. Suppose the lawyer also knows that the father is a good father who would provide good care for the children. What must the lawyer do? Legal ethics require him to protect the interests of his client—the mother. He may not consider the welfare or interests of the children—they are not his clients, and the mother is.

Suppose he does as the ethics of the profession require and wins custody for the mother. Will the lawyer have done right? Or will he have done wrong? Or will he "unintentionally" let slip some remark to the father's attorney that will open the door to discovery of the mother's faults? As a result, she could lose custody. Or will his defense of the mother be just a little bit weaker than it might have been if his heart had really been in the battle?

Such situations are daily fare for many lawyers. We feel that this chronic exposure of personal values, of the sense of right and wrong, to serious conflict must be very difficult to live with. The good lawyer must be perpetually on guard, lest his personal integrity be eroded by little sacrifices of honor; even the perpetual alertness must be wearing. The role of the good lawyer is, indeed, a difficult one.

We have seen a few lawyers who have constantly struggled to improve their honesty and forthrightness, who constantly have tested their motivation against sharp intellectual tests to assure themselves that their (sometimes risky) decisions were taken in the interests of their clients. We have been impressed by such men.

On the other hand, we have met lawyers who, one way or another, have failed to meet that terribly difficult standard. The most frequent area for criticism encountered by the authors has been the development of unauthorized "deals" between the wife's and the husband's lawyers. In one case, the husband's lawyer wanted a job in the wife's lawyer's law firm. An under-the-table deal was made whereby the husband paid the fees of the wife's lawyer and, in return, the husband's lawyer received a good recommendation to the law firm. The deal cost the husband more than a thousand dollars.

We caution you that *your own lawyer might not be totally honest.*[6] The lawyers' Code of Professional Responsibility is not so well written that it clearly indicates what is and what is not ethical behavior on the part of lawyers. There is plenty of latitude for bending the rules without getting caught.

By controlling "power of attorney" you have a strong means for keeping a lawyer honest. When you ask an attorney to handle your divorce, you confer upon him certain rights and privileges. In particular, unless you designate otherwise, he has the right to make agreements in your name, without your knowledge or prior consent, that are binding on you. However, you can limit your lawyer's power as you wish. We will provide suggestions later.

What Can You Expect from Judges?

Do not expect Solomon. Judges get to the bench in two ways: by being elected or by being appointed. When elected, it is usually by a public that knows too little to be able to vote intelligently. When appointed, the appointment frequently comes as a result of political favoritism. Orville H. Schell, past President of the Association of the Bar of the City of New York, indicated that in New York State, "our implacable enemy in the selection of good State judges is the politician."[7] Henry Foster, a scholar of matrimonial law, indicated that

> if courts are to do a better job in custody matters it is essential that such cases be referred to judges who have some knowledge of behavioral science and who are receptive to expert testimony and the recommendations of specialists.[8]

The training of a judge in the behavioral sciences (psychology, and sociology, for example) and in the other technical areas dealt with in the divorce court (accounting, medicine, and a dozen other fields) generally amounts to precisely nothing. Judges generally are trained only by becoming lawyers—spending three years in law school; in some states it is not even necessary to be a lawyer to sit on the bench.

This is not to say that you may not encounter a very smart judge. Judges develop savvy about people and their problems. However, it is our belief that few judges possess adequate knowledge of all the disciplines that are relevant to the issues of divorce and custody; their training simply does not provide for this. Nor is the problem helped by the fact that the judges who try matrimonial cases are generally the lowest paid and the least respected members of the bench.[9]

It takes a particular kind of personality to be a judge. Can you imagine what it must be like to listen to divorce cases day after day, to the lies, the tales of infidelity, the sob stories, and all of the human sewage that is brought to light? Can you imagine what it must be like to be able to destroy financial empires, break up families, dispose of properties, and modify the lives of adults and children with a flick of the wrist? That is a *lot* of power. Undertaken seriously, the responsibilities of the judge are enormous.

Part of the reason why the judge is nearly always "right" can be found in a fundamental difference between what the law views as true and what most people consider to be true. Most of us, in the educational process, have come to understand two different kinds of truth without clearly differentiating between them. One kind of truth can be seen in a simple example. If something is dropped, it will fall to the floor or to the ground. Is this true? How do we know it is true? The criterion that would be applied by a scientist is whether anyone could see the thing fall when dropped. If anyone could see it happen, then it really happened. This viewpoint is the one most frequently used and comes from the *philosophy of science*. Law, however, has developed along different lines over the centuries—from a *philosophy of ethics;* it is thus more directly concerned with whether something is right or wrong, or good or bad.

As a result of the differences between the two philosophies, the standards of proof have come to be different. In the courtroom there is but a *single* observer—the judge. *He* hears the witnesses, *he* looks at the evidence, *he* considers the conflicts, and *he* then decides what really happened. In a very real sense, this decision is defined as the truth of what happened and, since there are no other "observers" to the testimony and evidence, there is no one to refute his decision. Unless and until the judge's decision is reviewed by some higher court, the entire decision usually will be regarded as true. If the judge says you are an adulterer, you *are* an adulterer. That *fact* can be used against you in other legal proceedings. What all this boils down to is that in most cases the trial judge is the final trier of the facts.

The judge's decision is binding upon you. Unless his orders can be modified or appealed, you must obey them. The penalty for noncompliance is frequently up to the judge to determine and resides in the "contempt" power of the court. The contempt power is as great as it needs to be; you can be sentenced to life imprisonment for failing to obey a judge's order.

The most uncertain component of the way your judge will behave is a thing known as "judicial discretion." This refers to the fact that the law empowers the judge, in divorce and custody matters, to do just about as he pleases. His behavior is hardly at all regulated by either law or precedent. He can pay attention to some evidence and disregard other evidence; he can ignore the testimony of some witnesses and believe the testimony of others; he can just about disregard the entire trial, strip you of your assets, award custody of your children to your wife, and be completely legally justified in his actions. Judicial discretion is a great enemy of the American male in divorce and custody actions: first, because of the very uncertainty of unregulated judicial rulings; and second, because there are serious biases in the ways in which judges approach cases.

Most judges are at least forty-five years of age, frequently in their fifties or sixties, and they have the generational prejudices of earlier times. Lacking specialized training in psychology or other relevant disciplines, they tend to feel that motherhood is something to revere, that women are helpless and need protection, that mothers are superior to fathers as parents. This may explain why women receive custody in over 90 percent of all divorce cases.

If you offend a judge, you can expect him to retaliate. Judicial discretion gives him weapons of retaliation that are infinitely more powerful than anything you can muster. The judge can wipe out your assets and put you in jail. He can damage you beyond belief. Never—repeat NEVER—offend a judge.

The Balance of the System

Apart from the general public, from whom you can expect apathy and indifference, the rest of the legal system considers divorce and custody to be Big Business. There are about 355,000 lawyers in America, over half of whom belong to the American Bar Association. This number is sufficient to populate Birmingham or Fort Worth entirely with lawyers. If you included their families—figuring at four persons per family—they would nearly fill up the city of Detroit with nothing other than lawyers and their families. About 500 lawyers belong to the American Academy of Matrimonial Lawyers.

Somewhat more than 500,000 divorce or annulment decrees are granted each year in the United States. Even if the cost were as low as $200, this would amount annually to about $200,000,000 in lawyers' fees alone.

However, Bloom points out that

> ... few divorces are provided just for minimums. One estimate is that we actually spend about eight hundred million dollars in legal services for divorce, annulments, and separations.[10]

That is a lot of money, so much money that the system has a powerful vested interest in keeping the system intact, in protecting and extending its power.

One method used by the legal system to protect its power is to keep the system closed. The legal system itself determines who can enter it. Moreover, the system has resisted the intrusion of outsiders such as social scientists into its domain. Yet the courts badly need the information that social scientists could bring to bear on the issues of divorce and custody.

The system also retains its closure by deliberately mystifying the field of law, making it appear to be more complicated than it really is, thereby forcing the public to turn to lawyers for relief. The Bar also forbade advertising by lawyers until this was outlawed by the Supreme Court; in consequence, the public was denied knowledge regarding particular lawyers.

You, yourself, could well encounter either or both of two common situations in which pressure is applied to close a client out of the legal system. One is likely to occur in the context of friendly, fatherly advice from your attorney. He will tell you not to worry about things, that you are in good hands, that he will take care of the problem. In the process, he will be encouraging you to stay out of the system, to leave your case in its hands. We remark that the lawyer doesn't have to live with his mistakes —you do. Don't get closed out of your own life.

The second situation which frequently occurs consists of one or more meetings concerning your case from which you will be barred. The most glaring example is the "pre-trial conference." Under the guise of saving time for the courts,[11] many states allow the judge and the two lawyers to get together to discuss the issues in the case. Especially if the divorce is contested, the two lawyers will discuss the legal issues of the case. They will talk about the evidences they have, the witnesses they have, and what the witnesses can say. The judge will add comments regarding how he might consider the evidences, the relevance of the testimony, and so forth. In effect, they are trying the case *in absentia*. You will not be permitted to listen to the discussion, much less offer your own input into your own case. Beware the pre-trial conference even when your lawyer is well armed and fully trustworthy. You can require your lawyer to refer all decisions to you, as we explain later in the book.

We know of no human system other than the legal system which can so dramatically increase its income by making mistakes. If a lawyer or a judge makes a blunder, there is only one way to correct the mistake—by going back to court with a lawyer and relitigating the matter. A judicial error opens the door to appeals court; a badly written property agreement invites contempt proceedings. With the divorce-mill approach to marital disputes, it is all too easy to make such errors, and all too easy to pay more and more into the legal system to rectify errors that should never have been made in the first place.

Money is also created by the organized bar when it acts to prevent the introduction of reforms that would reduce the roles of lawyers and judges. Wheeler remarked that

> ...beginning in 1970 and continuing into 1973 the A.B.A. has deferred action on the Uniform Marriage and Divorce Act, a stand which has generally been interpreted as a rejection of no-fault divorce. Most of the opposition within the A.B.A has come from its Family Law Section, some of whose members are suspected of acting out of fear that no-fault divorce will ultimately mean no-lawyer divorce.[12]

More than any other thing, the power of the system is furthered by the simple fact that there are no effective checks and balances. Theoretically, such checks do exist. The lawyer who does wrong can be disbarred, and the errant judge can be removed from the bench. In addition, if a legal error is made, there is always the right to appeal. However, these safeguards pose no constraints on the system. Appeal, as we have indicated, is a source of funds for the system. Removing a judge from the bench for his errors is almost unheard of. While the legal system argues that the judge did the right thing, there is *no proof* either to support or to refute such a claim. Access to the files of divorce cases (all of which are public property[13]) is often difficult. One may be allowed to enter the file room in some jurisdictions only if nothing is taken into the file room and nothing is taken out—not even paper and pencil to take notes on the findings.

The legal system is designed to produce decisions, not to produce justice. A requirement for justice would undoubtedly do away with the adversary method since it is so prone to ignore scientific facts and since it is so prone to encourage litigation. A requirement for justice would also remove the anti-male bias inherent in the system, a bias not likely to be removed since the system profits from those husbands and fathers who refuse the "roll over and play dead" approach to divorce. A requirement for justice would also do away with the tradition that the man must be the one who pays in the divorce action—for the wife's lawyer, for her alimony, for her bills, for her court costs, for his lawyers, for his court costs, and so on.

We have indicated that the legal system is the system of power, designed for its own ends. You, as an American male, faced with this power, are on the defensive. You must create your own offensive in order to win.

4

The Law of Divorce

THIS CHAPTER may seem unduly detailed. Nonetheless, it does little more than outline the complexities that exist in the legal world regarding divorce. The purpose of the chapter is to provide an overview of fundamental legal concepts and viewpoints, and to educate the reader in the basic terminology of legal writing. While the contents are believed to be accurate and sound, the law varies dramatically from one state to another, and can even vary appreciably within a single state in terms of the way the law is applied. In addition, the law can change quickly, and thus the contents of this chapter will be subject to revision. You, the reader, have the task of learning about the law as it is applied in your own jurisdiction in order to understand how it relates to your own case.

Divorce Procedure in Brief

The divorce process is initiated when a person approaches a lawyer and says, "I want a divorce." In practically all the states, one must have grounds for the divorce, meaning that certain conditions must exist which make the continuance of the marriage inadvisable. The reasons for which the person presumably went to the lawyer and said, "I want a divorce" become the legally sanctioned reasons, or rationale, for which a judge can cancel the marriage.

The lawyer listens to the story of what is wrong with the marriage and then *drafts* (meaning, "carefully writes") a paper which claims that sufficient reasons ("grounds") exist to allow the marriage to be cancelled. The paper names the particular legal grounds being used (mental cruelty, adultery, or whatever) and provides some examples of events or circumstances which illustrate the nature of the problems. If, for example, "extreme mental cruelty" is claimed, the paper may provide examples of how the husband chronically belittles and is otherwise cruel to the wife. The paper drafted by the lawyer is called the *claim* or the *complaint*. The person who went to the lawyer is the *claimant, complainant,* or *plaintiff*. Once prepared, the claim is filed with the court. Once the claim has been filed (generally by paying a small fee and providing the Clerk of the Court a copy of the claim), the process of divorce is underway. Generally the lawyer, or his assistant, is the one who actually delivers the claim and pays the filing fee. The fee is later recovered through the lawyer's charges.

The next step is one of *notification*. Each party to the divorce action (husband, wife, and sometimes certain other people) must be notified that a lawsuit for divorce has been filed. This is done by providing a copy of a *summons and complaint* to each affected individual. The summons and complaint says two basic things: first, that a lawsuit for divorce has been filed and that the recipient is involved in this lawsuit; second, it indicates the nature of the claims that have been made by the claimant. The person who delivers the summons and complaint to the affected individual or individuals is sometimes called a *process server;* the act of delivering the document is referred to as *service,* or *notice,* and once the affected individual has received the summons and complaint, he has been *served* or *notified*. (The process server is frequently a policeman, sheriff, or other party associated with the law; he receives about $15 (more or less) for each service he performs.) The papers usually are delivered in person, and are signed and dated by the server and the recipient. The server also retains information which proves that the party was, in fact, served. Service can also be accomplished by registered or classified mail, where the return receipt proves that the proper party was served the papers. In some cases, a party can be *served by publication* of appropriate notices in local newspapers. This is also called *constructive service* and *service by construction*. Service by publication is sometimes subject to claims of improper service. It should be apparent that proper notification can be vital to an affected party; without knowledge that he is involved in a lawsuit, he may be unable to prepare for it. In some cases, notification is a mere formality, as when the wife goes to a lawyer and files for divorce at the insistence of the husband.

If the wife is the claimant, the husband becomes known as either the *respondent* (the one who will respond to the charges in the complaint) or the *defendant* (the one who will defend against the charges). If the husband has filed the suit, then the wife becomes the respondent or defendant. Once the respondent/defendant has been served, he (or she) seeks out a lawyer of his (her) own, explains the situation, shows the lawyer the summons and complaint, and they begin planning what they intend to do about the lawsuit for divorce.

The respondent has several options. First is to do nothing at all. This would result, in some cases, in a simple, uncontested divorce. The plaintiff would be awarded a divorce against the defendant and the marriage would be no more. The respondent would not be awarded a divorce against the plaintiff, but the marriage would no longer exist.

Second, the respondent can answer the charges claimed by the plaintiff. In this approach, the defendant attempts to disprove the claims of the plaintiff. If the defendant is successful, the plaintiff will have his or her grounds for divorce refuted and a divorce will not be granted against the defendant. They will still be husband and wife.

Third, the respondent can answer the charges made by the plaintiff and additionally can make some claims of his own. If he is completely successful, the respondent will be awarded a divorce against the plaintiff and the marriage will be no more. If neither party refutes the other's charges, each may be granted a divorce against the other.

Under the third option, in which the respondent forwards charges of his own, he becomes known as the *respondent-counterclaimant* or the *defendant-counterclaimant*. The charges, or counterclaims, made by the counterclaimant are similar to those made by the original claimant or plaintiff; they indicate the grounds which the counterclaimant believes are sufficient for winning a divorce, and illustrate something of the events and circumstances that will be the basis for the counterclaim. The claimant will be notified that the defendant intends to counterclaim, and will be provided a copy of the counterclaim itself (the paper drafted by the lawyer in response to the complaint).

Both the claim and the counterclaim can allege as many different grounds for divorce as the parties wish, provided the grounds can be proven by evidence. Thus the wife may sue the husband for divorce, alleging that he committed adultery and that he was mentally cruel; the husband may counterclaim and allege desertion, physical cruelty, and adultery—assuming that these grounds apply in the state where the suit was filed.

Frequently, the next process to occur, after all parties have been notified of claims and counterclaims, is the process called *discovery* or pre-trial examination (PTE). Discovery is the means by which the lawyers for each side find out how good the other side's case is, what the issues are, and how much money, property, and possessions each party has. Discovery takes place well in advance of the divorce trial and is performed in one or both of two ways: through depositions and through interrogatories. A *deposition* is a statement made under oath, just as if the party were on the witness stand in the courtroom. The people present consist of the discovering lawyer (who asks the questions), the lawyer of the party *being deposed,* the party being deposed, and a court reporter. There may also be others present, such as the spouse of the party being deposed. In taking a deposition, the deposing lawyer asks a question, the party being deposed gives an answer, and the court reporter takes down, verbatim, both the question and the answer.

The lawyer representing the party being deposed is there to prevent the deposing lawyer from taking liberties with his client, such as asking questions not germane to the case or badgering his client. Any remarks and objections voiced by this lawyer are also recorded by the reporter.

After the question-and-answer period is concluded, the reporter will prepare a typed transcript of the questions, answers, and any comments of the lawyers. All parties will receive copies of the transcript . . . if they ask (and pay) for them.

The second mode of discovery is through a questionnaire, frequently a lengthy one, called an *interrogatory.* The questionnaire prepared by the wife's lawyer is sent to the husband, and vice versa. Each questionnaire requests similar kinds of information: the facts that underlie each of the claims (or counterclaims) made, the names and addresses of persons who may serve as witnesses and what each of them might have to say at trial, and the financial condition of the parties to the divorce (sources of income, holdings in stocks, bonds, properties, business partnerships, savings accounts, checking accounts, income tax statements, etc.). By law, the parties to a divorce action *must* participate in the discovery process and *must* furnish the information requested, whether the mode of discovery be through depositions or through interrogatories or both.

There is frequently a lapse of several months, and in some cases, years, between the date of filing and the date of trial. Some matters may have to be dealt with by the court during the interim period. Such things include requests for temporary alimony, temporary custody of children, and temporary child support, and are called *pendente lite* (pending litigation) hearings. Such hearings result in *court orders* which require one or both of the parties to perform in certain ways (such as paying alimony or child support). Failure to comply with court orders can cause a judge to cite the offender for *contempt of court,* which can result in stiff fines and/or jail sentences.

When the hearings are out of the way and discovery is complete, and whether the *separation agreement* (an agreement between the parties regarding disposition of assets, custody, support, and alimony) has been attained or not, ultimately the case comes to trial. During the trial, both parties, their lawyers, one or more witnesses, the judge, a bailiff, a court clerk, and a court reporter will be present. What happens next depends on how completely the complications have been cleared away. If all complications have been cleared before the beginning of the trial (the most common situation), the claimant will be asked to take the witness stand and will be sworn in. The claimant's lawyer will question the claimant, asking questions designed to establish the claimant's right to bring the divorce into the court. This first round of questions is called *direct examination.* With the claimant still on the stand, the defendant's lawyer now stands up and asks whatever questions he wishes (*cross-examination*). Following the cross-examination, the first lawyer may again question his client (*re-direct*), and following this the second lawyer may ask additional questions (*re-cross*). When both lawyers are satisfied, the claimant is asked to step down. If the claimant has witnesses, these will next be called and examined by the two lawyers. *The claimant's side of the case is presented before the respondent's side.* Then the entire process is repeated for the respondent's case, beginning with direct examination of the respondent by his lawyer, then cross-examination by the opposing lawyer, etc. When all witnesses have been called, when all evidences have been presented, when both lawyers are satisfied that they need ask no more questions, each lawyer in turn summarizes his side of the case to the judge. If the case is simple, the judge may pronounce his decision at that time. If it is complicated, he may wait until a later date and produce an oral decision or a written decision. The judge's decision will grant or deny the divorces requested, will affirm, reject, or modify agreements reached between the parties, and will probably make some pronouncement regarding disposition of assets, children, support, and alimony. The trial is then over.

While in some states—Pennsylvania, for example—custody, divorce, and other matters are handled as separate hearings, for most people the above description is suggestive of the typical events involved in divorce and custody. For others, there are later activities. Hearings to modify or to enforce custodial arrangements, or to modify or enforce payments of alimony or child support are sometimes encountered. And for some who feel that the trial judge seriously failed to perform properly, the next step might be an appeal of the case to a higher court in an attempt to get the trial judge's decision *reversed* or *remanded*. Reversal indicates that the *appellate court* (court of appeals) believed the trial judge wrong, and that the higher court mandated the opposite conclusion. For example, the trial judge may have awarded custody to the mother. On appeal, the appellate court might reverse the lower court and award custody to the father. The appellate court alternatively might remand the case. This is a directive from the higher court to have some, or all, of the case retried at the trial level. Most commonly, the appellate court *affirms* the decision of the lower court (indicates that the trial judge's decision was proper in all respects).

Legal Orientations and Practicalities

Divorce, historically, has been abhorrent to the courts. The legal tradition has been that divorce was to be avoided except in the most dire circumstances. In most states this view still exists, but in much weakened form. Whereas, before, a divorce might be denied, today it might be easily granted, but not without some tsk-tsking at the thought of another family breaking up.

But no matter how favorably the people in the judicial system may look upon divorce, the laws generally require that grounds be asserted and proofs presented. The crux of the matter lies in the *standards of proof* and in the judge's *discretionary power*. In domestic law the standards of proof—statements regarding what will (and what will not) be considered evidence, or what will be sufficient (or not sufficient) to justify granting a divorce—are poorly developed. This provides a sense of vagueness as to what a judge must consider and what he can disregard in listening to the case.

The judge's discretionary power is the right the judge has to weigh evidence as he sees proper (he can believe some of it and disregard some of it if he pleases), and to make personal judgments in the absence of facts to go on. He can make decisions on the basis of what he may feel to be true; he does not have to have iron-clad evidence to prove what the situation actually is. Judicial discretion is nowhere greater than in domestic relations law.

For the judge, the first practical matter to be addressed is whether a divorce should be granted at all. The court feels some obligation to uphold the integrity of the American family. A couple married for only two weeks or so may find it difficult to get a divorce, the court holding that marriage is not a matter to be entered into frivolously. On the other hand, there is little to be gained by forcing two people to live as man and wife if they cannot stand each other; in fact, keeping them married might be ultimately harmful.

If the judge feels that a divorce should be granted, the latitude provided by the standards of proof and judicial discretion will almost certainly allow the judge to find sufficient grounds in the evidence presented. If the judge feels otherwise, the evidence must be incredibly persuasive—if not completely dispositive—in order to prevent the judge from denying the divorce.

If the judge decides that divorce is the solution for the instant case, he then reaches his second practical concern: what to do with the property and the money. Frequently, the law has something to say about how property and assets should be divided. While the law varies from state to state, the ground rules are similar. Properties held by the wife prior to the marriage and not put into both names after the marriage, and especially properties excluded from joint husband-wife ownership by an agreement signed prior to marriage—such properties remain the wife's after the divorce. Similar rules apply for the husband, although in many states there is a feeling that the wife has a right to share in the husband's holdings, including those that he owned prior to the marriage. As for properties and assets acquired after the marriage, generally these should be split down the middle, or as the parties may decide for themselves. But again, the judge may feel that one party is disadvantaged by the arrangement and may feel that the other's share should be reduced. His available latitude allows him to make this decision as he pleases.

He then comes to the third practical issue: how to provide for the continued support of the husband and wife. He wants neither of them on welfare. If he feels that both parties have honestly stated their financial needs and that they have accurately indicated their capabilities to earn incomes, he may feel that his decision is fairly straightforward. Or is the husband lying about his income? Or does the wife have a trust fund she can get by asking for it after the divorce? The judge's latitude enables him to adjust the predictable cash flows as he deems proper, and, if he feels the wife (or the husband) has lied, he can adjust the cash flow in punitive ways. He's not supposed to use alimony in this way, but he can. And sometimes he does.

Then the judge is ready for the final practicality of divorce: what to do with the children, and how to provide for their support. The judge is the personal embodiment of the *parens patriae* concept, the concept which indicates (in this context) that the state is a parent and protector of its minor children. Among his concerns is the welfare of the children of the marriage that is about to be dissolved. He feels they should have sufficient personal care, good food and clothes, proper medical care, and good educations. They should not be on welfare. He knows it takes more money to support older children than younger children. He is supposed to judge each case on its individual merits, and if custody is contested, he is supposed to determine whether *this* father or *this* mother would be the better custodian for these children, but he also believes that generally, mothers are more experienced and more capable of dealing with children than are fathers. Besides, if the mother gets custody, the father (who is generally the superior wage earner) is more free to work and to provide money to the children. Again, the judge has the latitude to set up an arrangement that he feels will answer these needs.

These are about the only practical concerns involved in divorce. The vaguely defined standards of proof and broad judicial discretion allow the courts to adapt their decisions to fit the particular needs of immensely varying cases, all of which have to be adjudicated under somewhat outdated and brittle laws. Perhaps this is why some believe that domestic law would not be workable without judicial discretion.

However, and this is the point, the application of latitude allows judicial action that is not predictable from the statutes and cases. Divorces must be argued in the courtroom in terms of law, but decisions must be made in terms of the practical necessities of particular cases *as these are perceived by the judge.* To the novice and the skilled lawyer alike, this duality of orientation induces a kind of unreality in the realm of divorce law. Be aware of this phenomenon whenever you hear of a case that seems to have been decided in some way that goes against your understanding of the law.

Pendente Lite *Hearings*

Pendente lite (pronounced "pen-den-teh lee-teh") hearings are those that are interposed between filing for divorce and the divorce trial. Such hearings deal with requests that the court order someone to pay alimony or pay money for child support, or that the court award custody of children to one party or the other. The court orders that result from *pendente lite* hearings are temporary orders which have effect only until the divorce trial; consequently, such hearings are sometimes referred to as requests for temporary alimony, temporary child support, or temporary custody. *Pendente lite* hearings are most frequently requested by the wife to secure support for herself and/or the children, or to secure clear legal custody of the children for herself.

For the American male, *pendente lite* hearings present a serious threat. They occur rapidly. The time from the date of filing for the hearing until the hearing itself may be no more than two weeks, or perhaps as little as three days. This frequently allows the husband little opportunity to assemble a proper defense against his wife's demands, even though the usual formalities for legal notification must be observed. The wife's lawyer, on the other hand, can usually take time to put together the foundation of a strong *pendente lite* case *before* he files. The husband must advance a hastily constructed defense against a carefully planned assault, and the result is frequently that the husband takes a serious financial beating.

A second source of threat resides in the fact that the *pendente lite* hearing is relatively informal. Generally, only the lawyers and the judge discuss the issues, frequently in the judge's chambers. Arguments are advanced from affidavits as to the wife's financial need on the one hand, and the husband's inability to pay more than he is currently paying on the other. Frequently, neither the parties nor other witnesses are questioned before the judge, and often the judge does not bother to study the affidavits. Instead, he relies on discussion with the two lawyers to get a feel for the situation. The in-chambers discussion frequently involves arguments relating to the divorce trial, and the judge uses as yet unproved allegations as a basis for determining how much, if any, support he should order for the wife.

> *Example.* Jim sat outside the courtroom in the hallway while his lawyer, his wife's lawyer, and the judge discussed the *pendente lite* matter brought to the court by his wife. While the wife was employed full-time and earned about $12,000 a year, Jim held a job which earned close to $17,000 a year. His wife felt that she had a right to some of Jim's income, and argued in her affidavit that she was nearly starving and that she faced terribly high expenses owing to a serious medical condition. After the in-chambers discussion, the judge and the two lawyers moved into the courtroom and in five minutes of formal hearing the judge ordered that Jim pay $100 per month as alimony *pendente lite* for his wife. She had asked for $400 per month. Jim's lawyer, an excellent negotiator, told Jim how things had gone in chambers:
>
> "Well," said George (the wife's lawyer), "this poor, sick woman was left to scrape by while her husband took up with this broad."
>
> "Four hundred," said the judge.
>
> "Just a minute, your Honor," said Bill (Jim's lawyer), "there's more to this than meets the eye. She may have an illness, but it doesn't seem to prevent her from working. In fact, during the past six months, she hasn't missed a single day's work."
>
> "What does she make?" the judge asked.
>
> "About ten thousand dollars a year," replied George.
>
> "More like twelve," offered Bill.
>
> "Fifty," said the judge.
>
> "Just a minute," replied George, "here's this guy who makes

> fifteen or twenty thousand dollars—nearly twice what his sick wife makes, and he's spending it on this other woman he's shacked up with."
>
> "Two hundred," said the judge.
>
> "Yes, your Honor," interjected Bill, "but the wife is no Pearl Pureheart in this case. You will notice that we are counterclaiming on adultery, and I think we've got a pretty good case."
>
> "One hundred," said the judge.
>
> "Yes, but . . ." George interjected.
>
> "One hundred," repeated the judge.
>
> And a hundred it was. Jim asked Bill how well the judge had reacted to the affidavits which the parties had submitted, and he replied, "Well, when we got there, the judge said, 'I've looked at this stuff,' pointing to the pile of papers, 'now what is this all about?' "

The results of this hearing were quite favorable to Jim, but undoubtedly would have been much less so if Jim had not, over the past several months, been systematically preparing to disprove his wife's allegations of financial need at the divorce trial. Because of his advance preparation he was able to brief his lawyer thoroughly, accurately, and quickly and to overcome his wife's excessive claims of financial need. Such outcomes are rare, however. More typically, the husband is not well prepared, and the outcome is less favorable.

In Jim's case, the judge did order an amount for support *pendente lite.* This is very frequently the case. The judge may feel that the case is more complicated than the brief *pendente lite* hearing can accurately disclose, but that where there is smoke —where the wife has pleaded for relief from her financial duress —there may be some fire, some true financial need. Hence, the judge frequently makes some alimony award even if he does not feel that the need is great. One man put it this way: the woman can generally get *pendente lite* support without presenting true proof of financial need, and without true rebuttal by the husband against her demands; the only real question involved is how much she will receive.

Because the outcome of the *pendente lite* hearing is a court order, this order may be (and frequently is) used later by one party or the other to sway the judge of the divorce trial. The order from the *pendente lite* hearing arrives in the divorce court with a persuasive power which greatly exceeds the care devoted to the issue during the *pendente lite* hearing. In fact, where the wife has received a goodly award, she will certainly argue during the divorce trial that the matter of alimony has already been examined with great care in a special hearing, and that the learned judge properly concluded that her financial needs justified the award. The divorce court judge can be powerfully persuaded by such arguments, for he dislikes overturning the rulings of his fellow judges. The power of the *pendente lite* support order can also work against the wife if the order itself has denied her demands.

> *Example.* In Jim's case, the outcome of the *pendente lite* hearing was a $100 per month alimony award to his wife pending the divorce trial itself. Jim's wife had to accept that amount during the interim period, but she had no intention of settling for such a paltry sum. She strengthened her arguments as well as she could and, at the divorce trial, again asserted her demands that her true financial needs were such that a proper alimony award should be between four and five hundred dollars per month. The judge, however, failed to agree. While he made some modifications to the conditions of alimony to provide for increased alimony should her medical condition abruptly worsen, he nonetheless retained the $100 per month alimony that Jim was required to pay.

In short, *the award set by a* pendente lite *court order tends to become permanent.* As in Jim's case, this may act to the husband's advantage. However, for a number of reasons there is a tendency for *pendente lite* awards to be excessive: because (1) the husband is frequently unprepared for the hearing; (2) the male judge frequently feels that he must protect the weaker sex against her more powerful husband; (3) the hearing itself is conducted with haste and informality; and (4) the *pendente lite* judge sometimes feels that he need not be too concerned for the effects of his decision regarding alimony because the whole matter of support will be more thoroughly dealt with during the divorce trial.

Even where the outcome of a *pendente lite* hearing strongly favors the husband, there is little reason for the husband to rest on his laurels. He may have won a battle, but the war is certainly not over. The divorce court may, at its discretion, modify the amount of the alimony award, and the trial judge may feel that the weaker sex needs greatly increased financial support.

The wife's lawyer may suggest to the wife that a *pendente lite* hearing be held to secure some amount of alimony—any amount—as a way of proving that she is qualified to receive alimony and, indeed, the *pendente lite* hearing is a good means to attain this end. In some states, if the wife is denied alimony during the divorce trial, she may not later return to the courts and plead for alimony (except by appealing the case to a higher court). In such states, if the wife's lawyer can get any amount of alimony during the *pendente lite* hearing, he provides strong assurance that at least some alimony will be awarded during the divorce trial. With it thereby established that the wife is deserving of some alimony, she may later return to the courts and plead for an increase in the amount of alimony she receives—a capability she might not have were she to be denied all alimony during the divorce trial.

For the wife's lawyer, the *pendente lite* hearing also can represent a tactical step toward a strategic goal: the reduction of the husband's will and capacity to resist his wife's demands. It is customary that the husband pay for his wife's legal expenses in addition to his own; thus, the instigation of a *pendente lite* hearing can add to the financial burdens of the husband. If successful, the alimony awarded to the wife will apply financial pressures in addition to those of the hearing itself, and if the *pendente lite* award is greatly excessive, the financial strain placed on the husband may be sufficient to crush resistance entirely. In addition, the threat of the *pendente lite* hearing will place large emotional demands upon the husband, and will require heavy investments of time and energy in his attempt to defeat the wife's demands.

In the sense of legal theory (and where the statutes permit men *pendente lite* rights), the relief afforded by *pendente lite* hearings should be as available to the needy husband as to the needy wife, but in practice, this is not the case. Even when the wife earns as much or more than the husband, it is unlikely that the husband will succeed in obtaining a court order that requires the wife to contribute to the support of children, even if he has custody of them at the time and is bearing all expenses for the home, the children, and himself while the wife has only her own expenses. The typical view of the courts is that the wife's financial obligations are secondary to those of the husband, not in addition to them. Generally, it is only if there is some compelling reason why the husband can no longer support the children at all that the wife's responsibility will be invoked. Similarly, in situations where the husband's income is dramatically lower than his wife's, his pleas for *pendente lite* alimony (in those states which allow it to husbands) will tend to fall on deaf ears. And even when the wife earns as much as, or more than, the husband, there is a likelihood that the husband will be required to pay at least some of his wife's *pendente lite* legal expenses, and he may end up paying alimony to her. However, in most jurisdictions, the well-employed wife is the husband's best friend. The more she earns, the less likelihood that she will succeed in *pendente lite* hearings, and the less likelihood that the husband will be adversely affected by requirements to pay her legal expenses; but the advantage of the well-employed wife generally does not extend so far that the husband will benefit by filing for *pendente lite* support.

As a caution, the husband should be aware of his legal requirement to support his family to the extent of his capability. As long as he has the capability of doing so, there is usually no similar requirement for the wife. If she wishes to exact support, she may provoke an argument with her boss and get herself fired, or work an arrangement to the same end. Thus, her income becomes virtually zero. If she can present herself at the *pendente lite* hearing as one who innocently lost her job and who, despite diligent efforts, has been unable to find employment, the husband may find himself in serious trouble. Proving his wife's complicity may be impossible. On the other hand, if he *can* prove that her loss of employment was a ploy and that her activities regarding employment amount to precisely nothing, he can expect that the hearing might result to his distinct advantage—she may be ordered by the court to actively seek *and find* employment, she may receive no alimony as an inducement to look for work, and her complicity will have been documented.

The husband's plea for *pendente lite* custody of his children, under some conditions, may be advantageous. The first condition is that he wants to have the children for himself to raise and love and care for. The second condition is that the wife does not seem to want to care for the children, seems incapable of caring for them properly, or has left them with the husband for too long a period of time or for the wrong reasons. The third condition is that the local courts be reasonably favorable to fathers who seek custody of their children. Proving that the wife who wants custody of her children should not have custody, but that the husband should have them instead, is a difficult and expensive task; it is treated at length in the next chapter. The things that must be done, the considerations that are involved, and the likelihood of success are similar in the *pendente lite* hearing to those same factors in the divorce trial custody hearing. The husband's custody during the interim period may demonstrate that he is an active, capable, and loving father, and that the children flourish under his care. Especially if there is a long period of time between the *pendente lite* hearing and the divorce trial—because the courts are often reluctant to disturb an established custody—the husband's likelihood of getting to keep the children, after the divorce, is enhanced.

Pendente lite child support payments are not deductible for income tax purposes. On the other hand, if properly done, temporary alimony (that is, *pendente lite* alimony) *is* tax deductible. The conditions tend to be met if (a) the word "alimony" is used in the court's order; if (b) the payments are to be made on a periodic basis (weekly, monthly, etc.); and if (c) the time for which payments are to be made is indefinite (as, for example, "payments shall be made until such time as this Court shall deem fit to alter this Order"), or is in excess of ten years. Lump sum payments of alimony do not qualify, and if the *pendente lite* order specifies a combination of a lump sum alimony and a periodic alimony, only the periodic component can be deducted.[1]

If the husband wishes, his lawyer can be instructed to do two things: first, to the degree possible, the lawyer can attempt to keep child support from being called "child support" in the court order. If the other side can be made to agree, much of the child support might be called alimony, thereby allowing the husband to deduct it. Second, the husband's lawyer can examine the court order and object to its style if it does not clearly set forth the alimony in such a way that it will be deductible to the husband. Frequently, the judge will be easier to convince that this should be done than will the wife's lawyer. Alimony which is deductible to the husband is considered taxable income to the wife, and her lawyer may try to prevent any such inroads against his client. The judge, however, is often of a different view; he is less involved with the nickels and dimes of the parties' finances, and is more concerned with the overall financial situation. Properly approached, he may feel that the shifting of child support into the alimony column of the balance sheet is of reasonable benefit to the husband, of little loss to the wife, and of no danger to the children.

There are two risks associated with this arrangement. In one case involving alimony (not temporary alimony) the husband paid substantial alimony to the wife but no child support, despite the fact that they had children. When the children matured and left the home the husband correspondingly reduced the amount of alimony he paid the wife. The wife sued for the balance of her alimony and the judgment went against the husband. The court said that the amount he had been paying was alimony, not child support, and could not be reduced because his children had grown up. This risk need not be of particular concern in a matter of temporary alimony, provided it is handled properly at trial.

The second risk is that the trial judge, seeing a lack of child support in the *pendente lite* order, may feel that this oversight should be corrected by adding child support to the already elevated alimony. This risk should be fairly easy to avoid by proper handling of the matter during trial.

Finally, temporary child support has income tax implications regarding which parent can claim deductions for the children. The considerations involved, however, exceed the scope of this work.

Alimony, Child Support, Property Distribution, and Legal Fees

The first question generally directed to the lawyer is, "How much is the divorce going to cost?" For the American male, this is indeed an important question, but when put so simply, it is also a naïve one. There are a number of factors which influence the costs of divorce actions.

Those factors within the control of the parties depend heavily on the communication between the husband and wife, on their willingness to trust each other and to compromise their desires in order to facilitate understandings and agreements with minimum involvement of lawyers and other aspects of the judiciary. As we earlier indicated, the adversary divorce system works against such good relationships. Nonetheless, as a source of financial concern to both husband and wife, factors within their own control are more important than all the others put together.

If they can keep their wits and work productively together, the husband and wife will hold costs to rock bottom. If they fail to do so, costs can explode into the thousands of dollars. It is not unusual that a family with a $30,000 annual income, representing the combined income of both husband and wife, will experience legal fees and related costs in excess of $35,000 (or even more) when they become embroiled in a custody dispute. To invest such sums of money in the legal system when amicable agreements might be attained by other means is wasteful.

However arrived at, if husband and wife can put together a workable set of agreements without recourse to lawyers (except for having them prepare the typed copy of the separation agreement so that it is in proper legal form), the cost of the divorce, from the viewpoint of legal fees, will be in the neighborhood of $300 (plus or minus $200) for each of them. If they bicker back and forth through their lawyers, both lawyers will make a lot more than $300.

If the divorce is headed in the direction of a contest, since the husband is so frequently required to pay the legal expenses of both sides, the threat of excessive legal fees becomes quite real. The husband cannot dictate that the wife go to a particular lawyer. If she is vindictive, she can select the most expensive lawyer in town and use him to the utmost, thereby running costs out of sight. If her lawyer wants to play "let's break hubby," he can use the discovery process as a deadly weapon. By insisting on repeated, lengthy depositions of the husband, the husband's employer, the husband's friends, his neighbors, *et al.,* he can increase legal expenses to unbearable proportions. Because depositions require the presence of both lawyers and a court reporter, the cost of taking a deposition runs about $175 per hour. Since the husband cannot prevent his wife's lawyer from deposing whomever he wishes, as many times as he wishes, for as long as he wishes, the picture can be very grim. If it is clearly obvious that the lawyer is using discovery as a form of harassment, it might be possible to get a court order limiting additional discovery, but the chances of success are slim, since the lawyer has the legal right to find out all he needs to know to properly represent his client, and he is generally the only one to decide how much is enough.

The wife's lawyer can also increase the costs of the divorce by parading a lengthy string of witnesses through the courtroom, pushing the trial over several days when the trial could as easily be completed in a few hours. Lawyers' fees while in court are generally higher than their fees for work done in their offices.

Distribution of property. The law is not specific regarding how property should be divided; instead, general guidelines are used to obtain what the court feels is an equitable division. Property is generally divided into two classes: items of personalty (your clothes, toothbrush, and the like), and assets (stocks, bonds, cash, business holdings and partnerships, other objects, and real estate). Assets are divided between the husband and wife. Items of personalty are not.

For a working rule of thumb, consider that anything which has value (monetary or otherwise) to *both* you and your wife, and anything which could be sold (converted to cash) is considered an asset. Valuable jewelry, for example, probably will be considered an asset, while cheap costume jewelry will not. There is frequently room for debate over whether a given item is personalty or an asset; the outcome of such debates can make a difference in how well (or poorly) the husband makes out. For example, if the wife claims that the $2,000 silverware set is her personalty, and if the husband fails to challenge her claim, then the $2,000 worth of silverware will be removed from the pile of assets before the bargaining begins; alternatively, if the husband successfully challenges, the silverware still might be given to the wife, but it would be treated as a transfer of $2,000 in assets to her. Because the husband should be treated equitably, he will generally be awarded a matching $2,000 which he would not have received had he allowed the silverware to remain her personalty.

While there are some differences in states with community property laws, the thrust of property division is the same everywhere: to divide the property between husband and wife in an equitable manner. Again speaking generally, assets acquired during the marriage are usually divided equally between the husband and wife, while assets held prior to the marriage remain with their original owners after the divorce.

Things can go the other way. For example, where a couple married and later bought a house, they may be required to sell the house upon divorce, and to divide the proceeds equally between them. However, had the husband owned the house prior to the marriage, it might seem logical that, upon divorce, he would keep the house. This is *not* always the case, because the courts may feel that during the marriage, the wife's keeping of the home, or her working and contributing financially to the maintenance of the home, has created a dollar interest in the property for her, regardless of whose name is on the title.

Moreover, the husband has a duty to support his wife both during and after the divorce, and housing is an important aspect of support. You can now see how, from certain viewpoints, the ownership and division of property becomes confused with the problem of alimony. This confusion is especially pronounced where there are children, for the support of both wife and children can be powerfully influenced by transfers of property. It is quite common that, where a husband owned a house prior to marriage, upon divorce the wife gets the house in order to have a place to raise the children.

ALIMONY AND CHILD SUPPORT. Alimony came to America through the traditions of the old English ecclesiastical courts as a way of providing for the support of the wife after a marital separation. At that time there was no corresponding protection for the husband. In consequence, we have a well-established, nearly common-law history regarding alimony for women, but not so for men. Unless a state has a specific law which provides alimony for men, men there cannot receive alimony.

Alimony for the wife is not specifically set by law. The amount of alimony which will be awarded by the court depends on the judge's subjective impressions, which are based on a number of factors. Some of the factors are: what the wife's financial needs are; how old she is (the older she is, the more likely that alimony will be provided); how much money she earns; what her job promises to do for her in the future (if she is a rising star where she works, the probability of an alimony award is reduced); how many young children there are if she is to have custody (the presence of young children makes it hard for her to work, so she needs financial support via alimony); the condition of her physical and mental health; the degree to which she was responsible for the breakup of the marriage, and how well the husband can convince the judge that she is blameworthy (repeated, open adultery may anger the judge so much that she will be denied alimony); the age of the husband; his health; his ability to pay alimony; his income, holdings, savings, etc.; what his future earning prospects are; the degree to which he was responsible for the breakup of the marriage, and how well the wife can prove he is blameworthy.

In legal theory, in most states, the issues which *should* determine whether (and if so, how much) alimony should be paid to the wife are but two: the wife's financial needs, and the husband's ability to pay. Older criteria are still occasionally encountered but are nowhere as persuasive as they once were. One such criterion is the idea that the wife should be supported in the manner of life to which she became accustomed through marriage to the husband, or that she should be permitted to retain her "station" in life. These are dropping away from frequent usage because, for most families, the finite and relatively fixed earnings of the husband can be stretched only so far, and it is more expensive to operate two households than one. A family that made out pretty well on $900 per month finds that, after a divorce, both new families must adopt a reduced standard of living. Where rent used to be about $275 per month for the single family, now it is about $200 per month for *each* family. Also, where they used to get along with one refrigerator, one electric iron, one washing machine, one clothes dryer, etc., they now need two of everything. Not only is the cash outlay for purchasing such equipment twice as great, but the incidence and cost of equipment repairs is doubled as well. Because the husband frequently is the one who must adjust to solitary living, and because the husband is frequently not properly trained in homemaking, cooking, and related skills, he sometimes is dependent upon laundry services, TV dinners, convenience foods, tailors, and other goods and services which used to be provided by his wife without cost, but which must now be paid for. This also increases the cost of living for *both* families.

After all is said and done, if there is to be alimony at all, there are unwritten rules which serve as guidelines for the amount to be assessed. In Pennsylvania, for example, it tends to be one-third of the husband's gross income (before taxes) as of the time of divorce. Other rules prevail in other jurisdictions; you can ask either a lawyer or a men's rights organization what to expect as to the risk in your jurisdiction.

The best protection for the husband is a wife who has a good education, a good job, and a desire for personal independence—in short, she neither wants nor needs alimony. In that position, she generally does not request alimony and, in some cases, will outright refuse it. Her position is of great importance, but it is not the sole governing criterion. Recalling that the state is the third partner to your marriage, the state holds the position that agreements between husband and wife regarding the wife's support are subsidiary to the state's continuing interest in her welfare. The judge is free to provide alimony to the wife even if she doesn't want it; if that happens, the man must pay. There are cases in which this has happened and in which the wife has later instructed the husband not to pay the alimony to her because she really doesn't want it. Interference by the judge is most frequently found in those states where, if the wife does not receive an alimony award at the time of the divorce, she cannot ever later return to the court and ask for alimony. In such situations, the judge may award some trifling alimony ($10 or so per month) merely to qualify the wife for greater alimony in the future should the need arise.

Alimony generally terminates upon the death of the husband, the remarriage of the wife (in some states by law; in other states this consideration must be present in the court's divorce order), or the death of the wife. Upon her death, alimony does not pass to her heirs, and, unless there are agreements to the contrary, upon the husband's death, the wife has no access to his estate for continued alimony. Alimony does not terminate upon the retirement of the husband; unless there are agreements to the contrary, the amount of alimony stays the same after the husband retires and his income drops to retirement level.

Awards for child support tend to follow principles similar to those for alimony except that it is rare for child support to be assessed against a wife, even when the husband has custody and the wife's financial situation is greatly superior to that of the husband. This is because of the tradition that the father is primarily responsible for the children; the responsibility of the mother is not invoked unless the father is unable to provide for their welfare. There is no law, however, against a mother voluntarily contributing to the support of the children under such circumstances, and the father should attempt to effect such agreements.

Child support generally terminates upon the child's attainment of legal age, the child's marriage (especially if the child is female, since upon marriage, her husband is responsible for her support), the child's death, and with increasing frequency, upon the completion of the child's education, even though the child may be over twenty-one years of age when schooling is finally completed. It is, as yet, rather rare that the father is required to continue support of his children beyond four years of college.

The continuing drain on the father's financial resources by alimony and child support represents serious dollar losses and results in a long-run reduction in standard of living, quality of life, and ease of retirement. When the court feels that the wife and children are in strong need of support, it takes the position that the alimony and support should be as high as they possibly can be without forcing the husband/father to prefer to be jailed rather than pay, and without forcing him to pull a disappearing act.

There has been a recent and continuing trend to relate the amount of support to the husband's increasing income and to the consumer price index. Since the consumer price index has risen more quickly in recent years than has personal income, the burden of support can represent an increasing threat, even when the husband/father's income is reasonably increasing. We have encountered males who live in barns and wear rags, even though they earn professional incomes, and we encountered one case in which, by the time the escalation clauses, trusts, insurance programs, medical provisions, etc., had been added to his support requirements, the total alimony and child support actually exceeded his gross income.

If a case is to be contested, the chances are that litigation will occur as a result of the inability of husband and wife to agree on matters of support, custody, and distribution of assets. Because the topic is, indeed, complicated and variable over jurisdictions, and because the risks are so severe, we urge the reader to engage in serious study of these issues within his own jurisdiction. Procedures for doing legal research are described in Appendix A of this book.

Separation Agreements

Separation agreements are not agreements to separate, and in some jurisdictions they are referred to as "settlement agreements." The separation agreement is an agreement entered into by the husband and wife which describes how properties and other assets are to be divided, who will have the children, what rights to visitation the noncustodial parent will have (including a visitation schedule), as well as a description of the kinds, amounts, and schedules of payment for support.

The law generally does not specify the exact form for separation agreements. Their contents usually can be as the husband and wife wish them to be. The law has, however, visited a number of opinions on what cannot be in a separation agreement. The voluntary dissolution of a marriage by a husband and wife is against public policy; consequently, a separation agreement will be voided by the courts if it contains statements which indicate that the couple are planning to divorce. The choice of wording is critical, and a lawyer should be consulted to make sure the agreement will meet the appropriate standards. The date of the separation agreement is also important. In some jurisdictions, the separation agreement cannot be entered into if the couple are still living together, and in other jurisdictions they first must have filed for divorce before the separation agreement will be legal.

In most jurisdictions, the wife cannot waive her rights to alimony. In a particular case, if the wife does not want alimony, the separation agreement can indicate that the wife neither needs nor desires alimony, and that she ask for no alimony. It generally cannot, however, indicate a waiver of her rights to alimony and, in all cases, the court has the final right to determine whether alimony is necessary.

Custody arrangements for children also can be developed as the parents wish, but here again the court has the final say. Especially if the arrangement seems bizarre to the judge, he may interfere with the agreement and modify the arrangement.

The separation agreement represents an advantage to the husband, for in the development of the agreement he has greater opportunity to seek an equitable settlement than at any other point of the divorce process. More is said about this in a later chapter.

A court order is a written command that someone do something. How such an order comes into existence may be of interest. There are a number of variations on the theme of development. A common method is to have a lawyer draft the terms and conditions of an order. The result is presented to a judge, in some manner connected to a hearing, so that the judge ratifies the draft and signs it. At that moment, it becomes a court order.

A second method is for the judge, in hearing or in chambers, to roughly outline to one or both lawyers the substance of what the order should contain. One of the lawyers subsequently drafts the order, perhaps passes it by the other lawyer for inspection and approval, then passes it to the judge for signature. Once signed, it is an order.

A third method is for the judge to become much more involved and to prepare some (or all) of the terms and conditions of the order. Sometimes the judge will pronounce what he expects the order to contain during trial so that it can be retrieved verbatim from the court transcript. In whatever way the judge effects the expression of his wishes, one of the lawyers will follow it to draft the order. The draft may bounce back and forth for a while between the two lawyers, perhaps with input from the parties, until a text has been agreed upon.

During the process of settling upon what the terms and conditions of the order should be, if the judge is the one who has initiated the terms and conditions, the lawyers are free to modify the wording, or to add terms and conditions as they may wish (so long as they both agree upon them). However, they are not free to change the substance or intention of the judge's order. Generally, the interests of the parties in what the judge said the order should contain will serve as a basis to prevent liberties from being taken with the judge's desires.

When the order is drafted to everyone's satisfaction, it is submitted to the judge for signature. An "order" without a signature is not an order at all, and it cannot be enforced.

Failure to comply with a court order risks the judge's wrath; he can punish those who do not comply through his *contempt power,* a virtually unconstrained power he has to levy heavy fines and jail sentences on those who defy the courts.

Even if the terms and conditions of the order are excessive (for example, requiring a husband to pay his wife $1,000 each Monday as temporary alimony, an amount which is impossibly high on a $15,000 annual income), the abused person has the right to appeal the terms and conditions of the order to a higher court to force the judge to modify the order or to obtain a more favorable order from the higher court. Nevertheless, *the abused party must abide by the terms and conditions of the original order until such time as they are modified by the court.* Failure to do so not only risks the court's contempt power, but the court will frequently refuse to listen to any arguments, on any topic, from the abused party until he is in full compliance with the court order ("those who refuse to obey the court are denied its protection").

This can represent a serious disadvantage to an ex-husband/father, since he may not have enough money to meet the terms of the court order and also instigate legal action to modify the order so as to reduce the burden. This double bind has driven many men to flatly refuse to pay, and to submit themselves to jail willingly, rather than to kill themselves trying to make enough money to meet the conditions of the order. And sometimes, such dramatic action has been sufficient to alert the court to the true severity of the order, and the terms and conditions are softened—but this is rare. In one case, a man was sentenced to jail "until he had paid the arrearage in full." The man had no job, no savings, no income, few possessions, and no friends and relatives. He was summarily jailed and kept there more than two years before a lawyer discovered that the man was living what was, in effect, a life sentence at the whim of a judge. The lawyer undertook the appeal of the contempt order out of the kindness of his heart and won the man's release. Had the lawyer not have come by, the man might still be in the county jail.

Stopping Your Wife from Divorcing You—The Male's Defenses

If your wife files for divorce from you, you may wish to prevent her from obtaining the divorce. Frankly, unless your rebuttal of her claims is a superior one, the chances of success are slim. Nonetheless, there can be, in certain circumstances, advantages to blocking her divorce.

Suppose, for example, that you suspect your wife is having an affair with another man. She has filed for divorce against you on the grounds of mental cruelty. As yet, you have nothing with which to prove her adultery, but such proof could well be vital to your side of the case. You need time for her affair with the other man to ripen, to allow her to get careless, and to give you the opportunity to gather the huge quantities of interlocking evidence which will prove her adulterous behavior. If you can successfully prevent her divorce you will have purchased at least a year of time within which to accomplish your purposes. After she has lost her divorce case, you can file your own. But remember, the probability that you can successfully block her divorce is small.

A second kind of advantage to blocking her divorce is simply one of threat. If you can convince her that you can successfully block her divorce, leaving her still married to you, she may feel that her entire future will be poured right down the drain, especially if she wants to marry her lover. In order to get out of the marriage she may be willing to do nearly anything for you, including forfeiting alimony and property. But again, the chances of actually blocking her divorce are slim.

A third kind of advantage is psychological. If you successfully prevent your wife from divorcing you, and if you later initiate suit against her, *you* will be the *plaintiff* and *she* will be the *defendant*. Every piece of legal paper that comes before her will remind her that she is the defendant, a word that carries a sense of wrong-doing. She will face the psychological burden of convincing herself that she is not a true wrong-doer. She will hate the word *defendant,* but will not be able to prevent it being applied to her by all and sundry. It will ring in her ears and echo in her dreams. While the onus of being a defendant is as serious to a male as to a female from the legal point of view, it seems to be psychologically more disturbing to the female. When a couple plan to divorce, the lawyers will frequently suggest that the husband become the defendant as a "courtesy" to the wife; and there have been cases in which, when a husband refused to be so generous, the wife became so enraged that the otherwise simple divorce went into a full-blown contest. There have been other cases in which the wife, realizing that she could not prevent the husband from filing and making her the defendant, was willing to bargain away her property and alimony rights in return for the courtesy of being the plaintiff.

Apart from such advantages, there is little to be gained by attempting to block your wife's divorce. There are some men who would prevent their wife's divorce because they still love her or need her. But this is a partial fiction. The wife generally can walk out anytime she wishes, regardless of how the husband feels about it. And even if she continues to live with the husband after losing her divorce, the husband's victory is Pyrrhic. Who wants to live with icy silence for the rest of his life?

Attempting to block the wife's divorce may not be a particularly wise course of action, especially since the expense and likelihood of failure are both high. However, if the husband intends to refute the nasty things the wife will say about him (which can influence child support and alimony, the disposition of property and other assets, etc.) *he must be prepared to defend against her charges.* The methods of defense are exactly the same as those which would be used to bar (prevent) her divorce. The legal terms applied to the methods of refuting the wife's claims are *bars* and *defenses.* In the paragraphs below, we detail the most commonly accepted defenses. Defenses are only applied in contested divorce and, as we have said, wives and lawyers win in the courtroom. The male does not. However, if there is more than a faint probability that the case will become contested, the husband must be prepared to defend his position to the utmost.

JURISDICTIONAL DEFENSE. The wife will be barred from obtaining a divorce if the court does not have *jurisdiction* over the matter. Three concepts are involved. When a court has jurisdiction, it simply means that the court has the legal right to hear a particular case and to make binding decisions upon the parties. A justice of the peace (J.P.) can marry a couple (the J.P. has jurisdiction over such matters), but he cannot divorce them (he has no jurisdiction in divorce). A Nebraska court cannot divorce Texas residents (has no jurisdiction over Texas residents). This brings up the second and third concepts: *residence* and *domicile*. Domicile (sometimes "domicil") is the older, common-law term, upon which the law is based in most states. It refers to the "home where one intends to live indefinitely." Intention is an important component of domicile. In the days during which the term was evolving, the concept made some sense because people tended to be born, live, and die in the same region. Today, owing to the high mobility of the American people, the term makes little sense but the slow-changing laws are still tainted with it. High mobility has caused the states to adopt *residence* as an alternative to domicile, or as an operational definition of domicile, in order to make the laws work. Residence refers to the place where one lives, either a street address or a geographic region (such as a city, county, or state), and is qualified in terms of a specific duration. In most states, legal residence is established if one lives within the state for one full year, meaning 365 consecutive days. Residence refers to the home, the place where you sleep, the place where you eat breakfast and supper; it does not refer to the place where you work. If you work in Kentucky and sleep in across-the-border motels in Tennessee, you are a Tennessee resident.

Not only is residence gained in most states by living there for a year, but it is also lost in most states after a year of continuous absence. If you have established residence/domicile, the courts of that state have jurisdiction over your (or your wife's) divorce. This makes for some interesting possibilities.

Your wife cannot get her divorce unless she has established residence in a state. Here, the husband may be able to apply what is just about his only advantage in the law of divorce: under the common law, the man is the determiner of where the family will live. According to the law, if the man moves to a new location, provided the new location does not pose a threat to the family's health, safety, and welfare, the wife is obliged to follow the husband. In fact, for her to do otherwise is, in the law of many states, grounds for divorce. The wife who refuses to follow is guilty of desertion. (Women's liberation organizations have been trying to get rid of this obligation for years.)

A possible way to bar a divorce, then, is to prevent the spouse from establishing domicile or residence by instigating a series of frequent moves from one state to another. Of course, this depends upon the varying jurisdictional requirements of the states wherein one lives (some states provide instant domicile for certain grounds for divorce). However, given the proper setup, one can continue to move from one state to another at sufficiently frequent intervals to prevent jurisdiction from being established over either the husband or the wife. Under such conditions, the wife cannot file for divorce because of her lack of residence and domicile.

Unfortunately, it also depends upon the wife being stupid, which is not likely to be the case. While the husband busily moves around the country, the wife may decide to forego the adventurous life of mobility. She merely stays behind while the family moves on, establishes domicile in the state where she is at the time, and then files for an *ex parte* divorce against her husband (if she can find suitable grounds, and she generally can).

The interpretation and application of residence and domicile, the degree to which the courts place emphasis on one or the other, as well as the subtle distinctions that have been generated over years of case law, can be found to differ substantially among the various states. Careful examination of the statutes and case law in states of interest should be performed before attempting to implement any of the possible variations on this theme.

As applied to *custody* cases, the law of jurisdiction, residence, and domicile operates quite differently, especially after a divorce. Many states will take jurisdiction over a custody hearing without a requirement for residence or domicile, so long as the affected children are physically within the state.

(From the viewpoint of advanced legal strategy, jurisdiction is an area of law which has not been fully explored; there are many interesting wrinkles that might be worked by bringing the laws of two or more states (or nations) into conflict, leaving the courts foundering in a confused morass of indecision regarding whether they can or cannot act on a given matter. A discussion of such conflicts is beyond the scope of this book.)

THE DEFENSE OF DELAY IN BRINGING SUIT. About a year after your marriage to Alice you met Maria at a party. You were attracted, recalling the freedom you had before marrying Alice, and an affair ensued. As with many affairs, the attraction in time wore off, and Maria became a part of history, carefully buried away, because now you had become more settled in your ways and had, for several years, been contentedly living with Alice. Then, horror of all horrors, Alice found out about Maria! Not being the forgiving type in such matters, Alice's first act was to read you the riot act, and her second was to visit a lawyer. Seemingly within minutes, you found yourself holding a wad of paper titled "Summons and Complaint." As the case came to trial, and despite your personal trepidation, your close-lipped lawyer seemed blithely confident. And during trial, he carefully examined you on the last date you had seen Maria. He also carefully examined your wife on the last date for which she could establish that you and Maria had seen each other. Having gotten the testimony he desired, your lawyer turned to the judge, mentioned that the last association between yourself and Maria was apparently seven years and three months prior to the date of filing, and, under the provisions of Code blank-blank-blank, as modified by blah-de-blah-blah, a divorce should be denied the plaintiff wife. Divorce denied. *The statute of limitations had run out!* Many states set forth statutes of limitations on certain grounds, most frequently adultery.

In the absence of statutes of limitations, a second legal concept can sometimes (but rarely) be invoked: the concept of *latches*. This simply refers to situations where a partner has waited too long to file suit; it is up to the judge to decide whether too much time has passed. Usually, the judge will hear the divorce case and will not apply latches against the wife, *unless* by granting the divorce to her, he feels that some severe harm would come to the husband. Such harm is difficult to show, which tends to make latches an ineffectual defense. There is some evidence to suggest that the wife can more effectively apply latches against the husband than he can against her. Apparently the courts seem to feel that under certain circumstances (such as one involving an elderly couple of modest means where the wife has no job skills) the wife would be unduly disadvantaged by the divorce and the husband's claims would be dismissed if the judge felt he had waited too long.

THE DEFENSE OF IMPROPER NOTIFICATION. The importance of proper legal service of the summons and complaint was earlier mentioned. In the view of the law, it is essential that the defendant be notified of the charges against him, and that he have adequate time to answer. The law prefers that strong evidence be gathered to document the fact of proper service. The most sure way to do this is to put the papers (summons and complaint) in the hands of an officer of the law whose job is then personally to contact the defendant and physically place the papers in his hands, concurrently obtaining and recording such information as the time, place, and date of service.

If your wife is divorcing you, don't be surprised to receive a telephone call from a deputy sheriff asking when he might drop by to serve papers on you. This might be your first indication that your wife has filed. A second method of contacting a party for service is to send a uniformed officer to the man's place of employment; this is embarrassing, but it does accomplish the service. In some metropolitan areas service is accomplished by process servers who do nothing but chase people down to serve papers on them. Personal delivery of service is, without doubt, the preferred mode of delivery because of its certainty. Officers of the law are preferred deliverers, not because of legal requirements (nearly anyone except the parties can deliver a service), but because they are trained collectors of evidence and are not likely to botch the job.

Service need not be accomplished by face-to-face physical contact. It can be accomplished by registered mail, return receipt requested, in which case the signature on the receipt indicates proper service. It can be accomplished by publication in some states, by posting a legal notification in a local newspaper for a certain period of time, but this method is seldom used because of the uncertainty that the defendant will actually obtain true notification, and because of the increasing frequency with which charges of improper notification via publication are winning in the courts. Service can sometimes be accomplished by simply handing the papers to the defendant's lawyer.

With the understanding that the intention of proper service is to make sure, and to document, that the right person receives the right set of papers, let us now consider some examples of improper notification. Giving the papers to anyone other than the intended party is improper; in serving you, the server cannot leave the papers with your friends, your relative, or your mistress—he has to give them to you. Slipping the papers under your door is improper personal service if the server does not actually see you (or hear you) within, or if you are not at home. Serving on you papers actually intended for someone else is improper. (In one case, a man proved improper service against the sworn testimony of the process server (who said he had personally served the defendant at his home) by showing records to prove that on the date of the supposed service, and for a couple of days before and after that date, he was in the county jail.) Undue delay between filing and accomplishing service is also improper. Most states have statutory or procedural requirements regarding the maximum delay that will be tolerated. If it is required to serve the defendant within fifteen days of filing, service on the sixteenth day is improper and may enable the action to be delayed, or may enable other remedies.

Now, with a feel for what is proper service and what is not, how can this be applied to prevent a wife's divorce? Suppose John's wife takes a lengthy vacation with relatives while John stays home to mind the business. Six weeks later, his wife returns to say that she has spent her time in Reno, has established residency there, and has divorced him. Now that she is a free woman, she intends to marry her lover (about whom John knew nothing at all), and John can go to blazes.

Not quite so fast. John may feel like doing a little detective work. Suppose he discovers that personal service was rendered upon him by his wife through having a gentleman friend receive the summons and complaint by registered mail. The friend signed in receipt of the service and, on the basis of a valid service, the Nevada court granted the divorce. Now, in his own state, John institutes a separate suit to have the divorce set aside as a void proceeding based on service obtained by fraudulent means. The divorce is declared void. John and wife are still married. Now John may be free to move against his wife on the ground of adultery and to save much of his property and income owing to his wife's marital fault and her fraudulent history. John has been careful, however, to keep up the appearance of being married to his wife, despite her Reno divorce. Had he behaved as if he were no longer married, the court might have considered that he had accepted the validity of her Reno divorce.

If you are never home when the process server drops around, if the registered letters never get to you, and if you have no lawyer, the whole legal practice may grind to a halt until you are served. This induces a delay which may be advantageous to you. It also tempts the devil, for it may represent "avoidance of service," which could be actionable.

THE DEFENSE OF CONDONATION. You have been having a fling with another woman and your wife has found out about it. The funny thing is that she doesn't seem to mind. She has even told the woman next door that, as long as you bring home the paycheck, she doesn't give a damn whom you sleep with. Now, however, she has discovered a man to her own liking, and she wants a divorce. "Jack," she announces, "I'm going to divorce you. Adultery. I've known about this affair of yours for some time and I have all the evidence I need. Thanks for the good times, and I'll see you in court."

Not so. She can file all right, and she can charge you with adultery. But (provided the defense is available in your state) you may be able to deny her divorce because she condoned your adulterous behavior, as evidenced by the statement made to the next-door neighbor. Since she has condoned the behavior she cannot now object to it. However, if you continue the affair in question (one additional act of adultery), you allow your wife to object to your (new) adultery and provide her with grounds. (You would also provide her with grounds by a single act of adultery with any other woman.)

THE DEFENSE OF RECRIMINATION. Recrimination, a defense left over from the Victorian era, is slowly dying but still in force.

You and your wife have been fighting for years. Finally, in an angry huff, she moves out. You beg and plead for her return, but to no avail. After a year and a half, you have finally quit trying to get her back and have found female companionship more to your liking. Your wife finds out about your new girlfriend and is delighted. You have now done just what she has been waiting for: you have provided her with grounds. She files against you on grounds of adultery. You counterclaim on grounds of desertion. If your state has the defense of recrimination, the court may find you guilty of adultery and her guilty of desertion, and, since you are both guilty of misbehavior, neither of you should profit by your misdeeds. Relief denied. No divorce to either of you. You are still married.

The doctrine of recrimination has been referred to as the

doctrine of "unclean hands" in some jurisdictions, and means simply that, if both parties have valid grounds for divorce, then no divorce can be granted to either of them. In such states, there must be one good guy and one bad guy before a divorce can be granted.

THE DEFENSE OF CONNIVANCE. John did not have a "bad" marriage; he merely had a boring one. It was more fun to pinch the secretaries on the job than to exercise similar license with his wife. It was also more fun to "mess around" a bit after hours with a couple of divorcees at the office than it was to go home. At the signs of lipstick on the collar, John's wife merely muttered that she wished he would be more careful. Although John could never be quite sure, it seemed that his wife knew he was involved in adulterous affairs with other women. Yet she didn't seem to care; she never made any direct statement on the issue. Indeed, she seemed to take perverse pleasure in John's amorous affairs, and even seemed pleased that he placed fewer sexual demands upon her. After several years of such conduct, John was surprised to discover that his wife had filed for divorce against him on the ground of adultery. Not in all the years of their marriage had she ever complained about his affairs, and he was sure she had known about them. In trial, the wife's divorce was denied. She had covertly condoned John's actions, and may have actually fostered them by looking the other way.

Connivance is a rarely employed defense and is usually restricted to defense against adultery. Elements of the defense are similar to both condonation (which is more overt) and provocation (discussed below).

THE DEFENSE OF LACK OF EVIDENCE. When one party claims against the other for divorce, the burden of proof theoretically lies on the claimant. If she accuses you of physical cruelty, she must be able to prove her claim. If she accuses you of adultery, she must have the proof to back up her statements. Theoretically, the defendant need not open his (her) mouth unless the claimant can show that she (he) has a case. If the proof of the claim or claims is inadequate, no divorce should be granted. That is the theory. In practice, unless the defendant strongly refutes the charges, even relatively unsubstantiated claims may be accepted as true by the judge. However, standards exist, in relatively amorphous form, to define what kind of proof and how much of it is needed to prove a claim. If major elements of these standards are not met, the defendant's lawyer can move to dismiss the complaint for lack of evidence. If he is successful the divorce will be denied.

THE DEFENSE OF RECONCILIATION. In a rage, you slugged your wife, blacking her eye. There were witnesses. This is not the first time this has happened, but it could be the last, for she has filed on the grounds of extreme cruelty. The two of you are still living under the same roof—there seems no other place to go—but there is little talk between you. Your thoughts go back over the years with this woman, and for some reason, you can only see the good times. You can't understand why you get so hot under the collar on occasion. Your continued reflection takes on a sentimental, melancholy tone, and while your wife is out shopping you put together a nice candlelight supper for two, complete with a well-chilled wine, and you send the kids off to a babysitter. Just for old time's sake. A goodbye dinner. Let's part friends. Your wife returns and is obviously moved by your gesture and the dinner goes smoothly. So does the wine. And later, things work out well in the bedroom. A week later you and she have lunch at a restaurant. At the conclusion of the meal, you impulsively kiss her on the cheek, and as you are leaving to return to work, she reaches out briefly to caress your cheek.

But next week, something you do sets her off again. In an absolute fury, she telephones her lawyer and tells him to hurry things up. At the trial, she is surprised to discover that you have successfully set up a defense of reconciliation. Despite the fact that she had overwhelming evidence of extreme cruelty, she took you back. The two of you had reconciled your differences, and her grounds were forfeit. In practically all states where reconciliation is a defense, a single act of sexual intercourse between husband and wife which takes place after filing for divorce represents reconciliation. In many states, continuing to live under the same roof (which provides the continuing opportunity for intercourse) represents reconciliation. And in some states, reconciliation can be demonstrated by a witnessed tenderness between the husband and wife. Reconciliation represents a forgiveness of particular past wrongs. A single new wrong may be sufficient to overturn the reconciliation and reinstate the grounds for divorce. Your wife may forgive your sexual indiscretion with Mrs. Apple and thereby provide a defense based on reconciliation; however, if she later discovers that there was an affair with a Miss Baker, the grounds may be reinstated.

THE DEFENSE OF COLLUSION. You and your wife want a divorce.

But there are no grounds, so together you work out a plan. Good old Marcia, a friend from out of state, can be persuaded to climb into bed with you, clothed in a scanty nightgown. You and she will pose for a couple of candid photographs, with expressions of shock, fear, and anger—as if you had been caught together in a hotel room. With such "evidence" of your adultery, no judge would deny a divorce. And so you and your wife put together a case, based on dummy evidence. During the trial, the judge smells rotten fish—the case is too open and shut, too pat. He asks a few questions of his own, reminding you both that perjury can carry a stiff penalty. Your wife comes apart on the witness stand, confessing to the manufacture of evidence. Divorce denied on the grounds of collusion.

Here is a second example: Your wife has a lover and wants a divorce. Recognizing her intense emotions, you know that you can drive a bargain. You indicate that you will not resist her divorce, provided she relinquish her rights to the jointly held property. If she refuses, well, it might take a long time for her to get the divorce. After some agony, she agrees. To protect yourself against her changes of mind, you put the agreement in writing and have her sign. During the trial the judge notices the strange imbalance in the way the property is being divided—all to you and none to her. The judge questions your wife and finally discovers that the agreement exists; the next day the agreement is produced in court. Divorce denied on the ground of collusion.

Most divorces barred on the ground of collusion involve attempts by the parties to manufacture evidence or otherwise fool the court. Agreements made in contemplation of divorce, of which certain terms are contingent upon the successful attainment of a divorce, are frequently held to be evidence of collusion.

Collusive divorces actually represent the majority of all divorces. However, divorces must be approached with an attitude that does not smack of collusion. Every state that has extreme mental cruelty as a ground for divorce knows that, most of the time, the woman's presentation during trial is an exaggerated and well-rehearsed drama. The husband sits quietly at his table while she makes her speech. They have worked the approach out between them and the judge knows it. However, unless something happens to irritate the judge, he will decline to explore the possibility of collusion and will grant the divorce. If, for whatever reason, the husband wishes to torpedo the proceedings, he has a weapon at his disposal. He can expose the collusion to the court with the possible result that the divorce will be denied.

THE DEFENSE OF PROVOCATION. You want a divorce from your wife, but you do not have grounds. Since your properties are considerable, and since you do not wish to share them with your wife upon divorce (at least, no more than you have to), you wish to make your wife commit a marital fault of such severity that you will have grounds and will be able to bring charges against her. If you can make her look bad enough in the courtroom, perhaps the judge will feel like trimming her share of the settlement in your favor. You know your wife very well, how to raise her ire, and you do so skillfully, especially at parties, where you cause her to get drunk, hostile, and aggressive. There are lots of witnesses to the scenes when she slaps you or shrieks invectives across the room. After each such scene you appear to be solicitous, amazingly understanding and polite, as you invite your wife to regain her composure and to get together with you to talk out your problems. Onlookers see what a kind, understanding husband you are and what an absolute bitch she is. What a shame to see a nice guy like you saddled with something like that! After several such scenes you announce to your wife that you have filed suit against her on the grounds of cruelty. You have an excellent case with many witnesses.

She is stunned, helpless. In talking about it with a neighbor, she hears the neighbor say that in her own observation that you baited your wife into an explosion—perhaps the wife should contact others who were at the party to see if their perceptions are similar. She does so and lucks out. One of the guests at a party was a clinical psychologist, who clearly saw the way in which you goaded your wife into a rage. On the witness stand, he says as much. Divorce denied on the defense of provocation. You provoked her misbehavior; the fault was yours, not hers. You get no divorce. Your wife might concurrently be able to proceed on a counterclaim to prove extreme mental cruelty against you; she well may win, too.

Provocation frequently appears as a defense against the claim of desertion. Desertion is denied on the basis that the defendant was forced out of the home by the actions of the plaintiff; true, the defendant did leave the house and remained away against the entreaties of the plaintiff for more than the statutory period of time, but this action was provoked by the unbearable and dangerous behavior of the spouse.

THE DEFENSE OF COMPARATIVE RECTITUDE. Comparative rectitude is a somewhat enlightened revision of the unclean hands doctrine. If both parties are found guilty of a severe marital fault, under the unclean hands doctrine, no divorce can be granted against either party. Under the doctrine of comparative rectitude, the party who is most in the right can be awarded a divorce, the party most in the wrong cannot, even though the faults committed by both are sufficient, in and of themselves, to warrant a divorce. For example, if the husband routinely beat up his wife, she has extreme cruelty as a ground. But suppose, also, that she had an open adulterous relationship with another man, and that she taunted her husband by constant remarks about how much better her lover was in bed than was her husband; then he has a case of very flagrant adultery against her. Under the doctrine of comparative rectitude, he would be awarded the divorce and she would not. Under the doctrine of recrimination, no divorce could be granted.

The summary of major defenses presented above does not cover the full scope of the bars to divorce that are available. Not all bars can be found in every state, and among those states that allow a particular defense, considerable variation in interpretation and application can be found. Variation can be found in interpretation even within a given state, from one county to another, depending on the local routines that have been established by the judges who hear the cases and the attorneys who prepare and present them.

The reader ultimately must determine how he will shape his case. It is his responsibility to discover what bars are available, to judge whether he can build a defense against claims by using them, and to evaluate how much energy, time, and money he should devote to such a defense.

5

How to Get Your Divorce—Grounds and Proofs

IN EVERY state in the Union, one must have grounds for divorce. The nature of the grounds that exist are described below. As with defenses, the statutes which "enable" a particular ground vary from one state to another, as do the cases which interpret the statutes. Not all grounds can be found in all the states. The only grounds available in California are irreconcilable differences and incurable insanity. In most other states, adultery is available as a ground. The presentation below speaks in generalities which the reader should relate to the particular circumstances of his own case.

The Ground of Adultery

Adultery refers to at least one act of sexual intercourse between a man and a woman who are not married, while at least one of them is married to someone else. Homosexual intercourse is not adultery (but is actionable on other grounds).

In divorce cases involving adultery there are four parties to the legal action: the state (the silent partner), the husband, the wife, and the *co-respondent*. The co-respondent is the person with whom the husband (or wife) is alleged to have committed adultery. The legal implications of adultery are serious for the co-respondent. For example, suppose a wife has been found guilty of committing adultery with Mr. John Q. Doe. If Mr. Doe is married, it logically follows that he also has committed adultery. The court proceedings from the trial of the adulterous wife represent *prima facie* evidence of Mr. Doe's adultery, and Doe's wife, with little effort, can easily prove an adultery case against him. For this reason, the name of the co-respondent always appears in the summons and complaint; he is (almost always) served with a legal notice that he is named in the action (that is, he too receives the summons and complaint), and thereby he has an opportunity to defend against the allegations of adultery.

To prove adultery is difficult, and it is more difficult to prove against a wife than against a husband. The courts seem to feel that a woman is more injured by a decision of adultery than is a male, and that it is more natural for a man to commit adultery than for a female, despite the fact that it takes two to tango. Adultery can be proved by direct evidence (eyewitnesses and photographs, for example) which clearly shows in an unimpeachable way that the marital partner was observed in an act of sexual intercourse with someone other than the spouse. Adultery can also be shown by inferential (circumstantial) evidence. To accomplish this requires proof of two kinds of facts: (1) that the defendant had the *motivation* to commit adultery, and (2) that the defendant had the *opportunity* to commit adultery. In short, that he (or she) wanted to commit adultery with a particular person, and that he (or she) had a situation in which any activity other than adultery would have been highly improbable.

For a simple example, a husband happened upon his wife who was embracing a man, and backed away from the scene unobserved. After watching his wife carefully for some days, he was able to get two men (a friend and a friend of his friend) to accompany him to a rendezvous where all three were able to get a good look at the wife's lover, and to obtain a good photograph of them kissing. On more than one occasion the wife had been observed kissing the man, thereby demonstrating a motivation on her part to engage in a sexual relationship.

As the affair progressed, the man's wife went on lengthy "shopping trips" and began visiting "friends" during evening hours. The husband bided his time until he was ready, then announced to his wife that he would have to make a three-day business trip in a couple of weeks. When the husband left the house for his "business trip," he went instead to a telephone and called his witnesses to stake out his home. At about 7 P.M. the wife left the house and drove to a restaurant where she was met by her lover. Both were observed by the friend of the friend, who casually followed them into the restaurant. After the dinner, they were followed to a hotel and observed signing the register. They went upstairs together at about 10 P.M. and were observed checking out at about eight o'clock the following morning. The presumption that the wife and her lover did not leave their hotel room unobserved during the night, and that they did, in fact, make love (they *could* have spent the entire night playing cribbage), together with expert testimony verifying the lover's signature on the hotel register and testimony by the observer-witnesses who saw the couple at dinner, entering the hotel, and leaving the hotel the next morning, constituted reason to *infer* the *opportunity* for adultery. The combination of opportunity and proof of motive was sufficient to obtain a divorce against the wife on the grounds of adultery.

Adultery, under the simplest circumstances, is very difficult to prove. The courts find this the most heinous of all marital faults and are reluctant to find anyone guilty. Their reluctance is enhanced by their concern for later legal ramifications. In New Jersey, for example, there is a criminal statute under which, if charges are pressed and the adulterous couple are found guilty, each can spend a year in jail. A finding of guilty may deprive a mother of her children in the state of Nebraska. And in many jurisdictions, a finding of adultery encourages the court to increase the share of property, assets, and income in favor of the injured party. Finally, the courts in jurisdictions where there are few grounds for divorce (and where divorce is correspondingly harder to obtain) have been faced with so many trumped-up cases of adultery that they tend to view all adultery cases as being based on collusion.

The Ground of Desertion

Desertion appears in a great variety of forms and embodies a corresponding variety of concepts across jurisdictions. In all jurisdictions it is a potpourri of things, frequently ill-defined. Only key concepts will be presented here to give the reader an idea of the kinds of things involved; the reader is urged to explore the definitions, concepts, and intricacies of "desertion" as it appears in his own state.

From a global viewpoint, a spouse is a deserter if he or she leaves home, deserting the marital partner and children, and stays away for a long time despite the continued and earnest entreaties of the deserted partner; the spouse no longer furnishes those things to the family that the law obliges him or her to furnish. Notice that there are a number of important factors embedded within this global definition. The states differ widely as to whether they consider each of these factors and, if they do, in the extent to which "desertion" is dependent upon each.

In some jurisdictions the key concept is abandonment of the marital home by one spouse. The abandonment involves going to live elsewhere for an extended period of time (from one to five years, depending on the state). Another concept is that of continued, willful (some states use the term "obstinate") absence; the spouse who remains at home has tried repeatedly, earnestly, and to the limit of his or her ability, over a considerable period of time, to convince the absent spouse to return. Despite all efforts, the absent spouse continues to stay away. A third concept is that of the provision of necessaries to the family by the husband and wife. The picture is further muddied by the concept of *constructive desertion* which can be found, in one form or another, in many states. Because of varying emphases upon these concepts, and upon specific interpretations of them in various jurisdictions, a spouse might be guilty of desertion in one state, whereas he or she might not be in another.

Willful and continued absence is readily understood by most; consequently, the emphasis of our discussion will be on the failure to provide the legal requirements to the marital home and on constructive desertion.

Both the husband and the wife have legal obligations regarding the family. By law, the husband is required to furnish his wife's necessaries (food, clothing, shelter, transportation, medical expenses, recreation, etc.) to the best of his ability. Failing to furnish *to the best of his ability* can be construed as desertion in many jurisdictions, regardless of whether they live together or apart. For example, the husband who allows his family to exist at a low standard of living as a result of spending most of his paycheck on buddies and booze can be found guilty of desertion, even if the family's standard of living is well above poverty level. The provision of sex to the wife is also a legal duty of the husband. Some jurisdictions have decided that the husband should provide sexual intercourse to his wife at least once per year.

The corresponding legal duties of the wife consist of supplying homemaking services (cooking, sewing, housecleaning, childcaring, etc.), and to provide sex to her husband (at least once a year). The wife has no support obligation whatsoever unless, for unusual reasons, the husband cannot work. This seems to be true regardless of how low the family's income may be. The husband has no legal right to compel his wife either to work or not to work. The courts currently consider that the economic contribution to the home made by the working wife can supplant, or substitute for, part or all of her domestic responsibilities.

Whether the husband is properly supporting the wife is readily documented through exploration of his income and standard of living compared to the economic level at which the wife is forced to live. By comparison, documentation of the adequate provision of sex by either party, and of the wife's proper performance as a housewife is much more difficult. The courts frankly don't consider the condition of the household to be particularly important, at least not in comparison to the importance of the husband's responsibility to bring home the bacon. To most intents and purposes, then, only the duties of the husband are enforceable in the courts. What this boils down to is that it is much easier for a wife to obtain a divorce from her husband via desertion than vice versa.

The law recognizes, in many jurisdictions, *constructive desertion*. This occurs, for example, when a husband is so mean to his wife that she has to leave her home. Under such conditions she may be able to convince the courts that, constructively, *he* has deserted *her*. In New York State, a leading case persuaded the court that whenever the wife was forced to leave the house, she took her home with her wherever she went, whether it was the street or anywhere else. Since the husband was not in that home, he had deserted her. A husband who forcibly evicts his wife from the marital home is guilty of desertion.

If the wife is not working and is in good health, and if she keeps house so badly that the husband's well-being is at risk to stay there, there is a slight possibility that he might be able to sue her for divorce on the ground of constructive desertion, even if it is he who actually leaves the home.

The husband has a common law right to expect his wife to live with him wherever he goes. If he moves to a new job, a new house, or a new geographic region, by law he can expect his wife to move with him. If she is tied to her mother's apron strings or to a particular locale and refuses to join her husband, she may be guilty of desertion. Alternatively, the health, safety, and well-being of the wife is legally considered a responsibility of the husband; he cannot expect her to move into an environment that would be dangerous or unhealthy (mentally or physically) for her. If a husband moves into an environment that is dangerous or unhealthy to his wife, and if she refuses to accompany him, he usually cannot sue for divorce on desertion; if he moves into such a hazardous environment voluntarily, the wife may be able to sue him on the ground of constructive desertion.

The Ground of Cruelty

Cruelty occurs in two forms, physical and mental. Earlier laws recognized only extreme physical cruelty, such as seriously beating the wife on a great number of occasions, inflicting physical injury. With legal progress, physical cruelty can now be just about anything that threatens or inflicts physical harm. A sense of deliberateness, or intention, is usually involved. For example, the husband who brings home roses when he *knows* his wife is seriously allergic to them can be guilty of extreme cruelty. A husband who baits his wife to the degree that she becomes upset and vomits can be judged cruel. Beatings and threats of beatings also qualify. Frequently, the laws refer to repeated, serious threats or acts endangering life or limb. The sense of repetition is important. Punching your wife *once* when she made you blow your cool will not qualify you as guilty of extreme cruelty as grounds of divorce.

With even more legal progress, the courts began to recognize that threats and physical violence were not the only things that could be cruel; continued badgering, verbal harassment, chronic nagging, belittling, and other forms of nonphysical cruelty have grown into such legal concepts as "extreme mental cruelty" and "indignities." Today, in many jurisdictions (and especially where the divorce is not contested), nearly anything can be construed as extreme mental cruelty sufficient to grant a divorce. Extreme mental cruelty is a great divorce catchall by which nearly any couple can get a divorce, provided the jurisdiction allows such cruelty as a ground. However, the standards of proof are tightened by the courts if the divorce is contested. In any uncontested case, the wife may say that you chronically belittled her in front of her friends, bringing her to tears. With one supporting (and lying) witness, and with you sitting with your lawyer making no defense, you may well have your divorce. Alternately, in a contested case, she may really have to prove such "extreme mental cruelty" by producing a string of witnesses who will demonstrate your cruelty; pitted against these, your own string of witnesses will demonstrate your earnest attempts to get along with a bitch of a wife. This may make it much more difficult for her.

Unfortunately, the law has not progressed to the point where a wife can easily be found guilty of cruelty in either form. Extreme mental cruelty and extreme physical cruelty are grounds reserved for women—not by law, but by custom and expectation. We know of men who were assaulted by their wives with kitchen utensils, sometimes with cast-iron skillets, so that they had to be hospitalized; we know of one case in which a wife would get her husband dead drunk when she was angry with him and, when he was too drunk to know what was going on, she would beat the hell out of him. When he awakened he could only vaguely remember how he came by his lumps and bruises. While such situations are known to occur, judges seem to feel that a man should be able to take care of himself and, moreover, that he should be able to do so without laying a hand on his wife (unless *he* wants to be judged "cruel"). Because such expectations blind the judges to the facts of particular cases brought before them, battered men are seen as the butt of jokes by the judiciary and their cases are dismissed out of hand.

This does not mean that it is impossible for a man to win a case on extreme physical cruelty; rather, that in order to win, the man must be determined and must be able to document for the court, irrefutably, *a history of severe, dangerous, acts or threats* against his person by his wife. If your wife brings her brothers over to your house to beat you up (yes, we have known this to happen), we recommend that you undertake immediate legal action against them on criminal charges—and don't be badgered out of it by the lawyers and court clerks who don't want to get involved in a "domestic quarrel." If necessary, import a lawyer who will file the case and prosecute it for you. Having succeeded there, a guilty verdict, plus fines and penalties, plus records of the court proceedings, furnishes (at little cost to you) much of what you need to press a case of extreme physical cruelty against your wife.

It is very, very rare that a man will win a case against his wife on the ground of extreme mental cruelty. The judges seem to feel that men are (or should be) immune to the psychological pressures that can be visited upon them by their wives. This is extremely unfortunate because, in fact, the typical woman is verbally more facile than the typical man. She is more capable of verbal attack and verbal defense than he is; and it is she, not he, who is master of the cutting remark. The stereotype of the nagging wife is well known in our culture and for good reason. Also, it is likely that the male is more readily damaged than the female as a result of psychological pressure brought to bear by the spouse. This factor may underlie a great number of wife beatings; when the male's shallow verbal defenses have been battered down, he resorts to his only available remaining defense—physical aggression. This, of course, can result in an immediate legal response by his wife, for wife-beating is illegal; driving a husband temporarily insane by nagging is not. Nonetheless, the judges tend not to listen to men who claim their wives are mentally cruel to them. In order to win such a case, the situation must be quite unusual. A man with a history of mental illness requiring periods of hospitalization (to demonstrate that his capacity to withstand psychological pressure is low), coupled with witnesses who can give glaring examples of her cruelty (such witnesses preferably including both his friends and hers, as well as strangers and psychiatrists), and where testimony and other evidence can demonstrate an association between her psychological harassment and his subsequent hospitalization—such a case just might be sufficiently persuasive to win.

If you discover that your wife is a lesbian and that she engages in homosexual relations with another woman you probably have grounds for divorce based on extreme mental cruelty.

The Ground of "No Fault"

The courts of most jurisdictions now feel that the couples who present themselves to the courts requesting a divorce are not especially bad people; enlightened judges have long despised the damage which can be caused by the adversary system. Today, most jurisdictions have enacted "no-fault" grounds for divorce to provide an alternative avenue that is not so condemnatory of either party. No-fault divorce comes in two forms: *separation* and *irreconcilable differences.*

"SEPARATION." In the sense of no-fault divorce, separation refers to the husband and wife having lived separate and apart for a certain period of time. The proofs required must clearly demonstrate that the marriage, in the sense of an emotional relationship, is dead throughout this period of time. Generally, this is accomplished by showing that the couple have lived in separate quarters, that they have met each other only on "official business," and that they have not engaged in sexual intercourse. Living in different rooms in the same house, and living in different apartments in the same apartment building have sometimes disqualified a couple for separation as a ground for divorce (the court feels that, if the partners live in such close physical proximity, some ghost of the marriage must still survive). But this is becoming more liberally interpreted, and varies from state to state. By all means, check out the cases in your own jurisdiction.

Being seen together in romantic settings—say, at dinner in a candlelit restaurant—or being seen displaying any form of affection toward each other also will disqualify the couple, as will a single act of sexual intercourse.

The intent of the no-fault laws is to provide a way of dissolving marriages that are dead, not to make divorce easy. When the laws were enacted, there was widespread concern that no-fault divorce would result in situations in which people would feel free to marry and divorce repeatedly, or in which people could legitimate a weekend shack-up by marrying beforehand and divorcing afterwards.[1]

Generally, before the couple can file for divorce, they must have been living in a state of separation for the statutory period. In the state of New Jersey, for example, the law requires an eighteen-month separation prior to filing. Owing to the normal time from filing to trial, two and a half to three years may elapse between the date of separation and the date of divorce.

"Irreconcilable differences." This term is a California invention. It means just that: there are differences between the man and wife which are important to them, and which they cannot reconcile. Because of the severity of these differences, they feel they cannot continue to live as man and wife. They want a divorce. Properly approached, irreconcilable differences is inexpensive, speedy, and sure-fire. Of all grounds for divorce, irreconcilable differences is probably the least painful, requires the least involvement with the legal system, and disadvantages the couple least in its consequence. It is almost impossible to bar a divorce in California, because, if one party wants a divorce and the other does not, *this disagreement represents an irreconcilable difference which is sufficient to grant a divorce!* The process is so simple that lawyers will handle the paperwork in an "uncontested" divorce for about $75; many people purchase a do-it-yourself manual or kit, fill out their own forms (contained within the manual), and process their own divorces. California has struggled mightily to get rid of the adversary system, with all of its evils, and has made great progress in that direction. The California system, however, has not completely succeeded in eliminating adversarial considerations, and these weigh heavily on divorces where there are problems of alimony, division of assets, or custody.

Living Apart (Separation)

In earlier days, in the absence of a clear case of adultery, divorce was virtually impossible to obtain. This did not necessarily force people to live together when they despised each other, for there was an available legal relief, termed *living apart* or *separation*. In some jurisdictions it was termed divorce *a mensa et thoro* (divorce from bed and board). This is a *legal* separation, attained as a result of a court hearing. It severs the interpersonal relationship, establishes alimony, divides some property, and awards custody and visitation privileges. The couple are legally permitted to live separate lives without legal divorce through such grounds as cruelty, desertion, and separation. They are still man and wife, and neither can form sexual liaisons with outsiders without risking divorce on the grounds of adultery. For as long as they remain in the state of legal separation, the husband is bound by his legal requirements to support his wife. His legal obligation to furnish sex to his wife is dismissed. All of the wife's legal obligations towards the husband are dismissed, except, perhaps, in some rare cases where the husband can no longer work.

Legal separation is not a divorce, but it remains a legal remedy available to those who might benefit by it, at least in some jurisdictions. We cannot understand how any man would benefit by it unless his religious beliefs simply forbid divorce. None of the man's legal duties are reduced by legal separation, yet he suffers loss of housekeeping services and the intimate company of a woman. Because it is more expensive to maintain two households than one, his financial burdens are actually increased, and it seems he obtains nothing in return except, of course, that he no longer has to live with a woman he can't stand.

Voidable Marriage

There is a legal distinction to be made between a *void* marriage and a *voidable* marriage. A marriage is *void* if it has no legal foundation or if it is technically faulty to such a degree that it can be presumed not to exist. If a man marries a second woman while he knowingly is still married to a first woman, he commits bigamy and the second marriage is void. By contrast, a *voidable* marriage is one which contains at least one technical fault, such that the court might, if it feels like it, render the marriage void through legal decision.

Suppose your wife suddenly vanishes. Instantly, you notify the Bureau of Missing Persons of her disappearance and hire private investigators to find her, but to no avail. For eight full years, she has been missing. Now you find a new romantic interest and, presuming your former wife to be dead, you marry the new woman. You and she have two or three children and then your old wife turns up, having spent years in a mental hospital as a result of amnesia. Not being particularly understanding of your new marriage, your first wife sues to have your second marriage (now distinctly voidable) declared void by the court. This kind of thing causes the judiciary to do some serious head-scratching. If the second marriage is declared void, the children will be rendered illegitimate. Certainly, you should not have remarried without having first obtained a judgment that the first marriage was no more. This might have been accomplished through an Enoch Arden statute, which declares a person legally dead after a sufficient absence, frequently seven years. Had your first wife been declared legally dead, the first marriage would be no more and you would have been free to remarry.

But you did not do this, and now the judge must declare one marriage or the other to be no more. The first wife's claim on the marriage generally supersedes all other considerations, but the presence of children may make such a decision odious. If there were no children by the second marriage, it probably would be declared void. In this case, however, since the first wife was gone longer than the Enoch Arden statute would require, the judge probably would see a means of declaring the first marriage void in order to protect the children of the second marriage. But don't count on it.

The void/voidable distinction is important to those who have been married for a short period of time and who want a divorce.

If other grounds are not available, it may be possible to have the marriage declared void. *Annulments* are characteristic of such actions. For example, a couple of teenagers of sufficient age to marry without parental consent got drunk at a party and, on a dare, were married by a justice of the peace. When they sobered up, they realized what they had done. They had not yet engaged in the usual wedding night ritual of intercourse. Had they immediately separated and moved as soon as possible to have the marriage declared a nullity, the court undoubtedly would have granted their request. In this case, however, the couple figured that they *were* married, and so they spent the weekend engaging in intercourse. They then went to the judge to have the marriage declared void. The judge reasoned that the couple had relied on the marriage in order to legitimize their intercourse and that they had done so while they were of sound mind. The marriage was declared valid.

A couple were married by a justice of the peace whose license had expired. The J. P. was, therefore, not legally authorized to perform the ceremony. The marriage, in this condition, is *voidable*. Later, the husband attempted to have the marriage declared void. Denied. The husband had relied upon the validity of the marriage by performing his marital duties, including intercourse with his wife. The marriage was declared valid.

A couple were married by a J. P. Only years later did the wife discover that her husband had set up the marriage and that the supposed J. P. was not a justice of the peace at all. He was, instead, an old friend of the husband who had performed the ceremony as a joke. The wife, upon the discovery, was understandably angry. She filed to have the marriage declared void. The husband, who had grown to cherish his wife, resisted the claim. The court saw things through the wife's eyes. The marriage was declared void.

Sometimes marriages can be annulled on sexual grounds. A couple married but, for the entire first year, the wife could not bring herself to have intercourse with her husband. In all other respects the marriage was normal. The husband sought the court to declare the marriage a nullity. The court agreed that, since they had never experienced sexual intercourse, the marriage was a nullity.

Either a husband or a wife may be considered impotent by the courts. A man is impotent if he cannot obtain an erection of sufficient stiffness to effect a penile insertion into the wife's vagina. A woman is impotent if for some reason (usually a physical abnormality) she cannot accept her husband's penis within her vagina; sometimes the vaginal opening or the vaginal barrel is too small to accept the penis without physical damage to the woman. In such situations, *provided* that the impotence was not known prior to the marriage, marriages frequently can be annulled. In situations where the impotence was known before the marriage, it is generally understood by the courts that the couple had planned a sexless marriage and the marriage will not be annulled. In some states, impotence is, in and of itself, a ground for divorce.

Other Grounds for Divorce

There are a large number of specific grounds for divorce apart from those named above. In states that do not have these specific grounds, generally they are subsumed within one of the headings already discussed. Alcoholism is grounds for divorce in some states if it can be proved to be intractable, uncontrollable, and chronic (over a year or more), especially if it can be shown to be responsible for embarrassing and damaging social and economic effects (a husband lost a big sale because of his wife's alcoholism). Notice that this could be subsumed under "cruelty" in other jurisdictions. Similarly to alcoholism, some states have drug addiction as a specific ground.

Insanity is a ground in some states. Frequently, the insanity must be considered incurable and requiring hospitalization. This is the one circumstance wherein the wife can take a financial beating. If she divorces her husband on this ground, she may expect to be hit with a stiff alimony which contains specific provisions to pay all his psychiatric and related medical expenses. Husbands, of course, when divorcing their wives on this ground, can expect similar treatment. Especially if violence is a component of the insanity, grounds of cruelty could be established in states that do not have insanity as a specific ground.

In some states, conviction of a serious crime resulting in a long prison sentence is sufficient to obtain a divorce. In other jurisdictions, the marriage is automatically dissolved if the sentence is greater than a prescribed number of years. And in still other jurisdictions, if the sentence exceeds a given number of years, the imprisoned party can be declared legally dead (as far as the marriage is concerned) and the marriage can be dissolved.

Default Judgments

With the exception of no-fault divorces, practically all uncontested divorces are achieved through default judgments. The most frequent ground used is cruelty (either physical or mental); due to the husband's courtesy, the wife files as plaintiff. The defendant husband does not counterclaim and, in fact, makes no defense at all to her charges during the trial. Because he makes no defense, the judge has only the evidence submitted by the wife and her witnesses. The only conclusion he can come to on the evidence is that the husband is, indeed, cruel. A divorce is granted.

Default judgments are *ex parte* divorces (discussed below), since the defendant does not appear at trial, either in person or through his (or her) lawyer; they are uncontested, since the defense makes no attempt whatever to resist the claims of the plaintiff. Of these two characteristics, the lack of appearance at trial is most important. In many conditions where the defendant is unable to appear for the trial, a default judgment may be entered against the defendant.

It is this feature that sometimes renders default judgments risky. With neither lawyer nor defendant present, the plaintiff may allege events that go beyond the previous arrangements, perhaps producing a harangue about poor financial circumstances or a lengthy description of the defendant's sins and evils. This may induce the court to award alimony and property to the plaintiff which clearly were not anticipated by the defendant. Once ordered, the judge's decision may be difficult to modify or appeal. Should the defendant object to the now excessive award to the plaintiff, he may be estopped from pleading for relief on the basis of his lack of appearance owing to his admission that he had earlier agreed (in a collusive way) not to contest the divorce.

Default judgments frequently come about as a consequence of both parties using the same lawyer. In many states some lawyers will undertake to represent both parties. In other states this is considered unethical; however, by cutting a second lawyer out of the action the parties can save several hundred dollars. The single lawyer for both parties actually represents the plaintiff before the court while instructing both parties regarding the way in which the divorce is to be processed. The defendant will readily and overtly receive service and will not contest the divorce. The plaintiff will procure one or two witnesses to corroborate his (generally her) testimony. If all goes well, the divorce will be secured with minimum fuss and minimal costs.

Alternatively, bad things have happened. Where the wife has secured a divorce on the ground of adultery in a default judgment, the husband/father has at least once been declared unfit for custody of his children as far as any later actions are concerned. And if things become acrimonious between the husband and the wife, the husband may be required to seek representation of his own very late in the proceedings, after he has fully exposed his finances and potential for resistance to the other side, thereby seriously weakening his case.

In most circumstances, however, a default judgment can be taken with confidence, especially if a few safeguards are observed. Two safeguards are especially important. *Before* the plaintiff files suit, the husband and wife should have completely agreed on the nature of the claims and the relief requested. Most typically, the judge will render a judgment by default, granting "the relief requested" with little amplification or modification. If the parties have worked out what relief is agreeable to them both, and incorporated the terms and conditions within the complaint, there is strong assurance that the judgment will go favorably to the defendant as well as to the plaintiff.

The second safeguard is a very well-developed separation agreement, setting forth all necessary details of assets, support, custody, finances, and so forth. The separation agreement should be signed by both parties before a notary public, and dated, to attest to the mutual consent of the parties and the formality of the agreement. The agreement must also parallel the relief requested in the complaint so that conflicts are not likely to occur later.

Especially if the resident state has a routine procedure for processing default judgments in divorce, with the above safeguards, there is little likelihood of anything going wrong.

Even so, the defendant should be carefully observant of the proceedings. If, for example, it seems that the preparation of the claim was slipshod, or if it was bulldozed through by the plaintiff and filed before the defendant's concerns were addressed, there may be cause for alarm. But notice that we have emphasized the importance of working out the nature of the claim and the requested relief between the parties *before* filing. If things start to go sour, the case is still young and there will be plenty of time for the defendant to seek out his own lawyer. Even in such an event, the case need not become contested; it may remain uncontested and may even remain a default judgment if the defendant's concerns can be settled prior to the hearing. In many cases, there is a slight shift from the default judgment approach to one in which, at trial, the plaintiff and her lawyer are present, as is the defendant's lawyer—just to make sure that the plaintiff does not attempt to push beyond what was earlier agreed upon. Since the defendant is represented at trial, the divorce does not "go by default" but remains, nonetheless, a brief and simple uncontested divorce.

Foreign Divorce

This term refers to divorce in a state other than the one where the parties currently live, or in a nation other than the United States. For example, all divorces in other states are foreign to Nebraska. Foreign divorce has achieved prominence through one particular manifestation, namely, *migratory divorce*. Migratory divorces are those in which one (or both) of the parties moves temporarily into a state that has a very short "waiting period" (the period needed to establish residence and domicile). Nevada, with a six-week residency requirement, has been a favorite state. Typically, one party moves into the foreign state, establishes residence there, and sues for divorce on some convenient ground. Such divorces are expensive (air fare to and from the foreign state, plus living expenses while there, plus the usual legal fees and court costs, although these are fairly low since the legal system is dealing with volume sales), but they are expedient to those who can afford them.

This brings us to the interesting problem of the *ex parte* divorce. An *ex parte* divorce is one in which the defendant is not represented at trial, either in person or through his or her lawyer. Default judgments are an example of *ex parte* divorce. However, the *ex parte* divorce has attained prominence in connection with migratory divorces, owing chiefly to jurisdictional and notification problems.

To work properly, a foreign *ex parte* divorce must meet the following criteria: first, the plaintiff must live in the foreign state for a sufficient time to clearly meet the state's requirements for residence; second, the defendant must be afforded proper notice (personal service upon the defendant in his or her home state is the best method; less preferable alternatives are service via registered mail with return receipt requested, clearly showing the defendant's signature, and service by publication in both the home state and the foreign state). It is even better if, during trial, the defendant shows up in person, submits himself or herself to the jurisdiction of the court, and makes no objection to the proceedings; technically, however, this is not an *ex parte* divorce, since the defendant is represented before the court.

In the *ex parte* situation, the plaintiff deliberately sees that the issues of residence and service upon the defendant are brought up, so that the court will formally take jurisdiction over the matter of the divorce. In such situations, provided the defendant does not answer the complaint, the courts are now clearly entitled to sever the marriage and to grant the divorce. With regard to issues of support, however, the waters become very muddy. Of course, the court may award alimony or not, as requested by the plaintiff; the difficulty resides in whether the terms of support will be respected in other states, and in whether, even in the foreign state, the ruling with respect to support might not be attacked.

Despite some inconsistencies in how the courts have ruled, there are some commonalities. It appears, for example, that if the defendant wife has been awarded alimony in her state (in consequence, for example, of a legal separation), then the *ex parte* order of the plaintiff husband cannot supersede or cancel the previous order for the wife's alimony. It also appears that, if there is no current order for alimony for the defendant wife, and if the plaintiff husband's *ex parte* divorce does not order alimony for her, the wife may nonetheless apply for, and receive, alimony in her own state if her state normally makes alimony available to wives upon divorce. On the other hand, if the wife lives in a state such as Pennsylvania or Texas, where there is no permanent alimony available to the wife, and if there is no current order for her support, and if the plaintiff husband obtains an *ex parte* divorce which fails to award support to the wife, then the wife may not then, or later, seek alimony, either in her home state or any other state at a later date.

In one case, the defendant wife had been living in Oregon where she was receiving separate maintenance. Recall that separate maintenance is distinct from alimony; it is for the support of a woman who is still married and it always terminates upon divorce, whether alimony is then awarded or not. The husband moved to Nevada and, well after the end of the time needed to establish residence, he filed for a divorce and had the wife personally served in Oregon. She made no answer to the complaint and an *ex parte* divorce was granted the husband. Since they were now divorced, the wife's separate maintenance was cancelled. She appealed the matter and lost.

Such complexities have resulted in frequent litigation as defendants attempt to overturn divorce decrees in order to secure alimony or modify the conditions of support. Obviously, if the entire divorce can be set aside, leaving the parties still married, the support issue becomes a whole new ball game. The defendant spouse usually will attack the validity of the *ex parte* divorce by challenging the propriety of the notification or by challenging the validity of the domiciliary condition. Since proper service of the summons and complaint can be effected by publication, there is generally little hope of successfully attacking the decree on the basis of notification unless fraud can be demonstrated. (For example, if the plaintiff has the service sent by registered mail to a friend in the same town as the defendant, and if the friend forges the signature of the defendant to falsely indicate a strong proof of service, this is fraudulent, and if the fraud can be proved by the defendant, it is possible that the *ex parte* order might be set aside.)

Most of the time, however, the defendant attacks the decree on the basis of domicile; the defendant alleges that the conditions of residency were not met in the foreign state so that the court there did not truly have jurisdiction, or that even where the technical conditions for residency were met, there was an obvious lack of settled, permanent domicile. Where the conditions of residency clearly have not been met, the order can be readily set aside by the home state, but where the domicile is an issue, it would appear that the outcome depends upon how strictly the home state requires actual domicile rather than mere technical residency.

Not to denigrate the *ex parte* divorce, if a divorce is needed, and if a person is not concerned about property, support, or custody, an *ex parte* order can be appropriate. Suppose, for example, you need a divorce but have no grounds. You merely relocate in Nevada, leaving your wife behind, stay for the necessary six-week period, and get a divorce. As long as you continue to stay in Nevada your divorce is legal and binding. Your (now) ex-wife may be able to approach the court to ask for property, alimony, child custody, and support, but the Nevada court will not overturn its own ruling about the divorce. You are a free man. (This approach could be a godsend to a particular Pennsylvania man who has been attempting, unsuccessfullly, to obtain a divorce from his wife for nineteen years!)

Appeal from the Divorce Decree

In any contested case, because of the broad discretionary power of the judge and the lack of exacting standards for legal process, there is the possibility of making an appeal to a higher court to make right an improper decision of the trial judge. Such appeals can ask the higher court to reverse all of the lower court's decision, or to modify parts of it. The burden of proof is on the party seeking the appeal to prove that either the judge ignored the facts or else he abused his discretion. Most appeals are based on an abuse of discretion, indicating that the judge went too far with his decision. Most of the time, the result of the appeal is that the husband pays the legal expenses of both sides, the lawyers make a lot of money, and the husband gets little out of it. (The minimum cost of an appeal is about $2,000, representing the legal expenses of his appeal and the wife's defense against it.)

If an appeal is to be undertaken, however, some facts must be known. Of considerable importance is the understanding that the higher court does not hear evidence. Instead, it looks at what the trial judge had to work with and decides whether, given those facts, the judge made a mistake in his application of the law. If the matter of divorce has ramifications that might conceivably warrant a later appeal, the husband had better get *all* the necessary facts into evidence at the trial level. Failing to do so means that he will not be able to introduce such facts at the appellate level.

The contents of this and the preceding chapter have been an overview of the complicated area of law regarding divorce. Certain rules can be repeated here in summary.

First, the man should not be so foolish as to provide his wife with grounds for divorce; even if she has such grounds, he should avoid providing her with evidence to further her case.

If there must be a divorce, especially if against the husband's wishes, or if it is likely to become a contest, the husband should push hard to file first to put his wife on the defensive—the battle of the defense is more difficult than that of the offense, and it is harder to live with.

No matter who has the best case, or how well prepared either side is, do not expect the major decisions to be made in the courtroom—they are more likely to be made in the judge's chambers in discussions with the lawyers or in consequence of pre-trial skirmishes.

Finally, in the world of contested divorce, preparation is everything. True, the courts tend to favor the woman, but if the man's preparation is markedly superior to hers, he will stand a distinct advantage. In the world of uncontested divorce, the separation agreement is king; this is the arena in which the male has the best opportunity to attain a reasonable and just settlement.

6

Custody

Do you want to keep your children? Unless your wife does not want them, you stand every chance of losing them to her at the hands of the court. This truth is a bitter pill to swallow; the psychological loss of a child is very like the loss of a child through death. And make no mistake about it, when one is reduced to visiting the children, one is physically and psychologically through as a parent.

If you intend to fight to keep your children, you face a serious, difficult, expensive uphill fight. Data collected by P. Clint Jones, probably the most authoritative source for such information, indicate that mothers are awarded 93 percent of all male children and 94 percent of all female children. His painstaking examination of more than 14,000 cases further suggests that there is no observable trend toward increasing awards of custody to fathers, despite the pervasiveness of this view among lawyers. However, Mr. Jones did encounter one bright note: in one particular California county, he found that when custody was hotly contested by the father, the father won the boys in 32 percent of the cases and the girls in 27 percent of the cases.[1]

In order to press successfully for custody, much must be learned and much must be done. Of primary importance is a self-evaluation by fathers who definitely want custody, or who have not yet made up their minds whether to fight. The Addendum to this chapter presents such an evaluation, and we recommend that it be given serious attention at this point. Having conducted a self-evaluation, those fathers who want custody should first learn the importance of the fathering role. Then they must learn how the law deals with custody, and what practical actions are necessary to build a custody fight.

We use the word "fight" advisedly. Psychological and social forces will cause even an indifferent mother to act the part of a she-bear willing to sacrifice all to retain "her" young.

How Necessary Is a Father, Anyway?

It is generally believed that a mother is necessary to the proper rearing of children, and that a mother is naturally fitted for the rearing of children by what is called the "maternal instinct." History and literature abound with tender images of mother-child relationships.

If there is such a thing as maternal instinct in human beings, the best scientists have been unable to find it. If anything, science is continuing to discover that man and woman are incredibly similar in structure and function. It is common knowledge that some women cannot breastfeed their infants. While it is not common knowledge, some men *can* breastfeed. Men have inactive lactation glands which under certain conditions can be activated.

In short, while there are biological differences between the sexes, these biological differences can be demonstrated consistently only in the procreative process up to the point of birth. From that point on, the biological advantages of one sex over the other, vis-à-vis childrearing, remain largely speculative.

There are, however, pronounced sociological and psychological differences between men and women with regard to childrearing. These differences tend to negate the importance of the fathering role unless one recognizes them for what they are—stereotypes. Our culture accepts as "normal" a mother who raises children and a father who works. It is precisely this stereotypical presumption—that the mother, not the father, will be at home to care for the children—which is so frequently mentioned as a basic reason for awarding children to their mothers. While this may be considered "normal," it is substantially inaccurate. Even in intact homes, over 40 percent of the wives are in the labor force, and among divorcees the rate is 70 percent. When a judge awards a divorce with custody to the mother, therefore, he incurs a 70 percent chance that the mother is not going to be home to care for the children. The overall labor force participation rate of men in intact families is 85 percent, and that of divorced men, 80 percent—only 10 percent higher than divorced females![2] It is nonetheless still not considered "normal" for a father to stay at home and care for the children while the mother works, nor for him to work and rear the children alone.[3]

Psychologically, there are important relationships between parents and their children. These relationships, in an intact family, are known to promote the proper mental, physical, and emotional growth of children. Upon a divorce, however, the family becomes no longer intact. Generally, since the mother keeps the children, they will be reared in a fatherless home. What happens to fatherless children is now becoming better understood.

The Fatherless Child

World War II removed a great number of fathers from their homes, and kept them away for extended periods of time. For the first time, research studies using reasonably objective techniques were applied to the assessment of the impact of father absence. Comparisons of children in intact homes with those in father-absent homes demonstrated that father absence resulted in children having inappropriate, stereotypical views of maleness. In short, they demonstrated the obvious: where there was no male around the house, neither boys nor girls had a clear understanding of what being a man, or relating to one, was all about.

Later research has employed better tools and better methods for applying them. It has been found that father-absent boys show an inverted profile of verbal and mathematical skills. Whereas a boy from an intact home frequently shows a mathematical level higher than his verbal level, the reverse tends to be true of father-absent boys, who show the verbal-higher-than-mathematical pattern that is more typical of girls. Preschool father-absent boys are more feminine, less aggressive, and more dependent than boys from intact homes. The sex-role orientations of father-absent boys are more feminine than those of father-present boys. Inappropriate sex-role development may be particularly affected by father absence during the first two or three years of life.

Such results are by no means restricted to the effect of father absence on boys. Father-absent girls tend to develop poor or inappropriate relationships with men; they are frequently man-hungry and promiscuous during their teenage and later years and may experience difficulty in marriage. Among working-class families, there is evidence that father-absence is associated with lower IQ scores in both boys and girls. It seems that the adverse impact of father absence has its most dramatic effect when the absence occurs during the early years of life. Also, while father-absent boys frequently show the effects of father absence before the age of eleven years, girls tend not to manifest directly observable damage until their teenage years when heterosexual relationships assume paramount importance. Father-absent children also show elevated incidence of juvenile delinquency.

But what about the corresponding impact of mother-absent homes? Frankly, there are so few mother-absent homes that the impact can only be theorized. There is no direct, objective research on the topic. In terms of what is really known, as opposed to what is speculated, we know that father absence has serious adverse effects upon the social, emotional, and intellectual growth of children. We do not know what impact mother absence has, if any.[4]

Jurisdiction and Custody

The problem of jurisdiction is the first issue addressed by the court in adjudicating custody. In the most common situation, where husband and wife are domiciled in the same state and are asking for an adjudication of custody at the same time as a divorce, the court has the necessary jurisdiction.[5] The states treat other situations in markedly different ways. Some states will take jurisdiction if the child is living within the state; others require one or both parents to be living or domiciled there. The principle of *parens patriae,* which requires the courts to protect the legal rights of citizens who cannot protect themselves (that is, children), usually makes it easy for the courts to take jurisdiction over a custody matter, even if the same court would be unwilling to hear issues relating to divorce.

Legal "Tests" for Custody

There have been three tests applied by the courts when adjudicating a custody issue. The *fathers' rights* dogma of the common law was the first. Under this test, the father received custody unless he was morally unfit. It was replaced by the *tender-years doctrine.* Becoming law in some states as early as 1860, the tender-years doctrine holds that young children of whatever sex, and girl children of whatever age, are to be awarded to the mother unless she is unfit. Because of the mysticism surrounding motherhood, the tender-years doctrine held sway for over a hundred years, and is still powerfully influential even though technically it has been replaced in most jurisdictions by the *best interest and welfare test.* Under this test, only the best interest and welfare of the children are to be considered in making an award in custody. In some jurisdictions, the statutes direct that no presumption can be made in favor of one parent or the other as to suitability; in practice, the judges follow the tender-years doctrine, feeling that the mother, not the father, is "in the best interest and welfare" of the children.

There are three important reasons why the tender-years doctrine is still so persuasive. First is the fact that cases tried today are dependent upon the legal precedents of cases tried years earlier. This inhibits fathers from being able to bring modern, scientifically acceptable (as distinguished from legally acceptable) evidence into the courtroom. Second is the cultural bias of most judges, men of mature years who remain imbued with the cant of earlier generations—that, somehow, mother is superior to father as a custodian. The third reason is that lawyers and judges are remarkably untrained in psychology, sociology, anthropology, and the other social sciences. While they may know the law, they know astoundingly little about the people they attempt to apply it to.

A quick review of some cases will reflect the ways in which judges have spoken about custody. A 1938 Missouri case, Tuter v. Tuter,[6] illustrates some of the mysticism associated with motherhood. In that case the judge said:

> There is but a twilight zone between a mother's love and the atmosphere of heaven . . . and no child should be deprived of that maternal influence unless it be shown there are special or extraordinary reasons for so doing.

If 1938 seems to represent an "old" case, consider the case of Brashear v. Brashear, a 1951 Idaho case[7] in which the decision included the following:

> Another rule has become firmly established in this jurisdiction, to wit: "... a child of tender age or a girl of even mature years can and will be reared, trained and cared for best by its mother. This conclusion needs no argument to support it because it arises out of the very nature and instincts of motherhood; nature has ordained it."

Later, the Kentucky case of Byers v. Byers[8] was decided on appeal. The 1963 decision read, in part:

> It is a fundamental rule that ... a child of tender years should be awarded to the mother. This is in recognition of the truism that maternal affection is more active and better adapted to the care of the child and best calculated to secure his or her happiness and well being.... There is no substitute.

Notice especially in Byers the mention of the child, the child's happiness, and the child's wellbeing. Kentucky was, at that time, a tender-years doctrine state. The Byers case represents a significant departure from the doctrine by beginning to identify the doctrine with the best interest and welfare test. A more clear-cut identification can be found in the 1960 Louisiana case of Dungan v. Dungan.[9] The decision there read:

> We recognize the law that the paramount consideration in determining to whom the custody of a child should be given after a divorce is the welfare and best interest of the child. Under this rule this court has consistently given the custody to the mother.

And in Pennsylvania, a 1973 decision, Commonwealth ex rel Lucas v. Kreischer,[10] thus expressed the wisdom of the court:

> In Pennsylvania, supported by the wisdom of the ages, it has long been the rule that in the absence of compelling reason to the contrary, a mother has the right to the custody of her children, over any other person, particularly so where the children are of tender years.... In fact, that the best interests of children of tender years will be served under a mother's guidance and control is one of the strongest presumptions in the law.

Some states have overtly rejected the tender-years doctrinal preference for the mother (California, Washington, Illinois), and have explicitly indicated that the children should go to the party who is better for the children—either the father or the mother. The limited statistical data that are available, however, display a pattern of awards to the mother which fails to distinguish such states from the others.

The most disturbing aspect of the tender-years doctrine is its insistence that the mother must receive the custody of very young children of either sex. As we have already indicated, numerous psychological research studies consistently report that at such young ages, father deprivation has its most damaging and long-lasting impact. Just how the courts can, in their wisdom, consistently award children to mothers in the absence of any objective evidence that this is a meritorious action, especially when there is so much evidence to indicate that it may well be inappropriate, is baffling.

Factors Influencing Custody

A thorough review of cases provides few guidelines to the actual reasons why judges award custody to mothers or fathers. Certain factors are frequently cited, and these may be suggestive of the judicial mind. (We and others have frequently suspected that the stated factors are merely an attempt by the judge to justify the award of custody to the party he preferred.)

AGE AND SEX OF THE CHILD. This factor constitutes the most frequently cited basis for making an award. Generally the context fits the tender-years doctrine. If awarding a boy to a father, the judge may indicate that the child was "of such an age as to require preparation for a career, which could best be accomplished by the father." Such wording is generally couched within the tenor of the best interest and welfare test.

THE CHILD'S PREFERENCE FOR ONE PARENT. This is frequently mentioned, and in some states, when a child reaches fourteen years of age the court *must* listen to the child's preference if he or she has one. This is not dispositive; it is merely one of many factors the court must consider in reaching its decision.

THE PARENT'S RELATIONSHIP WITH, AND DESIRE FOR, THE CHILD. Frequently mentioned, generally through remarks detailing who spent the most time with the child, who tended the child when he or she was ill, who was most active in the PTA or the Little League, and so forth. In reality, these considerations underlie all custody matters and probably should be the basis for custody awards rather than many of the others discussed.

THE RELIGION OF THE PARENTS. Often mentioned, but not usually in the sense of preferring one parent to another. The custodial parent has full power to religiously instruct the child as he or she wishes. Alternatively, if the court sees a particular religion as possibly endangering either child or society, such a religion may be an issue with regard to custody. A religion which required the child to participate in sexual intercourse with others, and a religion which required a child to miss one or more days of school each week were held to bar custody. On the other hand, a religion which prohibits blood transfusions, surgery, and other treatments, may not bar custody if the custodial parent will agree not to let the religion interfere with the child's medical care should the need arise.

PHYSICAL AND MENTAL FITNESS OF THE PARENT. This is a powerful factor. Age, as such, is not a factor, unless the parents are of considerably different ages. A father with some physical or mental disability is apt to lose custody. A mother with very serious physical or mental disabilities may also lose.

MORAL FITNESS. Formerly a favorite means for awarding children to the father. Moral unfitness of the mother was established if she was guilty of adultery, and the children could then easily be awarded to the father. Under the best interest and welfare test, however, moral unfitness is seldom used. In many jurisdictions, the considerations of what is in the best interest and welfare of the children must be confined to those things that demonstrably affect the children. The mere fact of a mother's adultery may not directly affect the children, and cannot be considered. In some states, *adverse impact* must be shown. If little Johnny sees mother in bed with a stranger, that *is not* adverse impact. If little Johnny is shocked or frightened to see mother in bed with a stranger, that *is* adverse impact, but how does one get such evidence to court? In a recent case, a father won custody away from his lesbian ex-wife when his teenage son described to the court his horror at finding his mother and another woman making love in his home.[11]

The difficulty of establishing adverse impact is increased by the tendency of the court to be lenient with the custodial parent. If the court wishes to award custody to the mother, and if the father has successfully shown the mother's drug addiction to have adverse effects on the children, the judge may still award the children to the mother, with the injunction that she give up drugs. In one case, an irate father moved to gain custody of his children away from the mother who had allowed her lesbian girlfriend to move in with her. Rather than change custody, the court made the mother move her lover out of the home. In another case, the father, who was the custodian, was accused of homosexuality by his former wife. While he admitted to having homosexual tendencies, he staunchly denied being homosexual. The court allowed him to keep the children, but required him not to entertain male visitors in his home.

DEATH OF A PARENT. If the wife dies before custody has been decided by the court, the husband's custodial rights to his children remain as they have always been—he has the sole care and custody of his children. If she dies *after* the court has ordered custody to her, the father must plead a change in circumstance and regain the custody of the children. This may be a problem where the mother has lived with the children and her parents for a long period of time. Upon the mother's death, father and grandparents have sometimes contested for custody, and sometimes the grandparents have won.

CUSTODIAL ANTE-NUPTIAL CONTRACTS. These contracts are sometimes advanced by fathers as a basis of receiving custody. Such a contract may be made at the insistence of a soon-to-be husband, who requires that the wife sign her rights to custody over to him in the event of a divorce as a condition of marriage. The courts disregard ante-nuptial contracts with respect to custody. Such agreements have no legal force.

A WELL-ESTABLISHED CUSTODY. This factor is a strong determinant of who will receive custody. The term refers to one parent having had sole care and custody of children for an extended period of time, at least a year and generally longer. In one case, a mother was awarded custody at the time of the divorce. Shortly thereafter, she left the child with the father while she took a vacation. When she returned from her vacation over a year later, the husband refused to yield up the boy. The court left the child with the father.

The reason underlying the absence of the missing parent may also be a factor. A mother who gives the children to the father for an extended period of time while she is hospitalized is less likely to lose custody than one who simply deserts her family or otherwise acts in a manner that flies in the face of the tender-years doctrine.

Probably of greater importance than the application of the well-established custody principle itself, is the fact that the father who has custody of his children for extended periods of time has the opportunity to demonstrate to the court that he is a capable father.

Traditional Custodial Arrangements

There are three commonly encountered custodial arrangements. The most common is *sole custody,* in which one parent is known as the "custodial parent" and the other has "reasonable rights to visitation." The second is termed *alternating custody,* and refers to situations in which the mother has the children for certain periods of the year and the father has them for the balance. Custody alternates in this fashion, year after year. Other terms are used to describe this form of custody in various jurisdictions. In one case, the mother was described as the "legal custodian" while the father was described as the "physical custodian." The mother was to have the children while the husband, who traveled extensively, was out of town. When he was in town, he was to have custody of the children. In some states, the term "co-custody" is used, and in others the term "joint custody" appears. Alternating custody is specifically forbidden in some states; in others, it is specifically accepted. The third custodial arrangement might be termed *splitting the children;* this refers to situations in which one parent is awarded custody of some of the children while the other parent is awarded the rest. "Joint custody" is sometimes used to describe this form of custody. Where the children are of close ages, the courts will not generally allow splitting the children between the parents. In some cases, where there are late teenage children and one or more very young children, for example, splitting the children might be permitted. More rarely, other forms of custody can be encountered.

Judicial Rights to Examination

In adjudicating a custody matter, the courts have the power to order examinations of the parties and the children. Such examinations may involve psychological, medical, or psychiatric evaluations. Guardians *ad litem* (temporary guardian) may be assigned to the case by the court, as may social workers, to conduct investigations of the homes and parties involved in the case. The parties are required to participate in such examinations when ordered by the court. In some jurisdictions it is legal for the investigator to render his report in secret to the judge, provided the parents give their permission. In other jurisdictions, secret reporting is illegal. On the whole, we feel that good judicial decisions can only be made if the judge has access to good information. However, there are a number of dangers implicit in the typical manner in which such examinations are conducted. These are addressed more completely below.

Practical Matters

The issue of custody is surrounded by a great body of law, much of it inconsistent. The confusion which results prevents even highly skilled lawyers from predicting how a case might turn out. Fortunately, the confusion can be sidestepped by dealing with custody in a very practical way.

The father must first address the decision of whether to fight for custody. If the answer is yes, he knows that the odds against his success are high, even if the mother is obviously of marginal quality as a parent. There are two avenues through which he may try to gain the custody of his children, both of which require a level of commitment resembling all-out warfare. Rather than undertake such extraordinary measures, some have argued that the father should do his best to hold the marriage together. That way the father has his children and his home, even if the home life is terrible. Keeping the marriage together for as long as possible also lets the children grow older, in the direction of the time where the children may have some say in the matter, and into ages where the tender-years doctrine is not so persuasive.

Of course, in many cases it is futile or undesirable to try to hold the marriage together. The two options are then: (1) to fight the traditional custody battle by preparing as strong a case as possible for presentation in trial; and (2) to apply nontraditional measures, which consist largely of techniques of escape and evasion.

The Traditional Custody Battle (Improved Version)

The issue of custody requires a different approach than that of a simple divorce, and there are a series of considerations that should underlie the entire scope of effort, from beginning to end. More tactical concepts appear in the pages that follow, and still more can be found elsewhere in this work, as well as in references and lawbooks we recommend. The strategic considerations, however, must be understood at the outset. They have less to do with specific acts than with the attitude of the father as he undertakes the fight to gain his children. Strategic concepts include the following:

- A custody fight is *always* fought in the courtroom. A lawyer must be found who is well experienced in trial. The lawyer would preferably be a specialist in child custody litigation, but such lawyers are rare; find the most experienced possible.
- The case to be developed is *constructive* in nature, building clear and factual evidence that the father is the superior custodian, and that the mother is lacking. This is in direct opposition to a *destructive* development, in which the husband attempts to derogate, shame, castigate, and otherwise bad-mouth his wife before the court. The court will be interested in why the wife is not the best custodian; the court will not be interested in your personal opinion of your wife.
- A winning custody case is always characterized by extraordinary thoroughness and attention to detail. Nothing is left undone, no avenue is left unexplored.
- A winning custody case is characterized by objectivity. The evidences presented by the father must be factual, clearly true, well corroborated, free of the taint of hatred for the wife. The arguments presented to the court must be characterized by extraordinary clarity and compelling completeness.
- In contrast to a divorce, in which data are gathered with respect to the parties and perhaps a co-respondent, a custody contest involves a greatly enlarged scope. Any place the child may live, any school the child may attend, any person who may touch, keep, feed, or care for the child is an object of attention. Much of the case may depend upon the history or character of the persons with whom the mother

leaves the child while she works; if defective in character, such persons weaken the mother's position even if she, herself, is not defective.

- Explorations of the character of "significant" people (the mother, her boyfriend, her parents and close relatives, babysitters she uses, et al.) are unassumingly thorough and attempt to construct a picture of the individual's past. This may include exploration for civil or criminal violations, dependency on drugs, driving fines and violations, medical problems, general reputation and character. To this end, police records, hospital records, credit bureau records, etc., are frequently explored.
- The winning custody case demonstrates through evidence a strong *history* of the father caring better for the children than the mother, and it demonstrates how, if father is awarded the children, they will *continue* to receive the benefits of his care in the immediate and distant future. The history is proved through witnesses, documents, photographs, and the like. The future is proved by demonstrating that the father has completely planned for the child's welfare, especially during those periods when he works, but at other times as well.
- Retention of a positive and dynamic attitude is essential to success. Even after you have experienced a losing skirmish, you can find something in it to exploit to your advantage. *Within every defeat there is a victory*. The winning father finds it.

The Eight Challenges

The father's first challenge is to *usurp the mothering role without relinquishing the role of father*. By whatever means available, he gradually begins taking on the responsibilities for all aspects of child care, including all domestic responsibilities, simultaneously "freeing" his wife from these responsibilities and binding the children to himself. If the wife is a lax or indifferent mother, such activities may be welcomed. Only if she is really bonded to the children is she likely to resent the intrusion into her domain. However, as time passes, the father's takeover becomes so complete that the children look to him for all their needs, thereby cutting the mother out of the picture, not only as the parent who does things for the children, but as the parent the children prefer.

To accomplish this, the father has to find ways to spend more time alone with the children. If mother belongs to an afternoon bridge club, father encourages her to go and enjoy herself; then he takes the children on an outing, or plays a game with them, or has a small party for them. He encourages his wife to take classes at night school, or to find a job, or to work full-time rather than part-time; such activities lessen her capability of demanding alimony and take her out of the home, thereby leaving the children with the father. Whenever there is a happening at the school, the father makes sure he is there, preferably to make himself known (by name) to the children's teachers as a concerned, friendly, interested, and interesting parent who is very much involved with his children. It is father who takes the children to the doctor, to the skating rink; it is father who thinks up delightful activities for the children; it is father who creates activities within the home which are at once rewarding and educational, or which promote the self-sufficiency of the children.

The father reads books on parenting and fathering, to become more skilled at the job of one-parent childrearing. Three such books are provided in the chapter notes. The book by Biller and Meredith is especially recommended.[12]

The second challenge is to *generate evidence for custody*. The father buys the children's clothes, and keeps and labels the sales receipts. He takes them to the doctor, and keeps and labels the receipts; he makes it a point to talk to the doctor so that the docor knows him on sight. He asks for special conferences with the children's teachers and discusses concerns over low marks in some subject; and perhaps, if his occupation is an interesting one, or if he has particular skills that might be useful in the classroom, he might offer to visit the classroom, to present a slide show, talk about his work, show the children a few magic tricks, or play a musical instrument. Father makes it a point to talk with the school's guidance counselors about the children's emotional or social development, or about concerns for the children's motivation in light of poor performance in some subject; he asks such people for their advice on how to improve the children's approach to their schooling. If the child has the slightest speech difficulty or "lip-laziness," the father contacts the school to see if special teaching is called for to facilitate speech development, and he monitors the child's progress through such therapy by contacting the special education instructor. The father may offer to teach a Sunday school class that the children attend; he may become an assistant in the local scout troop, and a standby coach of the Little League. When the children have a football game, the father is always there, cheering them on, bolstering their spirits when they lose, celebrating with them when they win. Later, these people—doctors, teachers, counselors, scoutmasters, pastors, Little League officials, and others—may be called to the witness stand in the father's behalf to demonstrate that it was the father, not the mother, who seemed interested in the children's welfare.

If the father has a girlfriend, he gives her up or takes measures to conceal the fact, since it might go against him in court if the relationship were brought up. He builds and documents a picture of himself as an excellent, all-around father, keenly interested in the moral, intellectual, emotional, and physical development of his children, and he works hard to spread this image as far as possible.

The third challenge is to *develop a list of reasons for why he should have custody.* Knowing that he can win only by being the obviously superior parent, he must be able to say on the witness stand, in simple, straightforward terms, why he is superior to the mother. He must be able to demonstrate to others that the mother is defective as a parent and that he is not. He cudgels his brain daily on this knotty problem, trying to turn up effective illustrations of how the mother has mismanaged the children, or has been too harsh with them, or has allowed a minor cut to become infected, or has failed to get the kids fed on time, or has failed to provide balanced meals, or has allowed the children to stay up too late, or has not gotten the children to school on time. He labors diligently to find additional illustrations of everything she does wrong, no matter how trivial or how significant, and he adds these to his growing list. Simultaneously, he works on his own good points, trying to set down in detail all the things he does for the children. If things between husband and wife are acrimonious, he makes it a point never to say anything bad about his wife in the presence of the children; in the presence of others he is observed instructing the children to be respectful and obedient toward their mother. He is alert for any signal that indicates that the mother is saying bad things about him in front of the children, and tries to establish witnesses who can be used to prove that she is trying to poison the minds of his children against him.

The fourth challenge is to *stay in the home with the children.* From the outset, he plans to keep himself in the house, and to keep the children with him. If husband and wife cannot live together, then he insists that it is she who must move out, but that the children must stay in their own home (never mentioning that they are then going to be in his sole custody) so that they can continue to attend their school, see their regular friends, and keep up their usual activities; he explains how important it is that the children be afforded every psychological advantage during these trying times of divorce, and that a dislocation from the neighborhood would take needed supports from them.

If he is lucky, the wife may become angry enough to try to teach the husband a lesson. She will simply leave the home and let the husband contend with the children for a while. That will put him in his place. So she leaves, and the father is the sole caretaker of the children, just as he wished. Father now faces the fifth challenge: *to get temporary custody*. As quickly as possible, he files a motion for custody *pendente lite*. The fact that his wife left the marital home is evidence that she is disinterested in the children (as would be said of him had he left); moreover, the father is concerned that the wife will try to remove the children from the home, which would be psychologically distressing to them because of their deep ties to friends and the neighborhood. If the wife has a boyfriend, the father complains that he fears she will move the children in to live with her lover, and that this would be an improper atmosphere for the children. If he is extremely lucky, the father will receive custody *pendente lite*. This represents a great victory, for it guarantees him the undivided custody of his children during the entire period between now and the trial, as well as the right to prevent his wife from entering the house. This leaves him in command of the books, papers, and financial records of the family, as well as the family possessions. "The courts are reluctant to disturb a well-established custody," rings in his ears. He will have tried to obtain custody *pendente lite* as early as possible, in order to give himself as much time with the children as possible; having obtained temporary custody, he now introduces every possible delay into the proceedings (without the opposition being able to show the judge that his delays were intentional) in order to stretch out the period of his sole custody.

If he loses custody *pendente lite* to his wife, he seeks to turn the situation to his advantage by exploiting the fact of the wife's temporary custody. During this period he carefully but unobtrusively monitors his wife, her visitors, her activities, her housekeeping, and the manner in which she deals with the children.

He looks for periods in which they are unattended, or when the house seems to be a shambles, or for gentlemen callers whose reputations may be imperfect, and he documents, documents, documents. A stranger knocks on her door, "Is this the Jones residence?" "No," answers the wife. The stranger thanks her and leaves; later he describes to the judge the mess he saw within. Quiet examinations of the care the children receive are obtained by talking with the neighbors. If things are truly bad within, if the children are being left unattended, the father notifies his lawyer, who calls for a social welfare investigation to be performed without prior warning. Their report later appears in court.

He also demands as precise an accounting of how the mother spends the child support money as he can get. If there is any misappropriation of the monies, he quietly but persuasively documents her squandery. Judges do not like mothers who spend the child support checks on luxuries for themselves.

The sixth challenge is *to increase the pressures on his wife.* If the father has been either smart or lucky, it will have been he who filed for divorce. If no-fault grounds were available, he probably will have taken this approach since it is the least harmful approach for everyone. His wife may be known as the defendant, but that may have only mildly ruffled her feathers, since "no-fault" removes much of the sting from the status of "defendant." However, if there are other grounds available in the jurisdiction, the father now gives these serious consideration. Of the available grounds, which one comes closest to meeting the criteria: (1) that a plausible case could be built on such a ground, and (2) that the proofs of the case would involve factors relating to adverse impact on the children? If the wife is involved in an affair, perhaps adultery meets the criteria. If extreme cruelty is available, perhaps the way she slaps the children around is but one aspect of her cruelty toward her husband. If he is lucky enough to have an available ground that meets these criteria, he next modifies his claim or counterclaim to include the new "fault" ground in addition to the old "no-fault" ground. This is a relatively simple matter for him, but it will require a lot of work on her part to prepare a refutation of the charges. Unless she prepares carefully, the proof of the ground will imply that facts against her custody also will have been proved. If the wife is the defendant in the case, she now begins to feel the full impact of that term, and the losing psychology begins to take its toll.

By now, the battle for custody will be in full swing. For the first time, the wife will feel threatened with the loss of her children. If the husband has temporary custody, he allows his wife limited but reasonable visitation, firmly insisting that she live up to the terms of the court order; if she violates the order, he warns her only once that the next violation will bring about a complaint to the court. If she violates the order a second time, he carries out the complaints, hoping to document her willingness to break the law.

If adultery is charged against the wife, the lover is next deposed. Both wife and lover will find this an unpleasant and stressful experience. But the husband does not stop there. It may be possible, depending on the outcome of the deposition, to charge the lover with interference with the family, or to charge both of them with criminal adultery. The husband applies every means to cause his wife to spend her financial resources, to keep events moving faster than she can cope with them, to keep her constantly shocked, threatened, and off balance. If he is successful, the wife's capacity to resist will be badly deteriorated well before the trial. Her development of her side of the case will have been erratic and incomplete, because of the need to deal with oncoming problems, and because her stresses were so great that she couldn't think. She may have developed other psychological responses to the stresses: insomnia, fatigue, ulcers, depression. Kept in this condition up to the point of trial, she may come unglued on the witness stand, shouting and screaming accusations at her husband across the courtroom, thereby demonstrating that she is ill-equipped to handle children under conditions of stress.

Sometime during the course of meeting these challenges, probably within a month of the trial, the father will face the seventh challenge: *to control the development of expert psychological data.* In many, if not most custody battles, psychiatrists, psychologists, social workers, and others become involved. There seem to be three situations which give rise to the involvement of such people. First, the wife may make some statement against the husband, or may set events in motion to jeopardize the husband's image as a psychologically sound, loving, capable father. The father may feel that he must develop a defense against such happenings. Therefore he attempts to gather psychological evidence to support his contention that he is as he says he is, not as she says he is. Submitting one's self to interviews by psychologists or psychiatrists, taking psychological tests, having psychologists or social workers visit the home, and so forth, are means to this end. In one case, for example, the wife contacted a child welfare bureau and accused the husband of child abuse. Even though the charge was entirely fabricated, the child welfare bureau conducted an investigation of the father and the children. While the investigators failed to discover any evidence of child abuse, their report was less than glowing. Such a report, having been prepared by "expert" state officials, can carry great weight in the courtroom. The father resorted to psychological experts to vindicate himself from the statements made in this report.

The second situation that seems to call for psychological data-gathering arises from the husband's feeling the need for additional facts in support of his case; if he can demonstrate that he is psychologically intact and emotionally well involved with his children through the introduction of psychological evidence, he may add relevant and positive data to his presentation in court.

The third situation is brought about by the court. We mentioned earlier that the court has the power to order investigations into custodial matters in most jurisdictions. Where the courts have such power, they frequently exercise it in cases of contested custody to gather "objective" third-party evidence for the decision they must make. Most frequently, such data are gathered by social workers belonging to a child welfare unit of the state, or by a guardian *ad litem* who has been appointed to protect the legal interests of the children and to distinguish the interests of the children from those of the parents. The court can also order psychological and/or medical evaluations of the parties and/or the children.

The first two situations are adversarial in nature; the husband gathers (or causes others to gather) evidence that he can use in court to support his case or to destroy his wife's case. The third situation is not adversarial; a third-party evaluator enters the court almost in the sense of *amicus curiae* (friend of the court). Such parties theoretically have an unbiased initial position from which they are to develop a recommendation for custody in the light of their investigations.

In reality, all these experts will tend to take a biased approach to their tasks. Bias is inherent in their training and tends to predispose their thinking and actions along certain paths, though without awareness or intention. The seventh challenge for the husband is *to detect and document these biases,* and to modify the approaches that the experts use so that their investigations will be fair and honest.

In some cases, this may involve nothing more than exercising a little thought in the selection of expert witnesses. For example, the husband may have been accused of mental instability by his wife, and he may wish to generate evidence to counteract this false allegation. To whom does he turn? To a psychologist or a psychiatrist, right? Right. Of the two, the psychiatrist is the better source because his profession is better respected by the courts, and his testimony will tend to have more impact. Now suppose the wife has accused the husband of being unable to understand and deal with the needs of small children. To whom does he turn? A psychologist or a psychiatrist, right? Wrong. He should turn to proven good parents and get them to observe how well he performs. Expert parents can be expert witnesses and they don't cost much for their work. The psychologist also will be useful, *if* he is trained in developmental psychology or child psychology. The worst choice of the three for the husband is the psychiatrist, because his or her psychiatric training is likely to be influenced by the theories of Sigmund Freud, which see the mother as the source of conscience development in the young child. A parallel can be noted between Freudian theory and the tender-years doctrine; in fact, Freudian theory has been used as a justification for the doctrine for the past forty years or so. Fortunately for men, many aspects of Freudian theory which relate to custody issues have been challenged in recent years by psychological research. Unfortunately for men, many psychiatrists and psychologists are not yet aware of how seriously Freudian theory has been damaged by such research, and they still believe as they were taught. Thus the father seeking custody will avoid if possible being evaluated by Freudians.

To find fair and unbiased investigators, it may be necessary to *interview the experts* before they are hired. Three things should be established by such an interview: first, whether the expert has the needed qualifications for the job; second, what the father wants the expert to do for him; and third, whether the expert is willing to do the job, and, if he is not, whether he can recommend another expert for the job.

In conducting the interview, the father must make sure that the expert understands the adversarial nature of the data to be generated; the expert's primary obligation will be to find good things to say about the father. (The other side has the responsibility to find out the bad things through cross-examination.) The father should be apprised of all findings, good and bad, and he and his lawyer should decide whether the expert witness should ultimately be used. The expert witness hired by the father should not feel compelled to produce a clear, balanced picture of his findings unless it is the father's intention that he should do so. In adversarial actions, the court expects each side to "put its best foot forward" and each side has a right to do so.

Court-ordered investigations, because of their "disinterested third-party" nature, frequently prevent either party from selecting those who are to conduct the investigation. Nonetheless, there are things that can be done to improve the quality of such investigations. First, the father should demand a formal statement of the investigator's academic and experiential qualifications for conducting such investigations (for example, a personal résumé), and these should be available for study prior to the investigation. The mere fact of a person's being employed by a child welfare bureau, or licensed as a psychiatrist, is no assurance that his background relates to the investigative role assigned by the court. There are three advantages to having such background information on the assigned investigator: (1) if the investigator is unqualified, a bid can be made to replace him; (2) the background information makes it possible for the father to undertake verification of the investigator's past (perhaps to recover his college grades or the courses he has studied, or to interview people involved in the last few cases the investigator worked on); (3) such information provides avenues for attacking the witness on the stand if his work is unsatisfactory.

Second, the father should insist on a formal *written* report of the findings, to be submitted simultaneously to the court and both parties at least ten days prior to trial. This prevents surprises. Further, the report should be specified to contain the methods used to conduct the investigation (psychological tests, specific diagnostic procedures, interview methods, and so forth), the places visited, the people interviewed or examined, the questions asked of each and their responses thereto, and a statement of all findings and conclusions in the investigation. This level of detail allows weaknesses and strengths in the approaches to be brought out in trial. Thus equipped, the father will be able to refute ill-founded statements and destroy the credibility of an incompetent investigator.

Third, the father should deny any attempt to keep certain data privy to the judge. No data which may persuade the court should be allowed to reach the judge unless the source of that information can be put on the witness stand and examined. This also applies to situations where a child may be interviewed by the judge in private; do not disallow the judge his conference, but assure that the entire conversation is either tape-recorded or that a witness is present throughout the conference for later examination on the witness stand.

Fourth, the father should insist to the court that the investigation be conducted so as to render direct and objective comparisons between the parties regarding their suitability as custodians. Lack of insistence on comparability and objectivity is perhaps the greatest weakness in current procedure. In a custody trial, the entire process is directed theoretically toward determining which parent is best for the children; this seems to require the most direct possible comparisons between mother and father to be made in the most objective manner possible, yet this is almost never attempted. Lacking comparability in the evidence presented, the courts are forced to compare apples and oranges to attain a decision; lacking objectivity, biases in viewpoint and methodology are transmitted through the data to the judge.

Objective psychological tests are characterized by the fact that the results would tend to be the same no matter who administered the test, so long as it was administered under reasonably standard conditions. Frequently, the tests are self-administered with test questions printed in a booklet, answers recorded on an answer sheet, scoring accomplished by use of scoring keys (applied by scoring machines, computers, or people), and interpretation of results made by trained experts or, in a few cases, by computer. In such tests, there is little way for a biased investigator to affect the results. The MMPI (Minnesota Multiphasic Personality Inventory), used to diagnose some forms of mental abnormality, is an objective test which has been used in custody cases.

Such tests are probably more objective than *projective psychological tests,* such as the Thematic Apperception Test (TAT) which requires personal administration, subjective scoring, and subjective interpretation of the results, even though a trained expert may not be particularly subjective in his approach.

At the bottom of the heap, we would classify the uncontrolled interview, where the investigator simply looks things over, asks whatever questions come to mind, and subjectively formulates his opinion of what the situation is. Still, the uncontrolled interview is probably the most frequently applied method for gathering data for presentation in court.

While we express a preference for the more objective approaches because they tend to reduce the impact of personal biases in the investigator, it must be understood that no single psychological test, method, or procedure is infallible. To get a clear look, several different methods should be applied, even if they vary across the scale of objectivity as a result.

Comparability is an absolute must, and *comparability can only be attained by getting the same kind of information from both the husband and the wife*. If an investigator administers a psychological test to the husband, the investigator should also administer the same test to the wife. If the investigator asks a question of the husband, he should also ask that identical question of the wife. If the investigator makes up a rating scale to apply to evaluating the wife's housekeeping, he should apply that same rating scale to the husband's housekeeping.

Objectivity and comparability sometimes can be enhanced by separating those who gather data from those who interpret them. For example, suppose the same person administered the MMPI to both the husband and the wife. That person would know which test answer sheet belonged to which party. If, however, he handed the answer sheets to a second party to score and interpret the tests, the second party might be kept in ignorance of which answer sheet belonged to whom. His subsequent interpretation would therefore probably not be contaminated by a personal disposition to favor either the man or the woman.

The eighth challenge to the father is *to deal effectively with the judge*. Both the father and his lawyer should be alert to any behavior on the part of the judge which seems inappropriate or which seems to depart from sound courtroom procedure; this could give them a basis for appeal if the case is lost. In some cases, the father may wish to argue with the judge, not to become involved in a fight, but to insist on a better approach than the one the judge has suggested. The father's lawyer may have to work up a little nerve for this, since it can be very risky if not well handled. Alternatively, if it later develops that the father loses the case as a direct result of the judge's refusal to allow certain evidence to be admitted, or to allow valid evidence to be collected, the basis for an appeal may be at hand. In certain cases it can make a difference if the judge thinks that the father is sufficiently litigous to appeal the decision if he doesn't like the way the judge behaves.

The final result of rising to these challenges probably will be that the father will lose custody. He may be in a position to know this early in the trial, or even before the trial begins. Somewhere along the way he may get an offer from the other side, offering him liberal and reasonable visitation rights in return for dropping the custody battle. They may indicate that to continue the exercise would be wasteful of time and money, especially money, and that they are prepared to be *very* reasonable. After all, the reasoning will go, you should realize that a sound and active parent such as yourself can have a strong, positive influence on the children's growth through the exercise of visitation rights. Such visitation would not require you to compromise your job, yet would afford you every opportunity to be with your children, since they are willing to be very liberal.

Chances are that you will ultimately have to accept such an offer, or will have terms of visitation dictated by court order. But at this point, be cautious. The liberality they refer to, that huge amount of time they plan to make available to you, may be nothing more than the application of a well-proven tactical maneuver: mollify the husband with references to generous visitation time, and so get him to drop his demand for custody. If the husband agrees, the custody matter is concluded. Then, and only then, does the husband see what the other side actually means by visitation time: one weekend a month and one major holiday each year. If the wife moves out of state, he may lose even that. For this reason, the husband should make no concessions until the other side provides, in writing, the proposed terms of a visitation schedule.

If the visitation schedule they offer is suitable, the father may wish to drop the custody battle and save some time and money. Alternatively, if the visitation schedule is unsatisfactory, there may be a small chance that the husband could do better by fighting the custody battle to its conclusion. If the other side is perfectly sure of winning the case, they are making an offer for visitation for only two reasons: (1) you are a nice guy and your former wife doesn't want to see you hurt, and (2) they want to preserve your finances in order to have more left for your wife to spend. If these motives do not fit the case, the only remaining possibility we can think of is that their case may not be as good as you think it is. Perhaps they are afraid of what you can do in the courtroom. You might wish to probe this possibility in a communication to the other side:

> I am in receipt of your offer regarding a visitation schedule; however, the offer was not exactly in keeping with my serious determination that the children should have the benefit of the best custodian. My case has been carefully prepared to demonstrate that I am in the best interest and welfare of my children, and I am prepared to try my case before the court. However, I am a reasonable man, and will be willing to listen to any reasonable discussion you may wish to advance.

Such a communication seeks to explore whether they may wish to change their proposed visitation schedule dramatically in your favor. If they do, you can infer that they are concerned about what you might be able to do in the courtroom. If they do not, you will have learned nothing, but will have given nothing away. The choice of whether to fight or to yield is then, as it nearly always is, solely yours.

The Nontraditional Approach to Custody

Most fathers are unaware of the fact that until a court has ordered a change in the custodial rights of the parents (that is, until a *court order* has been issued), both parents have undivided and complete custodial rights in the children. This means that it is legal for either a mother or a father to take the children wherever she or he wishes. It is legal for a father to take the children away from the mother and move with them to Europe, and it is legal for her to do the same. It is legal to do so even if the other parent strenuously objects.

However, once a court issues an order which prevents the children from being removed from the state (or other locale), or once the court has made an order for permanent or temporary custody, then the custodial rights of the parents are accordingly modified. To act against the terms and conditions of the order is illegal and actionable; the court can respond to violations through its contempt power which, as we have earlier noted, is a fearsome power indeed. He who violates a court order does so at his peril.

The essence of the nontraditional approach is to take the children into a different jurisdiction, leaving the wife behind. In short, the husband takes the children and scrams. This is not so simple as it may seem. The first hurdle is to prevent the wife from following the husband into the new jurisdiction and filing for custody there. If she does so, the planning and expense of moving will have been for nothing. The husband will face approximately the same risk of losing the children in the courts of the new jurisdiction as he would have in the old, except that the new judge may not like a father who is unwilling to trust the courts.

To prevent their wives from locating them, many fathers have changed their names and the names of their children, changed their occupations and jobs, and fired their lawyers. Under the common law, a change of name is legal so long as the purpose is not to defraud. Lawyers are fired in order that the wife cannot seek an order for custody by serving the husband through the person of his lawyer.[13]

Having successfully pulled off a disappearing act, at least for the time being, the father faces the second hurdle. He must try to get an order for custody, either temporary or permanent, and do so as quickly as possible. The presence of such an order can effectively block procedures of summary judgment such as *habeas corpus*.[14] To obtain an *ex parte* order for custody is difficult except for a select few conditions (such as when the wife has moved, leaving no forwarding address, so that she cannot be served notice of the pending action), but sometimes one can find a judge who is willing to hear a custody matter even when neither the father nor the children are residents of the state.

A father might choose to move to one of the civil law countries in Europe such as Italy or Spain (as opposed to the common law countries such as the United States or England), thereby presenting a variety of difficulties to the wife. Among these are the difficulty and expense of trying to locate the husband by long distance, the expense of hiring reputable private detectives, the jurisdictional complications, and the expense of living abroad during the suit. At each step of the way the wife is forced to expend her financial resources, and sometimes her resources are simply not up to the task.

In the end, the nontraditional approach serves to generate time, preferably three years or more, during which the children are in the sole care and custody of the father. During this period the children grow more strongly attached to the father and less attached to the mother, and the custody becomes more established as time continues to pass. Even while a judge may seriously frown on a father who has vanished with the children for five or six years, he may well keep custody with the father in order not to damage the children. But on the other hand, the judge is entitled to consider all relevant details of the custody case, and in arriving at his decision he will certainly consider how the father came to be the single parent. If the case ever gets into the courtroom.

A Self-Evaluation of Issues Involved in Custody

A father who is certain that he does not want custody of his children has made his decision. For others, it may be fruitful to approach the decision from the viewpoint of an extensive self-evaluation. There are really two parts to the decision. The first part is to come to grips with the question in such a way as to fully understand the implications of the decision. The second part is to decide who is really the better parent, and the better custodian for the children. Having completed a thorough self-evaluation, if the decision is that the mother would be better for the children, bite the bullet and let them go to her.

We present below a lengthy set of questions designed to aid one's evaluation of himself as a parent and as a person. The questions should objectify the father's perceptions of himself and his wife as parents, and should clarify the relationships between himself and the children. Should the decision be to fight for custody, the questions may aid by revealing strengths and weaknesses in one's position.

As with any self-evaluation, one benefits in proportion to the effort expended. We suggest that several hours be devoted to the task, spread out over a week or so, and that one address the questions by writing out the answers. This should be done in private, and the written responses held securely.

The questions are presented in numbered clusters. It is neither necessary nor desirable that each question in a cluster be addressed. Instead, a general answer should be written which addresses the theme of the cluster of questions. One should write quickly, keeping the pen moving, and formulating one's answer as one writes. Over-thinking could prevent bringing inconsistencies of logic to the surface. While writing, be attuned to inner feelings that occur in response to the material; attend to issues under consideration where the pen stops moving. Such feelings and behaviors may be suggestive of sensitive issues, lack of data, lack of objectivity, etc.

The questions are not intended to force a decision regarding custody, but, rather, to stimulate productive thought about the primary considerations involved. Having completed one's response, one should review the work as a whole with a view toward assessing what has been learned. It is the learning that is fuel for the decision.

Thoughts about yourself

1. When other people think about you, what do they think? How do they see you? What is your image to your friends, your co-workers, your boss, your children?
2. What are your life goals? What do you want to be ten, twenty, and thirty years from now? Are you currently moving in that direction? Are you dedicated to a life of expanding your horizons? Are you comfortable as you now are? Pretend you are twenty years older than you actually are; write yourself a letter and mail it back in time to the present, to give yourself some advice regarding how you are doing things wrong and how you might improve what you are doing.
3. How do you now see yourself as a father? How dedicated are you to the role and its responsibilities? Do you feel you are an effective father? How might you be more effective? What fathering things do you do very well compared to other fathers you know?
4. How well would you work out as a combination father and mother? What mothering functions would give you difficulty? Why do you feel this way? Would your investment of self toward your own life goals interfere with the combined father/mother role of the single custodian? Or are they in harmony?

5. Imagine you have lost your children in custody; how does this make you feel? How would you deal with these feelings?

Your plans and concerns for your children

1. Are you satisfied with your child's progress in school? How would you like to see his performance improved? Is he placing too much emphasis on some subjects compared to others? Is his performance in keeping with his abilities? How far would you like to see him go in school?
2. What would you like him to be when he grows up? What kinds of occupations do you envision as being good candidates for his consideration? For a girl, do you consider it best that she plan for a working future, or a housewife/mother future?
3. How do you feel about a boy being taught to cook, clean, sew, etc.? How do you feel about a girl being taught to repair appliances, replace broken windows, use hand tools? Why do you feel this way?
4. How about the child's friendship relations? Does he have a sufficient number of friends? How do you know? What are their names? Does he seem to get along well with them, or are there unpleasant differences? Is he a central member of the group, or is he a tag-along? Does he seem to make friends easily, or does he have a difficult time?
5. How about opposite-sex relationships? What are their names? Are there girlfriends/boyfriends in the picture? Is the child at ease with age mates of the opposite sex? Are there signs of wallflowerism?
6. Interest patterns: What kinds of things does the child like to do? How about scholastic interests? Is the child curious? About what kinds of things? Does the child enjoy manipulative activities, taking things apart, putting things together, building things, etc.? Does the child undertake such activities on his own, or does he have to be coaxed into them? What kinds of activities does he initiate by himself? Does he like sports? As a participant or a spectator? What kinds of things does the child dislike doing? What school subjects, if any, does the child like/dislike? What kinds of games does the child play with his age mates? Are these intellectual, or problem-solving games? Competitive games? Games involving a high level of whole-body activity? Games involving fast reaction time? Games involving manual speed and

dexterity? How does the child amuse himself when alone? Reading? What kinds of things does he read? Mysteries? Animal stories? Adventure? Hero stories? Romances? Factual material?

7. Emotional development: Does the child seem to express emotions which are appropriate to his age and circumstances? Are his behaviors appropriate to his emotions? Does the child seem balanced in his emotions? Is he optimistic in outlook? Are there depressed periods, moods which seem to last too long? What seems to cause such periods? What seems to modify such moods? Are you a capable modifier?
8. Problem areas: Are there any problem areas which currently exist? What are these? What can you do to overcome these problems, or to help overcome them? Are you currently working against such problems? To whom can you turn for additional assistance if needed? Is this the best you can do? What more might be done? Why have you not been doing more? Is money necessary to solve some of these problems? If so, do you have adequate financial resources? If not, what might you do to bring more money to bear on the problem? Or, what other things might you do to get around a money problem?
9. Comparing your plans and those of the child: Review the child's performance and progress, his preferences and interests, his social characteristics—and compare these with the kinds of things you feel he/she should be aiming for, that you want him/her to be developing toward. Are they in harmony? Is there current conflict over such matters? How do you think the conflict can be resolved? By dealing with it directly? By letting the child grow out of it? By directly ignoring it? If there is no present conflict, might there be in the future? How will this be resolved when it occurs? What can you do to minimize or solve the conflict? What can you do to bring the child toward an understanding so as to alleviate or remove the conflict?

Your activities and relationship with your child

1. Sole custody situations: Have you had the children solely in your care for an extended period of time, say, two weeks or more when your wife was not available to care for them? In caring for, or dealing with, the child, what problems

arose? How were these dealt with? What would you do differently if you were to have the children for an equal period of time in the near future? Did the housework get done properly? Did the children behave properly? Were there discipline problems? Who fixed the meals? You? The children? Was the quality of food good? Was the diet balanced? Was there a reliance on convenience foods, including frozen main dishes or TV dinners? Who did the housework? How was the laundry handled? Was there ironing? If so, who did it? You? Were standards of hygiene kept up throughout this period, or did hygiene and sanitation slip during your wife's absence? Did the normal activities of the children continue on schedule, or did some of them have to be dropped because you lacked time to attend to them? Did the children always get to school on time? Who provided transportation for the children? How was your job affected by your increased homemaking activity? Were you less able to devote yourself to the work? Was your work criticized as a result, by either co-workers or superiors? How did you feel about such criticism? Did you have to take any time off from work? Did you suffer a drop in income? Did you find it hard to schedule and perform the activities of both home and job during this period? Did things run smoothly, or were there rough spots? If there were rough spots, what were they, what caused them, how might they have been avoided, how were they corrected?

2. In general: What kind of relationship do you have with your child? Is it a warm relationship? A loving one? Does your child imitate your behavior? In what respects? How does this make you feel? Are you proud of your child? In what way? What, if anything, does your child do which especially pleases you? What, if anything, do you do which pleases, delights, amuses your child? In the past twenty-four hours, how many opportunities did you have to praise or compliment the child? What did the child do which warranted it? Did you praise or compliment him for it? In the past twenty-four hours, how many opportunities did you have to correct or criticize the child's behavior? What did he do, and did you criticize him for it? When you criticize, do you explain what you don't like and also explain how you would prefer things to be—is it constructive criticism? When you punish your child, or discipline him, how do you

do it? A stern talking-to? A good bawling-out? A spanking? A whipping with a switch or a belt? Sending him to his room? Taking away his privileges? Giving him the silent treatment? Does the child seem resentful long after he has been disciplined? How do you feel about yourself in light of your responses to this question?

3. Special activities: Within the past ten days, what (nonroutine) thing have you done with your child which was educational (in any sense you wish to apply) for him? Within the past ten days, what special thing have you done with him that was recreational? Within the past ten days, what special thing have you done that was social? Within the past ten days, what special thing have you done to provide an experience that he would not normally have? When you undertake special activities of your own, especially those around the home, do you always plan for a way to have the child participate in the activity with you? Do you make it a point to involve him with you in activities to train him in self-sufficiency (how to make repairs, how to handle domestic responsibilities, etc.)? How do you feel about yourself as a parent in light of these responses?

Who, yourself or your wife, provides the greatest direct support of the following activities for the children or their welfare: The PTA; scouts; religious events; charitable activities; good-neighbor activities; taking the children to movies or drive-ins; to plays; to the dentist; the doctor; arranging get-togethers between your children and others from school or the neighborhood; taking care of a sick child at home; taking children to the zoo; to museums; to special children's events; to the circus; to the library?

Who, yourself or your wife, is the better parent, all things considered? How does this make you feel about yourself? What parenting things do you do better than she does? What parenting things does she do better than you do? What parenting things does she do that you do not do? What does she do that bears adversely on her parenting? What bears adversely on your parenting? What would you have to do to do these things better than she does? In which of these areas is the potential greatest in terms of preparing the child for adulthood?

If you were to win custody of the children, how would you function as a single parent? How would you schedule and execute all the necessary activities? Where would difficulties most likely arise? Would your job be a problem? How would you handle each difficulty? Do you have resources sufficient to the task? If you are the custodial parent, the children will occupy more than twice the amount of your time they now require; where can you find that kind of time? Are your thoughts regarding problems and solutions realistic? Are they within your physical, financial, and intellectual capabilities? What other resources can you bring to bear on whatever problems might arise? After the divorce, do you think you might someday remarry? Will you have difficulty finding a suitable woman if you have custody of the children? Would you insist that a new wife take on many of the mothering responsibilities for your children? Should she love your children? Why do you think she should love your children? If she is not to be responsible for much of the welfare of your children, how are you going to prevent her from being saddled by such responsibilities? If you do not remarry, and if you have custody of your children, how will you deal with your own problems of sexual deprivation? Will you live celibate? If not, will you entertain women in your home with the children? Will you take them to bed there? If so, will you try to buffer such activities from the children? If you seek the company of women away from your home, how will the children be taken care of during your absence?

As a result of performing these exercises: What have you learned about yourself? What have you learned about each of your children? What have you learned about yourself as a parent? What have you learned about things you should strive to improve? What have you learned about parenting weaknesses in your wife? What have you learned about the difficulties that lie ahead if you become the sole custodian?

7

Find a Good Lawyer

YOU MAY not need a good lawyer. If you are certain that the divorce will not become contested in any respect, if you and your wife have already come to the necessary agreements, if there is no possibility of trouble, then you do not need a good lawyer. You need the cheapest lawyer you can find. Call a few of them by telephone and ask what they charge for processing an uncontested, simple divorce. Choose the cheapest, just as long as he is competent to fill out and file the proper forms. Most lawyers are.

Alternatively, your situation may be not quite so rosy. If so, you may need a very good lawyer. There are seven methods which can be used to find him. The first is to pick up the telephone directory and turn to the yellow pages under the heading "Lawyers" or "Attorneys." The limited advertising that lawyers are permitted makes this a poor method. It provides little guidance in finding a lawyer who is skilled in the practice of domestic relations law.

The second method is to telephone the local or state bar association. Asking the person who answers the telephone to name a lawyer in your area who is especially skilled in divorce problems will generally draw a blank, but it is worth trying.

The third method is to go to a lawyer, any lawyer, and ask him the following question: "If you were not to be my lawyer, whom would you recommend to take my case?" If he equivocates by such statements as, "Well, they're all pretty good," or, "Well there's Lawyer A, and Lawyer B, and Lawyer C, and . . ." (running through the list of all local lawyers), then you definitely do not want this lawyer. He is not being responsive to your needs. But if he keeps his recommendations to one or two or perhaps three others, write their names down, then visit these lawyers and ask the same question. After interviewing a few lawyers, a picture should emerge—the lawyers whose names are frequently given as being good are apt to be good. The method is a good one, though it may overlook a crackerjack lawyer in a nearby town; you may be given only the names of the best ones in the in-group of your immediate locale. The method is also time-consuming, and, since you will have to pay something to each lawyer you interview, the expense may be high. Even so, the cost may be worth it, especially if your case is a difficult one.

The fourth method is to approach one or more of the judges who sit cases in divorce and custody. If yours is a contested case, try to locate those judges who try contested cases. The court clerk can probably identify the judges for you. After obtaining the identities of the appropriate judges, ask the clerk the names of the lawyers who most frequently and most successfully try divorce cases. Then approach the judges, one at a time, and, without explaining your case at all (the judges you talk to may include the one who will try your case), ask each judge to name those lawyers who are most frequently successful in preparing and trying cases in divorce (and/or custody) before him. The judges will frequently sidestep the question, or refuse to answer outright, for they don't wish to recommend against any lawyer. However, if you can get a straight answer, and if the answer is confirmed across several judges, you know you have some good input. This approach takes guts and time, but it is relatively inexpensive.

The fifth method is that of lawyer referral from friends, neighbors, relatives, and acquaintances. This is one of the most frequently applied methods, and it is also the least useful. If the individual's experience with his lawyer was pleasant, the lawyer will be seen as sharp, honest, and capable. If the experience was not pleasant, the lawyer will be seen as an incompetent shyster.

The sixth method is to locate and contact a men's rights organization, if there is one in your area (see Appendix C in the back of this book for a listing). Such organizations frequently compile dossiers on the lawyers in their area, showing their histories of success and failure in the preparation and presentation of cases. They may also know something about the performance of various judges in their locale. We do not know how complete, how accurate, or how effective such organizations are, but a number of men who contacted men's rights groups have reported favorable results.

The seventh method is to telephone the dean of the nearest law school in your state. Ask the dean to recommend a good lawyer for you. We know of one case in which this approach identified the *only* lawyer in the whole state who restricted his practice to domestic relations law. We know of another case in which a wife who had a terrible case was represented by this same lawyer, whose prestige was so great that the judge was apparently afraid to question anything he said; in consequence, the judge pooh-poohed every point made by the husband, regardless of its importance, and eagerly agreed with everything propounded by the prestigious lawyer, regardless of its triviality. The wife won a sweeping victory (and her husband roundly lost), despite the fact that she literally had no case.

You, of course, are not constrained to use only one of the above methods; we encourage you to use all of them. But put less reliance on the impressions of friends, relatives, and acquaintances than on other methods, and do not believe that the first lawyer you contact is the best, unless it finally turns out that way.

By applying these procedures you will be able to narrow the field down somewhat, to reduce the number of lawyers under serious consideration. In the winnowing process, delete from consideration any lawyer who is a personal friend. Your lawyer, as your doctor, should not be emotionally involved in your problems or he may lose a needed objectivity regarding your case. Moreover, it may become necessary for you to fire your lawyer (sometimes because he isn't performing properly, sometimes for a tactical reason such as halting the progress of your case in order to gain a temporal advantage). Many people find it difficult to fire a personal friend. If your lawyer-friend is knowledgeable about your case, you can always call him as a witness. You do not need, nor do you want him as your lawyer.

Your goal should be to assess the field of available lawyers in your area and to determine which is *best for your purposes*. Good lawyers are rare, especially if you are facing a contested divorce. It is sheer folly to fail to check thoroughly. Such a thorough check must involve a face-to-face interview with each lawyer who might be acceptable.

Interviewing the Lawyer

There are both tactical and strategic goals to be attained through the face-to-face interview. The overall strategic goal is the determination of whether *this* lawyer is *the* lawyer for your case. You will be associating with him for a year or more, he will spend a lot of your money, and some assurance is needed that your decision is a proper one. Regardless of how you feel about any lawyer, unless time is extremely pressing (and it almost never is), do not make the decision until at least a full day after the interview. Give yourself a little cooling-off period. Lawyers are terribly persuasive and can blind you with empty words which seem like powerful statements. After the interview, try to summarize what happened. Try to write it down on paper, to put it into words. Try to describe what he said, what you said, and then try to see if it makes sense. Or did he neatly sidestep the issues, provide you with empty arguments, try to snow you with fancy legal doubletalk? Having read at least the previous chapters of this book, you will have some understanding of legal language and will probably be able to tell if he is trying to snow you.

When you talk to a lawyer, first tell him your name and why you are there. Tell him that you intend to file for divorce against your wife, or that she is filing against you. If you have been served, show him the papers and give him a little time to read them. *Be sure to get them back!* Make clear that you are looking for a lawyer, that you have not decided whom to select, that, in any event, you will not make that decision today.

Avoid "legalese" in your language. Don't talk in terms of grounds, defenses, marital fault, extreme mental cruelty, and so forth. If you are filing against your wife, indicate what she has done that you feel is so bad it warrants a divorce. Describe this in summary form, in terms of her chaotic housekeeping and her affairs with other men, giving the lawyer an overview of the situation you are dealing with. Let the lawyer use the legal terminology. By doing so, you invite him to snow you, for you give him no insight into your now considerable understanding of the law relating to divorce. If he tries to snow you, you will not wish to hire him, since you won't know whether you can trust him to level with you in the future.

If your wife is filing against you, or if you can anticipate that she will counterclaim against your complaint, then confide to the lawyer *something* that is mildly damaging to your defense against her charges. It should be a *small* bad thing. Nothing serious. Since no husband is perfect, admission of a small fault cannot be damaging. Work out this small admission in advance of your first interview. In writing up your summary of the interview afterwards, make sure you date the summary and include mention of this small admission. You are doing this for a special reason. You may not want this lawyer, but your wife may want him instead. Even if she already has a lawyer, she may lose him or dismiss him in the future. If this occurs, she may end up with one of the lawyers you have interviewed. You may have interviewed the best lawyer in the whole state, only to find that, as much as you feel you need him, you simply cannot afford him. Your wife may feel no such constraints; besides, she knows that one way to break your spirit is to impoverish you, and she may see this lawyer who costs three times as much as any other as the perfect means to that end. Remember, you cannot dictate to your wife which lawyer she must use.

But you can deny her this lawyer. By virtue of the fact that you have conducted a lengthy conference with this lawyer, during which you disclosed information which could be damaging to your case under the protection of privileged communication between lawyer and client, if this lawyer accepts your wife as a client, you can immediately scream *conflict of interest* to the court. The lawyer *must* remove himself from your wife's case or face serious ethical discipline and other legal action. Such conflict of interest can spread to all the lawyers in the lawyer's firm; none of them can serve as your wife's lawyer. Your dated summary of the interview with this lawyer, which contains the notes describing the trifling indiscretion you admitted to him, is all that is needed. The lawyer's own records will disclose that, for a fact, he did interview you on that date, and you've got him where you want him.

For this same reason, you should insist on paying the lawyer for the initial visit. If he indicates that it is free, and that if you decide to use him as your lawyer he will then add the initial visit to his final charges, *don't buy it*. Insist that you would feel better if he would accept a check, and even if he continues to resist, force a check on him. If he states an amount (probably in the neighborhood of $35 to $50), make the check in that amount. If he refuses to do so, write the check in an amount from $15 to $25, *date it, sign it,* drop it on his desk, thank him for his time, and leave his office. He will undoubtedly deposit the check, and you will have the cancelled check as definite proof that he (or his firm) received payment from you on a certain date. Thus, even if the lawyer's records do not disclose your interview visit (or if he is unscrupulous enough to destroy such records), you have all the evidence you need to establish the visit, regardless.

During the interview, do not bother to ask the lawyer how he would handle your case. To get into discussions of tactics at this time is premature. However, if complications (such as matters of support or custody) are present, or are apt to be, by all means bring out your concerns and see how he reacts. He may provide you with some good suggestions for protecting yourself at this stage of the game.

Throughout the interview, keep your mind working at a double level. First, talk with the lawyer—to express your concerns and to gather information about your legal position. Second, assess the lawyer. Pay particular attention to whether there seems to be a sense of rapport between you and him, a sense of trust on your part, and a sense that he is honest. This is important, for dishonesty is a frequent complaint of men who have gone through messy divorces. Also try to sound out his willingness to fight for your case. The most frequent problem expressed by men in divorce is that their lawyers do not get up off their butts and *work,* that their lawyers have spent their money and given nothing in return. Try to determine whether this lawyer seems to be active, whether he seems to enjoy a good scrap.

Question him about the judges in your area who might try your case: their names, their judicial attitudes, how they deal with men who have cases such as yours. Do any of these judges have any particular pet peeves, things that really irritate them? Are there certain things that particular judges look for in the cases they try?

Ask the lawyer how easily he can control the timing of the case. What can he do to speed up, or slow down, the normal legal process in order to further your case? Does he know the court clerk well enough to pick the judge who will try your case? Can he easily get hearings postponed if this seems to be advantageous to you?

How well does the lawyer seem to know the law? At this early stage of your case he probably knows it a great deal better than do you; however, you now understand that there is a difference between what the law says it does, and what it actually does in the courtroom. Does the lawyer point this out in his conversation? Does he indicate that the courts are fair to men? If so, on what does he base this statement?

Find out if the lawyer specializes in any particular aspect of law. What proportion of his time is spent in dealing with domestic relations law? What proportion is spent in divorce and custody cases? How much experience has he had in dealing with contested divorces?

Toward the end of the interview, after you have had some time to feel each other out, ask him how serious he considers your problem to be, and what chance you have of winning what you want from the case. Be careful here. If he assures you that everything will work out in the end, he is probably correct, but he has not answered your question. If he guarantees you that you will win, hands down, that your case is superb, you must begin viewing this lawyer with a jaundiced eye. At this stage no case is certain. No lawyer with so little understanding of the full complexity of your problem can know how things are going to turn out in the end. A decent lawyer will point this out to you. However, based on what you have given him, he may be able to point out some of the strengths and weaknesses in your present position, and he may suggest how these could be reflected in the outcome of the trial.

And be wary of an old come-on: if the lawyer says something to the effect that "It really doesn't matter how things turn out at the trial, because we can always appeal," you know you do not want this lawyer. Your battle must be won at the trial level; the chances of winning on appeal are about 50 to 1 against you.

Last, but by no means least, find out what the lawyer charges for his time. Expect a figure in the neighborhood of $40 per hour, unless you have some reason to believe that the lawyer is really good (in which case his fees may be much higher). He may not be able to give you a fixed dollar-per-hour figure for his charges. Many lawyers charge according to the kind of work they do. The charge for an appearance in the courtroom may be higher than the charge for desk work in his office; the charge for legal research (if he is the one who does it) may be at still a different rate. He may have special charges for filling out forms and for filing them. If this seems to be the case, take your time and ask him the rate he would charge for each and every likely kind of service to you. Write these figures down. Regardless of how he charges, the final question should be, How much is my case apt to cost me? If the divorce is uncontested, open-and-shut, the figure may range from $75 to $500, depending on your jurisdiction. If there is any likelihood of contest, the only truthful answer he can give is that he doesn't know. He may be able to provide a ballpark figure in the neighborhood of a thousand dollars, but how hotly contested the case becomes is generally a result of disagreements that may come about between you and your wife. How long you two argue will be reflected in the legal fees of both sides.

This kind of interview should be conducted with each lawyer you visit. If yours is to be an open-and-shut case of uncontested divorce, you need not be too concerned for the quality of your representation. However, if the case is likely to be complicated, much will depend on the quality of your lawyer. If you have screened the available lawyers by using the procedures we recommend, you will have produced a small pool of lawyers who should be pretty good. You will have interviewed at least three of them—the three you found best. Now, working from the interview summaries and your memory of the interviews, compare and contrast the interviewed lawyers. Trade off good points and bad points and choose the lawyer you want to represent you. Don't be too objective about this appraisal; much may depend on how well you can get along with your lawyer, or how well you like or respect him. A bad interpersonal relationship with your lawyer is one sure way to lose your case. This is, incidentally, a two-way street; you must believe in him and he must believe in you. If your case is complicated, the two of you will work together, hand in glove, to build your case. You will be gathering the evidence and he will be assembling the legal building blocks; only when these two components are integrated will you have a case that will hang together in the courtroom.

Hiring Your Attorney

Now let us assume that you have decided which lawyer you want. There still remains the question of whether he will want you. If he doesn't like you, or if he feels your case is a real loser, he may not be willing to take your case (lawyers' reputations are built on winning cases and are damaged when they lose). If he doesn't want you, go to the next one on your list. Rarely is there any difficulty in this area. Lawyers like to make money, and they are almost always looking for more work. But you should, as a courtesy if nothing more, put the question to him.

Be careful of what you ask him to do. If your case is to be uncontested and quite simple, especially if you and your wife have already effected the necessary agreements regarding custody, support, property, etc., then you can ask the lawyer to "handle your case" for you. This simple statement grants him *full power of attorney*, the legal right to make legal commitments in your name which are binding on you. He can do so with or without your knowledge and with or without your consent. Once he agrees that you will do a certain thing, it is as if you, yourself, had agreed to do so. In the case of a simple, uncontested divorce there is generally little harm that he can do, even if he blunders.

Most lawyers prefer to work with full power of attorney, since this gives them the greatest latitude for action. They can effect decisions quickly, without having to consult with you, and they can work in the style they prefer. Naturally, this freedom of action is desirable from the lawyer's viewpoint. Were you in the same position you would want similar freedom.

But if your case is complicated, you cannot afford to provide full power of attorney. If your lawyer makes a mistake, it is you, not he, who will have to live with the consequences. The relationship between you and your lawyer must be modified to put you in the driver's seat. You must be the one to make the decisions, to say yes or no, to direct (or prohibit) certain courses of action on the part of your attorney. In a complicated case, the role of the attorney should become that of an esteemed advisor and legal legman. He should keep you informed of the situation as it changes and advise you of the probable implications of the changing situation. He should present to you the alternative courses of action that are available, together with his professional evaluation of the risks and benefits likely to be associated with each. He can also recommend the alternative he thinks is best, together with the reasons why he thinks so. *Then you must make the decision regarding what is next to be done.*

The outcome of your decision may be an instruction to your lawyer to prepare a particular set of papers, to conduct a certain kind of legal research, or to file or amend a complaint. Or it may be decided that you have certain things to do for yourself, evidence to prepare, witnesses to interview, or lists of assets to compile. Or your decision may be simply to do nothing, to let time pass and see what develops. In any event, *you* will be the one who makes the decisions regarding how the case is developed. You will not be working in a vacuum, for your lawyer should apprise you of all relevant details, and your decisions probably will be well founded.

To secure this type of working relationship with your lawyer there are certain specifics which should be worked out. In particular, the lawyer should understand and agree that he will make no agreements whatsoever with the "other side" without first discussing with you the nature and ramifications of the situation; it will actually be you who says whether "your side" will agree or not, and your lawyer will then return the decision to the other side. Your lawyer must understand and agree that there are to be no "memoranda of understanding" or other forms of understanding effected between the two sides, or advanced by your side, or accepted from the other side, without your *prior informed consent;* meaning that your lawyer must again inform you of the situation and its ramifications so that you will be in a position to make the appropriate decision. Your lawyer must understand and agree that he will not initiate contact with the other side on any matter related to your case without your prior approval of the purpose and substance of the communication. Especially, your lawyer must understand that there are to be no buddy-buddy chats between your lawyer and hers regarding how they will put the case together.

Your lawyer can feel free to receive information from the other side, but he will not give information to the other side without your prior informed consent. Your lawyer must agree to notify you, in a timely manner, of all acts of the other side of which he becomes aware. He must also understand that his dealings with you must never involve a hidden agenda; in particular, there must be no attempt to manipulate you to make decisions in certain ways, nor can there be any attempt on his part to cause you to accept a "proper view" of your case which would fit it (and your future) into a stereotypical case, trial, and legal outcome. In many cases, the American male simply cannot afford to be "reasonable" and accept a "proper view" of his case, for too often the "proper view" is that the husband should recognize the needs of his poor, defenseless wife who must now face the big bad world all alone—meaning, of course, that the husband should roll over and play dead, giving his wife whatever she wants.

Take care to emphasize to your lawyer that what you require is a highly interactive relationship with him, that you will not try to be a lawyer but that you want to take full responsibility for your own life by making the decisions that may affect you. You will expect your lawyer to be active on your behalf, and to recommend and advise you, as well as to perform the necessary technical legal functions throughout your case. As he will be responsible for those kinds of matters, you will be responsible for providing the facts and pieces of evidence needed to build a winning case. You may wish to put the nature of the relationship in writing as a memorandum of understanding between yourself and your lawyer, to become a part of your file. (You will, of course, keep a copy for your own file.)

If the lawyer has concerns about what you propose, he should be free to voice them, and the two of you should be able to come to an amicable understanding. This may involve some give and take on both your parts. However, your "give" should not go too far. You must not lose the right to *prior informed consent* as regards the dealings with the other side; you must not lose the sense of a highly interactive relationship with your lawyer; you must not lose the right to make the major decisions and all agreements for yourself; and you must receive photocopies of all documents in your case. If your lawyer cannot agree with these necessities, you have come to the wrong lawyer. Go to the second-choice lawyer on your list.

BRIEFING YOUR LAWYER. Now that you have set forth the ground rules for the relationship between yourself and your lawyer, the next step is yours. *Brief your lawyer.* Provide him with as much information as you can regarding your case. Give him not only the strengths, as you see them, but also the weaknesses. If you are homosexual and your wife has found this out, if she has threatened you with public exposure unless you do as she wishes, let your lawyer know. If you have been caught dead to rights by your wife in an adulterous situation, and if her proofs are strong, let the lawyer know. *He must know the problems he is likely to encounter and the weapons he will have available for attack and defense.* He must know what he is facing, even if it is acutely embarrassing for you to put it into words. Gird your loins and say what you must say. Few things are more sad than to observe a case go right down the drain during trial because the lawyer did not know there was a hole in his defense. No matter how much a bastard you think you are, there are people who have done things a whole lot worse than you. Your lawyer must know what the score is, and it is up to you to tell him. There is no other way he can find out. Without such information, he cannot prepare a proper defense, much less a decent offense.

What to Do with a Bad Lawyer

If you have followed the suggestions above, you will have established a working relationship with your lawyer which affords you considerable safety. Nevertheless, it sometimes happens that your lawyer does not do as he is supposed to. The cards-on-the-table nature of your agreement with him gives you the right to apply pressure against your lawyer if he gets out of line.

The first level of pressure is a verbal rebuke. Let him know that you are displeased with his actions, and that they are not within the spirit of the understanding between you. Ask him how he feels about it, and what he proposes to do differently in the future in order to avoid violation of the agreement. Lawyers seldom get this kind of treatment from their clients and it can have quite an impact, especially as the lawyer is asked to indicate how he will proceed so as not to violate the agreement in the future. This evokes a verbal commitment from him, and forces him to recognize that he has done so.

If that is unsuccessful, or if the violations continue, then it is time to let him know who employs whom. As it happens, *you employ him.* At any time you wish you can discharge him. Let him know that you are aware of this fact, and that unless he takes you more seriously, you will do exactly that. You also might ask whether he finds working with you so difficult that he would prefer to be relieved. If so, pay him off and go elsewhere.[1]

Frequently, your lawyer will refuse to release his files to another lawyer unless his bill has been paid in full. Normally, this would constitute quite a roadblock, in some cases preventing a client from going to another lawyer. In your case, this probably will not happen. You already have the full set of documents that comprises your file. (You required copies of everything from your lawyer at the outset.) All you have to do is to copy these documents and you have a set which can be given to a new lawyer. In the event the new lawyer says he must have a release from the first lawyer, indicate that none will be forthcoming for some period of time because of a disagreement between you and your former lawyer which may be actionable (that is, you may sue your previous lawyer) on the grounds that he violated the agreement between you. Moreover, you have no intention of paying the previous lawyer for work he performed in violation of the agreement. This frequently will be enough to cause the new lawyer to dismiss the requirement for a release. Such releases, incidentally, are required by lawyers for only one reason—as a courtesy to their fellow lawyers, to ensure that they get paid.[2]

Beyond firing your bad lawyer, you have two additional recourses. One is to contact the disciplinary committee of the bar association for your state. Write the chairman of that committee a letter stating what your lawyer did or did not do, and indicate that you feel this is not in accord with the ethical standards of the bar. Such a letter usually has little effect, but it does sometimes cause your ex-lawyer to receive a very uncomfortable phone call, and if many of his clients do the same thing, he may find himself facing a formal hearing which could result in his being disbarred, although this is quite unlikely.

The final recourse is difficult to put into action, but it is increasing in frequency and popularity. You may be able to sue your lawyer for damages as a result of his misconduct, or to recover fees you have paid while he performed in violation of your agreement. A successful lawsuit against your ex-lawyer will undoubtedly reward you with quite a bit of cash, but don't expect to find many lawyers who are willing to bring suit against one of their own. Even if you pass this hurdle, the suit is likely to be expensive.

8

Support, Property, and Custody Agreements

If your jurisdiction is not antithetical to dviorce, and if you and your wife have agreed to seek a divorce, the two of you have arrived at the most critical stage of the divorce process—that of the separation agreement. Embodied within this agreement are terms which affect your standard of living and the welfare of you and your children, not just now or in the immediate future, but for the rest of your lives.

The separation agreement dominates divorce. Practically all modern contested divorces are brought to the point of contest because the couple cannot agree upon the terms of the agreement; when the couple can readily come to a good agreement, the case is almost never contested. The agreement cannot be taken lightly, because its implications are too far-reaching.

Must There Be a Separation Agreement?

Separation agreements are not required as a matter of law, nor are they legally required before a divorce can be granted. However, the absence of a completed separation agreement risks two things: first, that the judge may take it upon himself to dictate the terms and conditions of such matters as custody and alimony (as he has a legal right to do, but which might result in a very unworkable set of conditions for the parties); and second, that unsettled issues will remain to cause later conflict between the divorced couple, with the result that they will return to the courts in order to settle matters which should have been settled earlier.

In a practical sense, not a legal sense, there should be a separation agreement, if for no other reason than to avoid such difficulties. For the husband, the development of the separation agreement is of particular importance, since it is here that he has an opportunity to establish his bargaining power. The law of the courtroom, owing to its bias in favor of the wife, is a bad place for the male to seek equity. In the development of the separation agreement, however, he stands a good chance of attaining an equitable arrangement by which both he and his wife can live in years to come.

It is further to the husband's advantage to develop a separation agreement, because frequently he must pay the legal fees of both sides. The lack of a separation agreement will undoubtedly cause the judge to explore such matters as custody and disposition of assets, and his deliberations will take time. Having a separation agreement in hand, prior to trial, reduces the judge's task to rubber-stamping the divorce decree. Courtroom time is reduced from days to minutes, and costs are correspondingly lower.

In the development of the separation agreement, the husband has an opportunity to control the disposition of assets. He cannot, of course, generally expect to get everything he wants; neither can he generally expect to lose everything he has. But there are many ways to divide a pie, and the husband here has a good opportunity to influence the way the pie is divided. He may be able to avoid selling off the old family homestead by trading off other items to his wife to satisfy her equitable requirements. Similarly, as regards the custody of children, the father here has the opportunity to influence the custodial arrangements. If the husband and wife reach an accord early enough, they may be able to put their plan into action, to try it out for a while and test its workability before the trial.

Purpose and Contents of the Separation Agreement

The purpose of the separation agreement is to specify how the assets of the family will be divided between the husband and wife; to indicate whether alimony for either the husband or wife has been agreed upon and, if so, the amount and schedule of payment of alimony; and to specify the nature of the custodial agreements for the children, the nature of visitation by the noncustodial parent, and the agreements reached as regards child support and related matters. The agreement can also indicate how the couple propose to pay for legal expenses associated with the divorce. The separation agreement, once signed by both parties, is a legally binding document, and its terms and conditions are enforceable in the courts.

CONTENTS OF THE SEPARATION AGREEMENT. For a more comprehensive discussion of the contents and form of the separation agreement, the reader is referred to Alexander Lindley's two-volume work[1] which is devoted to this topic. The overview we provide is necessarily incomplete.

The contents of the separation agreement, assuming that the husband and wife can cooperatively develop the agreement, can consist of just about anything. By nature, the contents tend to consist of financial concerns—dispositions of properties and other assets, and future provisions for alimony and child support. The agreements can be very general in nature, or they can be very specific. They can be as short as a page or as long as a book. It is up to the parties to decide how they want to word their agreement; if they wish, they can avoid most of the wording chores by asking one of the lawyers to write it for them—for a fee, of course. However, they cannot avoid being faced with the often distasteful task of saying how they will go about breaking up the home into two homes.

There are advantages and disadvantages to both long and short forms of agreements. Short agreements are necessarily written in generalities and lack specific guidelines regarding what is required of both parties. If one party violates the terms of the agreement, the other party may have difficulty proving it in court, because of the numerous interpretations that are possible.

On the other hand, the detailed, highly specific separation agreement is felt by some to invite future litigation. There are a couple of reasons for this. First, the detailed nature of the agreement tends to disallow flexibility: simple problems that might be solved simply, or by common-sense approaches, are deprived of solution by some trivial clause in the agreement. This sometimes results in deliberate violation of the terms of the agreement in order to effect a common-sense solution, which, in turn, results in litigation by the other party, who feels that the offender should be made to comply with the agreement. Alternatively, the pary who finds the agreement unnecessarily constrictive may be sufficiently irked to ask the court for relief through modification of the order.

Obviously, the best solution is to be found somewhere between these extremes. One wishes sufficient generality to permit interpretation of the terms, and one wishes sufficient specificity to make clear what is, and what is not, proper compliance with the terms of the agreement.

To develop the agreement requires communication between the husband and wife, and they should sit down together to write what they want the agreement to say. If they have trouble communicating with each other, the wife might take a first crack at drafting the entire agreement; the husband might then make whatever modifications he wishes and return the agreement to the wife for comment, further modification, and so on, until they have what they think they can agree to.

They should not be too concerned about the fancy legal prose that will ultimately be needed; rather, they should try to state, as clearly and unambiguously as possible, what they want to agree to. After they have written out an acceptable agreement, it should be given to the two lawyers for review. If the lawyers object to the legal implications of some of the terms the parties have used, the parties may wish to reword their agreement slightly. Having finally attained a consensus as to the contents of the agreement, the wife's lawyer should draft the legal version of the document. The husband, of course, will retain a copy of the rough draft which was sent to her lawyer. Why send it to her lawyer for drafting? Because then it is part of her legal expenses, not those of the husband (important if the parties have agreed to pay their own expenses).

When the wife's lawyer returns the separation agreement, now written in legalese, the husband should send a copy to his lawyer for review (to keep the wife's lawyer honest), and he should, himself, study the document to make sure that no significant changes have been made in the scope, coverage, and terms of the agreement.

Up to this point, he should not have signed the agreement or any of its preliminary versions. An early signature, either his or his wife's, can later be used to signify earlier intentions which can, in some circumstances, be important. For example: a wife instructed her lawyer to draft a trial separation agreement, which he did, incorporating into the agreement all the terms and conditions she wanted. The husband was not involved in this development. When the document was completed, the wife signed it and forwarded it through her lawyer to the husband's lawyer, and thereby to her husband. The alimony demanded by the agreement represented about 45 percent of the husband's gross income. The husband refused to sign, but kept the copy bearing her signature in his files. The case later moved toward contest and, in a pre-trial conference, the husband's lawyer showed the one-sided agreement to the judge. The judge realized that the demand for alimony was excessive and interpreted the wife's earlier position as greedy; his final award for alimony was much lower than that called for by the agreement.

Earlier intentions may play a part in interesting ways. For example, suppose that one particular clause of the agreement dealing with custodial visitation is onerous to the husband, but the terms regarding alimony are very attractive to him. His wife has signed the agreement, but he has not, because he hopes to bargain further for a better visitation schedule. For some reason, the wife becomes angered at the husband and she triples her demands for alimony. In the absence of excellent reasons for the change, she probably will not get the alimony she now demands because her earlier intentions signify the amount she was earlier willing to accept.

Naturally, if the husband sees that the agreement is highly advantageous to him, he should seek to obtain his wife's signature, even on crude, handwritten, preliminary versions, but he should not sign until he is quite sure that the agreement represents the best deal he can get. If the best is still not good enough, he should steadfastly refuse to sign, even against his lawyer's advice. This will tend to push the divorce toward a contest, but he may do better under the judge's decision than under an adverse agreement.

If both parties have entered into the agreement voluntarily, fairly, and without duress, and especially if both parties have had access to legal counsel, the chances are good that the judge will not modify the agreement. Agreements arrived at in this way are sometimes termed "consent agreements" and are valued by the courts. Judges seem to feel that consent agreements are generally more pleasing, more tractable, and less likely to result in future litigation than are orders created by the court. Judges also tend to enforce the letter and spirit of consent agreements with greater vigor than they do court orders, and they seem more reluctant to modify the terms of consent agreements than the terms of court orders.

Once the separation agreement has been dated and signed by both parties, its terms are legally enforceable and both parties are required to perform as the agreement indicates.[2] There are two avenues which may be used to enforce the terms of the order. One method requires that the separation agreement be provided to the court during trial with the request that the agreement be made part of the court's order in the divorce.[3] If this is done, breach of the terms of the agreement is simultaneously breach of a court order and is subject to the court's contempt power.

The second method does not incorporate the agreement within the court order. After the divorce, the terms of the agreement are enforceable through contract law. The offended party initiates a lawsuit against the other party for breach of contract. This method is seldom used because the divorce court judge finds it a simple matter to incorporate the agreement into his order "by reference" (in his order, the judge merely names the existing agreement and indicates that it is herewith incorporated within the order of the court).

It is likely that under the second method it would cost more to obtain a hearing and that the hearing would take longer to come up. We do not know whether the penalties for noncompliance would differ between the two methods. There is, however, one advantage associated with the second method. If the agreement is not bound up in a court order, it can be modified at will by the parties to the agreement. If the ex-husband and ex-wife wish to change the agreement, they can do so anytime they jointly agree that the change is needed. However, if the agreement has been made part of the court order, any attempt to modify the agreement must be done by returning to the court and seeking a "modification of the order." This is usually easy to accomplish if the parties are agreed on the change to be made, but it is the judge, not the parties, who has the power to decide whether the modification will be permitted.

PRECAUTIONS. While the contents of the separation agreement can be pretty much what the parties wish them to be, there are nonetheless a few precautions to be observed. In writing up the agreement regarding custody of children, judges will balk at anything they feel is bizarre. The judge will not countenance, for example, having little Johnny live with Mom on Mondays, Wednesdays, and Fridays, and having him live with Dad on the remaining days of the week. Clearly, such an arrangement would fail to provide a needed stability for the child. Some judges will not listen to suggestions for joint custody—for example, a situation in which Mom has the kids one year and Dad has them the next, or a situation in which Mom has the kids throughout the school year and Dad has them during the summer vacation. If you and your wife are planning anything out of the ordinary in terms of custody, you would be well advised to get a reading on how the judges in your area are apt to react to it, and to take special care in the wording of the separation agreement so that what you want will not seem offensive to the judge.

If the couple intended that the wife should have custody of the children, the father should be especially careful not to agree that the wife/mother should have custody, or that she is the superior custodian. Rather, the agreement should indicate that he intends to be a continuing part of the children's development, and that he intends to play a powerful role in this regard; he may also indicate that he believes that, for the present, the best interest and welfare of the children is that they live with their mother, but that if situations change, the parties may return to the court to obtain approval of his having custody. He does this against the future possibility that the wife will remarry and that the new husband will apply to the court to adopt the children. In some jurisdictions, a statement in the separation agreement to the effect that the husband agrees that the children should be in the wife's custody is taken as proof that the father is indifferent to the welfare of his children, and as justification for adoption over the father's objection. Even if the wife does not now live in such a jurisdiction, she cannot be prevented from moving into one after the divorce.[4]

The husband should be aware that his wife cannot relinquish her rights to alimony. This is because of the continuing interest of the state in the welfare of the parties, especially the wife. The instant she relinquishes her rights, the state reinstates them. What this means, in effect, is that the court will discard the separation agreement (either some of it or all of it), as a matter of principle, if the document indicates that the wife has given up or relinquished her rights to alimony. If the separation agreement is to be legally acceptable, it must avoid such terminology.

There is a simple way out. The agreement can state (in words to the effect) that the wife "does not need alimony, does not want alimony, and does not ask for alimony." Notice that this does not *forfeit* her rights; instead, it is one manner by which she *exercises* her rights, and generally this avoids the problem. If the divorce is showing signs of moving towards contest, and if your wife has a demonstrated history of trickery in legal maneuvering, she may "surrender her rights to alimony" in the agreement as a means of keeping you fat, dumb, and happy until the trial. At that time she may claim that the agreement was developed under duress, and she may ask that the agreement be abandoned in favor of a court order awarding her alimony.

The terms of the separation agreement are rife with implications for taxation. The husband must be aware of some of the consequences. If the house is awarded to the husband, either through the court order or through the separation agreement, what effectively happens is that the monetary value of the wife's equity in the property is transferred to the husband. This is treated as income to the husband. Need we go into the effect on the husband's income tax of receiving an additional $30,000 in taxable income as a result of his wife giving up her share of a $60,000 house? Alternatively, if the husband gives up his interest in the house, by order or agreement, the monetary value he is forced to relinquish is treated as a gift, not as a business loss, and it is not deductible. Alimony paid to the wife is deductible to the husband and is considered part of the wife's taxable income. Payments of child support are not deductible to the father; they are merely part of his continuing obligation to provide for his children. However, if he can show that he pays more than half of their financial support, he can claim them as deductions on his income tax. In the separation agreement, the husband may be able to gain an advantage by skillful wording. Suppose, for example, that there are three children, all given to the wife in custody. The husband can show that he has provided one-third of all child support, and that the wife has provided two-thirds of all child support. The husband has not actually provided more than half of the child support for any one child; however, he has paid enough to fully support one child, and his wife has paid enough to fully support two children. Under the "more than half" test, the wife can claim all three children as deductions; however, if the proviso is in the separation agreement, under such conditions the husband can fairly deduct one of the children, allowing his ex-wife to deduct only two of them, instead of all three.

The husband must be particularly wary of clauses advanced by his wife which provide for escalation of the amount of money he must pay under specified conditions. With increasing frequency, alimony and child support payments are being tied to the consumer price index. As inflation increases, so also do the dollar amounts that the husband must pay. Unless there are special considerations given to the formula by which payment is computed, the husband may be adversely affected. Let us consider a couple of "model" formulas for computing alimony or child support.

Model 1: *Fixed payments, no allowance for modification according to economic conditions.* The husband pays a fixed amount on a periodic basis, say, $100 every two weeks, for child support. If the husband loses his job, he must continue to pay $100 every two weeks. If he receives a small, but nonetheless constraining, cut in wages, he still must pay $100 every two weeks. We have known of men under the "fixed payments" model who have been subjected to adverse economic conditions to the point that they were gradually stripped of all assets and were nearly placed on welfare, although this is fortunately a rare occurrence. If the husband prospers, his former wife derives no benefit, nor do his children. If the husband prospers at a rate better than the inflation rate, his standard of living rises; the standard of living of his children will actually decline unless there is income from other sources.

Model 2: *Payments proportional to consumer price index.* Under this model, a current amount is agreed upon as the amount to be paid by the husband. At yearly intervals (or at monthly intervals) the amount to be paid is adjusted to reflect changes in the consumer price index. If, after a year, the consumer price index is up 10 percent, the amount the husband must pay is also increased by 10 percent. The $100 every two weeks becomes $110 every two weeks. There are some subtle effects inherent in the model, such as the fact that the consumer price index is based on urban prices, not on rural prices. Rural and farm prices tend to rise earlier than urban prices; a rural father, under this model, experiences a rise in his payments only after the price rise has been measured in the urban setting, and thereby he benefits from the lag effect in prices.

Such effects are small, however, and are not appreciable at the single-family level. Of greater importance is the fact that inflation, as measured by the consumer price index, does not accurately monitor either hours worked or wage rates. In recent years, there have been declines in the hours worked (people who earlier worked a forty-hour week have been shifted to a thirty-seven-hour week, for example) with little opportunity to recover the lost hours through overtime work. Also, the wages paid per hour of work have not tended to increase as fast as inflation. Actual earnings, in terms of dollars received and what they will buy, have therefore declined. Effectively, the husband/father has increased the dollars he earns by about 8 percent, but inflation has increased by about 10 percent. Under this model, he must pay his former wife or children the full 10 percent and suffer the 2 percent loss from his own standard of living. Should this loss continue over a ten-year period, since it is recomputed periodically, the loss in standard of living will magnify like compound interest; in ten years, his losses would be so severe as to produce a standard of living more than 20 percent lower than that of his former wife. Other things being equal, his standard of living would be less than 80 percent of what hers is.

Other escalations seem more direct, but frequently involve financial impact which cannot be anticipated. For example, the agreement may provide that the husband is to be responsible for all medical expenses of the wife and children, apart from the other provisions of alimony and child support. If the former wife becomes seriously ill, requiring extensive hospitalization, the husband may find himself paying not only for her extraordinary medical expenses (which otherwise would be paid for out of her alimony or her other financial resources), but also paying for the cost of a live-in maid or babysitter to care for the children during her hospitalization. Because of the fact that these medical expenses are not regular, periodic payments, they would not be deductible to the husband. Similarly, medical payments to the children would not be deductible to the husband unless he first was qualified to take the children as exemptions.

Future educational expenses for the children also are frequently written into the husband's obligations under the separation agreement. If the child will not go to college, the father's support obligation generally ends when the child becomes of legal age (eighteen or twenty-one, depending on the state), but if the child is college-bound, the separation agreement may require the father to pay for the first four years of college (or more, although this is infrequent). The costs of college education have risen dramatically in recent years, and when the father discovers that his four-year-old son will, in fifteen more years, be costing him about $9,000 after-tax dollars for each year of school (much more, if the child goes to a prestigious university), he suddenly realizes that he cannot make such payments. And if he has three such children, how is he going to come up with $27,000 after-tax dollars *for each year of their college?*

The husband should reject outright any agreement that the current wife or his children will share in his will or estate. At this time, while the two are still married, the husband cannot disown his wife. He cannot cut her out of his will; it is illegal. It is legal, however, to cut out the children entirely. If the husband agrees, through the separation agreement or as a result of court order, to name his wife or his children as beneficiaries of his estate, he may do a great disservice to his future happiness. He may remarry and have children by his new wife, and may find that the new marriage is beautiful, rich, and full of love. Won't that second family be surprised to discover upon his death that his considerable estate belongs entirely to people they have never met? If you now have a will, make no mention of it and ask your lawyer about reworking or revoking it. Pray that the matter will not arise during the divorce process, and as soon as the divorce is final, make a new will. If you do not have a will, wait until after the divorce to make one up.

Avoid clauses in the agreement which tend to tie financial obligations to *gross income;* tie them, instead, to after-tax dollars. The alimony formulas used by the courts are generally based on before-tax income. Especially under escalation rules, this works a serious hardship upon the husband. As the husband's income rises, not only does he have to pay his wife more in after-tax dollars, but he also goes into a higher income tax bracket. A severe business loss might not offset gross income under certain accounting procedures, and the husband may be required to pay on the basis of an artificially elevated gross income; were the monies tied to after-tax income, these losses would have been compensated and the former wife would not have been enriched to the husband's detriment.

The objective in the development of a separation agreement is to establish equity: a fair division of spoils now, and fair future support of the wife and children. It is not the purpose to enrich the wife or the children by impoverishing the husband/father. The husband/father must not view himself as an infinite source of funds to provide for the welfare of others. He must secure his own future and provide as well for the other concerns. The wife should understand that she has an ethical responsibility for the welfare of herself and her children, and that she does not have the right to be a parasitic alimony drone. Her ethical responsibilities are financial, as well as domestic, and she should accept her share of the responsibility to provide for the needs of her children. While this viewpoint is not law—for the law holds that all such financial responsibilities are solely those of the husband/father—she should recognize that often the husband simply cannot support two independent households, even if he lives alone and destitute. The courts have sometimes recognized this problem by ordering the wife to seek and find employment. For the wife who refuses to recognize her ethical responsibilities, this is a just conclusion; for the wife who willingly recognizes her responsibility, such an order is unnecessary.

Bargaining

The husband's ability to bargain toward a favorable separation agreement depends chiefly upon two things: the mutual willingness of husband and wife to resolve differences amicably and attain a workable agreement, and the power of the husband to force an agreement should the wife be unreasonable. It serves no useful purpose to wantonly destroy a favorable atmosphere, because a breakdown of communications represents a one-way ticket toward contested divorce. Under normal circumstances, neither husband nor wife deserves such an experience. If they have an amicable relationship, they should both strive to retain it in order to make all that remains easier to deal with.

As the term is used here, *bargaining* refers to the development of a power base from which the other side can be made to see the inevitable; when the wife understands that she can do no better, no matter how predatory she may be, she realizes that further efforts on her part will only cost more time and money.

All bargaining is based on three interacting principles: (1) each party has a possession; (2) each party places value on both the possession he holds and that held by the other, and (3) if the values can be brought into harmony, an exchange in possessions will occur.

The three principles must be interpreted liberally. A possession need not be material; it can be an idea, a piece of information, a physical object, or a person. A value need not be in dollars; it can be in terms of personal desire. Neither is it necessary that a value be positive; it can be negative as well. Trash has a negative value for its possessor; he must pay money to get rid of it.

Successful bargaining demands an accurate understanding of what you have to bargain with. To gain such an understanding, the husband must conduct an inventory of all family assets and possessions, including those of the wife and children. Begin by enumerating the worth of all income, savings, debts, securities and other holdings (partnerships, etc.), and all real estate. Financial holdings, debts, and incomes can be summarized next to reflect the relative incomes, expenses, debts, etc., of husband and wife separately.

Continue by listing all other property which the family owns (house furnishings, cars, clothing, jewelry, stereo equipment, appliances, tools, recreational equipment, etc.). This can be accomplished expeditiously by waiting until the house is empty, then walking from room to room, dictating household contents into a cassette recorder. When the tape recordings have been transcribed into a thoroughly detailed typewritten list, the husband should enter two separate dollar values for each listed item: (1) the probable amount of money which would be realized if the item were to be sold now in its current condition; and (2) the cost of replacing the item with an identical, but brand new, item at current retail market prices. More expensive items, such as real estate, jewelry, silver service, paintings, fur coats, etc., should be evaluated carefully. Informal estimates can often be obtained without charge, and formal appraisals by qualified experts can usually be had for a fee. The values of other items can often be established through the want ads of local newspapers and through the catalogues of agencies such as Sears Roebuck or Montgomery Ward.

Development of the inventory will take a lot of time if it is to be done properly and should be completed before bargaining begins, if possible. The inventory is a highly sensitive document. Its existence should be known only to the husband and his lawyer (a "need to know" basis). Should the wife or her lawyer learn that the document exists they will certainly demand it through discovery, thereby neutralizing any bargaining advantage the husband might have derived.

Before discussing the difficult bargaining involved in contested divorces, we present two approaches to bargaining for those couples who expect to have an uncontested divorce. The first approach is fairly simple and straightforward. It is especially suitable for younger couples who do not have many assets, or for couples who are more impressed with the usefulness of certain items than with their monetary values. Others may feel that the simpler method provides inadequate control over the dollar value of the items being divided. However, we suggest that the first approach be tried at least, because it is quick, reasonably relaxed, and effective. If, after trying it, either of the parties feels disadvantaged, then try the second, more complicated method.

The division of property and other assets is a permanent division. Once agreed to, the division cannot be questioned and cannot be retracted by either party. A deal is a deal. It is not concluded until both parties are satisfied that it is fair, but once that agreement has been made, it sticks.

Every piece of property and every asset acquired since the marriage is involved in the bargaining. Nothing is held back, not even your toothbrush. Certainly not your $25,000 in bonds cleverly secreted in a safe-deposit box. In amicable divisions of the spoils, the intention is to split things down the middle. Properties and other assets held prior to the marriage are exempt from the bargaining process, as are properties and assets which might be acquired after the date of the final divorce decree. Only the assets and properties acquired during the marriage are involved in bargaining. Of course, there is nothing to prevent one party from "purchasing" an asset or property from his spouse by trading items he had owned before they were married.

> *Example:* Mary and John were divorcing. Before they were married, Mary owned an excellent typewriter which she brought to the marriage. After they were married, John bought a middle-quality stereo sound system. During the division of the spoils, Mary traded her typewritter to John for the stereo system. This was Mary's wish; she could not be compelled to bargain with her typewriter since she owned it prior to the

marriage. The stereo system, however, was purchased after the marriage and was therefore subject to bargaining as a piece of property held in common between husband and wife.

A clear and explicit agreement must be attained regarding the disposition of all the properties and assets that are subject to bargaining. If there are any caveats or conditions, these should be openly understood by both parties to prevent misunderstandings.

Example: Mary left John, taking with her most of her personal effects. She moved into a furnished house, and left practically all of her own furniture, objets d'art, etc., in the house she owned with John. It was her intention to let John have the use of these things until the house was sold, then to take possession of half of the furnishings (or their value), leaving the balance with John. Unfortunately, she failed to communicate these things to John. When the house sold, John stripped the house of all possessions and moved into another state. Since the divorce had been granted, it would have taken a new lawsuit to force John to return her share of the possessions. The cost of such a suit made any attempt to regain the possessions impractical, and besides, she didn't know where John was living. Five years later, Mary still complained about how she was "ripped off" by John; but she wasn't, really. She failed to make explicit her wants and intentions. Although John was not available for comment, we suspect he felt his ex-wife had abandoned the possessions to him. As far as he was concerned, they were his and he took them.

AMICABLE DIVISION OF THE SPOILS (SIMPLE METHOD). Obtain a few sheets of paper and divide each into three columns. Title the first column, "Things I want"; the second, "Things for bargaining"; the third, "Things for (your wife)." Working from a complete list of possessions, enter each item in its proper column, according to whether it is something you want, something you feel your wife should have, or something to be bargained for.

After all items have been placed in their proper columns, give the sheets to your wife. She should now modify what you have done by circling any items she feels are misplaced, drawing an arrow from the circled item to the column where she thinks it should be.

When your wife has completed her task, the two of you should get together to bargain. The things you wanted which she did not feel were misplaced are yours. Things you felt she wanted which your wife did not feel were misplaced are hers. All other things are shifted into the "bargaining" column.

What happens next is loose-footed horse trading. Let your wife pick whatever she wants from the "bargaining" column, then you take your turn, and so forth, until all items are divided between you. Maybe the two of you are now satisfied. If so, fine. If not, discuss what it would take to correct the dissatisfaction. Both should realize that the division of the spoils, by whatever method, will leave you feeling somewhat dissatisfied. Remember that you are not trying to achieve perfect inner peace, but to make an arrangement that you both can live with. Trade a few items back and forth to even up any inequities, but don't overdo it. You may be merely prolonging the inevitable.

Having divided up the properties, next assemble all monetary assets. These assets include real estate holdings, business proprietorships, shares of stock, bonds, debentures, paid-up insurance policies, partnerships, and cash held in checking accounts or savings accounts. The total monetary value of all these holdings is to be divided in two, half for you, half for her. Stocks and bonds should be valued as of current market value. Real estate can be appraised (for a fee) or its value estimated by a real estate broker. All outstanding debts should be liquidated before dividing the monetary assets. All credit card accounts in both names should be closed and new accounts opened (if you want them) under the separate names of the parties. From this moment on, the debts incurred by each party are his or hers to take care of.

The two of you may face emotional difficulties when it comes to the house. Getting together the down payment for it may have taken years of concerted effort. There may have been many happy times shared within its walls. You may find the shop you installed in the basement full of fond memories of relaxation. She may remember the fun she had redecorating the family room and the many joyful times when friends dropped in for coffee. But now the divorce is under way. Your first consideration is, or should be, to make a complete and clean break with each other, leaving no details to drag on you in the future.

The house could be a serious source of contention unless you both approach the question realistically. If one of you wants to keep the house, it is necessary to buy out the other's interest in the property. If a fair market value of the house in currently $60,000, and if you still owe $22,000 on the mortgage, your equity in the property is $38,000 which should be split between you. Each of you has $19,000 invested in the house; thus, if one of you wishes to buy out the other, pay him or her $19,000. Part, or all, of the $19,000 may come from other possessions already acquired through bargaining which might be traded back. A loan might be acquired from a bank to handle the rest.

If one of you owned the house prior to the marriage, figure out how much the house has increased in value over the period of the marriage. If the house was worth $40,000 at the time you married, and if it is now worth $60,000, it has appreciated $20,000. Each of you deserves $10,000 of that appreciation. The original owner can buy out his or her spouse with a payment of $10,000. For the spouse of the original owner to buy out the other's interest, it would take $50,000—the value of $40,000 brought to the marriage by the original owner, plus half of the increase in value of the house over the period of the marriage.

If neither of you wants to purchase the house from the other, or if the cash to do so cannot be raised, *then sell the house,* and divide the proceeds. Forget how painful it is to sell, just sell it and divide the money equitably.

The presence of children adds other considerations. In dividing the property and assets, the parties must, absolutely must, set aside their selfish interests to secure the welfare of the children. It is frequently assumed that the custodial parent has a right to the house and that the other party must relinquish his or her right to whatever equity he or she may have in it. While in some cases this may be the best approach, in many cases it is not. If yours is a typical family, your finances have been strained nearly to the breaking point. You have not lived within your income, but have lived on the borderline of debt. This probably has been reflected in the purchase of your home; instead of buying a house merely adequate for your needs, you probably bought the largest one you could afford. From an investment viewpoint, this may have been wise; but in considering other expenses, it means that the mortgage is probably as high as the family can afford.

Moreover, after the divorce, the noncustodial parent is going to have to set up housekeeping all over again. What about his or her needs for a washing machine, pots and pans, a vacuum cleaner? It may be necessary to buy furnishings—rugs, a bed and bedding, a dining table, etc. Beyond these "one-time" costs, there will be continuing costs for rent or a new mortgage, utilities, food, and clothing. Where is the money for all this to come from? Is income going to rise in the near future so as to meet these burdens?

If so, perhaps it is reasonable for the noncustodial parent to donate his share of the house to the benefit of the children. But if income will not predictably rise to meet these expenses, such an arrangement could be an invitation to bankruptcy. Perhaps it is better to sell the house and apply the proceeds toward the purchase of a smaller house for the children and the custodial parent, as well as toward establishing a home for the noncustodial parent.

AMICABLE DIVISION OF THE SPOILS (COMPLICATED METHOD). This method does not provide the parties with equal dollar value after the possessions are divided; rather, it attempts to provide each party with a sense of having received equal personal value. In this method, the current monetary value of possessions is the basis for bargaining, but leeway is provided to allow each party to exert particular bargaining pressure for those items of cherished or sentimental value, where mere dollars would be inadequate.

Several steps are involved in the process. The first of these is to obtain two photocopies of your list of possessions. Set one copy aside. Some of the items on the list will be of no personal value to one, or perhaps both, of the parties. If neither party wants an item, strike it from the list. All remaining items are of value to at least one of you. For each remaining item, determine if it is something you would have to replace for your own use, if it should be awarded to your wife as a result of bargaining. For example, if your wife were to be awarded the vacuum cleaner, would you have to purchase one for your own use? The same kind of determination should be made from the wife's viewpoint. Any item that would have to be replaced must now be subjected to further scrutiny. What would it cost to replace the item? Would it have to be purchased new, or could it *easily* be found in good condition second-hand? If a new purchase would be necessary, circle the "replacement cost" figure on the list; if it can easily be found second-hand, circle the "current market value" figure on the list. For any item that would not have to be replaced, circle the "current market value" of the item. Apply this evaluation to every item on the list until a value has been circled for each. Don't become finicky about these decisions; perform the task quickly between you and be done with it. The numbers you have circled represent the "cash values" of the items.

Many of the items on the list will be exempt from bargaining. The guidelines for exemption presented below are arbitrary and may be changed to suit you; however, you and your wife should agree on the guidelines before bargaining begins. As with the simple method of dividing the spoils, items owned by either party before the marriage are exempt; these may be struck from the list. Other exemptions include items of personalty, certain kinds of tools and gifts, and items used by children. Guidelines for these exemptions follow.

Items of personalty include clothing, items of personal hygiene, cosmetics, costume jewelry, etc. Such items are to be struck from the list.

Possessions used by either party for the exclusive purpose of earning an income are also to be stricken from the list. The automotive tools used by the husband-auto mechanic qualify for removal, as do the expensive gowns used by the wife-cocktail hostess in her work. Possessions used by both husband and wife jointly for the sole purpose of earning an income are not removed from the list. For example, husband and wife may both be writers who share the family typewriter in the preparation of their manuscripts. The typewriter would not be removed from the list.

Gifts received from outside sources are treated as items of personalty provided they are of direct benefit only to the recipient. The wife's fur coat, given to her by her mother and of direct benefit only to the wife, is considered personalty and is removed from the list. The wife's electric mixer, given to her by her father but of benefit to the family at large rather than solely to the wife, is not considered personalty and stays on the list. The husband's car, given to him by his father and used by the family, is not removed from the list. His radial saw in the basement workshop, given to him by his father, is of direct benefit only to the husband who uses it in his hobby of woodworking; as personalty, the saw would be struck from the list. Alternatively, a saw used by the husband almost entirely as a tool for the repair and maintenance of the house, or for the creation of objects of general benefit to the family, would stay on the list. Ceremonial gifts are excepted from this consideration and are considered personalty. A valuable grandfather clock, used by the family at large but awarded to the husband for his salesmanship on the job, is considered personalty and is removed from the list. The gold filigree wine set presented to the wife for her work in a local civic organization is considered her personalty and is removed from the list.

Extravagant personal possessions—unless the parties *agree* otherwise—are not considered personalty. The wife's fur coat purchased for her by her husband, the husband's $1,000 wristwatch he purchased for himself, the wife's $12,000 diamond necklace, and the husband's gold-plated golf clubs would not be considered personalty. Such items would remain on the list.

All possessions used exclusively by the children (clothing, furniture, toys, books, tools, room furnishings, etc.) are assigned to the children and deleted from the list.

All items still remaining on the list are subject to bargaining. Add together all the cash values of these items and divide the total cash value by two. If the total cash value of all items remaining on the list is $12,000, each of you has a right to $6,000 of it—more or less. This value, half of the total cash value of the possessions, is called your "personal purchasing power."

Next, take the remaining photocopy of the list and conform it exactly to the list you have just developed by deleting the same items and by circling the same dollar values. When both copies of the list are identical, give one to your wife and keep the other for yourself.

The next step is to allocate your purchasing power to the items on the list that you want.

Each of you now has enough personal purchasing power to buy half the items on the list. You and your wife do this privately and separately. The allocation will not be fair if either of you knows in advance how the other is allocating his or her purchasing power.

The winner of the bargaining for any particular item is determined by the relative amounts of personal purchasing power allocated to the item by you and your wife. The party who has allocated the greater amount of purchasing power wins the item.

Certain items have sentimental or personal value far beyond their cash value. To accommodate this phenomenon, you can allocate as much of your personal purchasing power as you want to any item. By bidding high enough, you ought to be able to secure for yourself a particular cherished possession. But in so doing, you will forfeit more of your purchasing power than would normally have been required.

To illustrate how the system works, suppose the vacuum cleaner had an agreed on cash value of $60. Your wife allocated

$25, and you allocated $20 of purchasing power to it. Your wife is the winner of the bargaining and the vacuum cleaner is hers; she has received the full cash value, $60 worth. Now consider a grandfather clock you purchased at auction. The cash value of the clock is $450. You cherish that old relic, but unfortunately, your wife likes it, too. You decide that to get the clock you will forego some of the purchasing power you might spend on other assets, so you intentionally overbid on it. You allocate $600 of your purchasing power to the clock. Your wife allocates $400 to it. You are the winner of the bargaining and the clock is yours. You have received $450 of the family's assets, but it cost you $600 in purchasing power.

The above examples illustrate how bargaining works under this method. It should be obvious why you and your wife must be separate and private when you make your allocations. When you have completed the task, check your figures to make sure that you have not spent more (or less) than you have to spend. Husband and wife now come back together to compare their biddings on the listed items.

It often happens that husband and wife will each allocate equal amounts of their purchasing power to one or more items. It can also happen, despite earlier precautions, that there will be some items on which neither husband nor wife make a bid. These are special cases that require additional bargaining. First, however, complete the division of spoils for the items that have been bid for. This should handle most of the items. Next, add up the cash values of all special case items and divide by two to obtain new amounts of personal purchasing power. Husband and wife next allocate their new purchasing power over the remaining items, as before. Repeat the process until all items have been awarded.

There is little advantage to be gained by bidding very low on undesirable items, since these items should be able to be sold for approximately their fair market value. There is also little to be gained by squandering one's purchasing power unnecessarily through excessive overbidding on items of sentimental value. Finally, we emphasize that each of you has only enough purchasing power to "buy" about half of your combined possessions. The allocation should be judicious.

It may be instructive to prepare a few dummy examples of ten or so items, to assign fictitious cash values to each and allocations of personal purchasing power for husband and wife, just to see what happens. You will quickly discover a disparity in the dollar value of items gained by each party. One party generally comes out ahead in terms of dollar value. When this happens, the other party generally comes out ahead in terms of getting the items that he wanted badly. Neither party need feel that he or she has lost. The person who received most in terms of dollar value may be able to sell those items of small personal value, thereby turning their market value into cash; the person who got most of what he wanted out of the bargaining should feel satisfied.

BARGAINING IN CONTESTED DIVORCE. Almost by definition, there is little or no bargaining in contested divorce. Instead, what passes for bargaining consists of continuing attempts to force concessions from the other side while yielding as little as possible of one's own position. Because both sides are similarly engaged, the "bargaining" takes on the characteristics of a small war. We know of one man who shot and killed his wife as a result of an argument over a separation agreement.

The war is protracted, sometimes lasting for years beyond the final divorce decree. It can become a consuming war into which the parties throw themselves with every ounce of vigor; their lives are spent shoveling money into the legal system to correct presumed or actual inequities. Underlying the entire effort may be nothing more noble than human pride, a foolish pride which demands that one consume oneself merely trying to get even for some relatively minor fault that happened years ago.

The ultimate objectives of such wars are generally associated with money. These objectives are sought through various predictable strategies: by forcing out-of-court agreements, by provoking judicial action, by causing the other side to so completely expend its financial resources that resistance must be abandoned, and by applying sufficient psychological stress to the other side as to render resistance ineffective.

Most often, the war is fought within the boundaries of the law; nothing is done that is actually illegal, although ethically or morally there may be cause for concern. Frequently, however, the actions of one or both parties are of questionable legality, so that it might require a judicial decision to clarify the situation. And sometimes, the acts are out-and-out illegal. Here are some examples.

> The wife threatens to smear the husband's reputation by putting the history of his indiscretions in the hands of the press.

The press quite likely will pass the story up out of concern for liability, but the husband does not understand this and is terrified. He gives the wife most of his property and a very generous alimony. Nothing is illegal.

A wife shows up at the husband's office, where she screams at the husband and accuses the husband's secretary of being his mistress. He has not been having an affair, and the wife knows it. It is merely a tactic. Nothing is illegal. Similar events have taken place with the wife breaking into an important business meeting of the husband, or intentionally getting mildly drunk and flying into a rage of accusations at a business party. In none of these events was the wife's action illegal.

A wife swore out a nonsupport charge against her husband who had, she claimed, failed to pay her any support at all during a two-month period. She also went on welfare. During this period the husband had written checks to his wife in excess of $600 for her support. The husband was subsequently jailed on the nonsupport charge. The whole thing was a ruse to obtain personal service of papers on the husband in order to have a hearing regarding custody and alimony. Once the husband had been served the wife dropped the nonsupport charges. The wife was criminally liable for falsely swearing that the husband had not been supporting her. She was also criminally liable for swearing that he was her husband for, in the same jurisdiction, she had earlier obtained an *ex parte* divorce from her husband without his knowledge. The husband was unable to find a lawyer who would press charges of perjury against his ex-wife, possibly because the wife's lawyer was recently a member of the county prosecutor's office. The husband was unable to obtain legal redress for the wrongs done him, despite the fact that it cost him several thousand dollars in legal and other fees.

John and Mary were divorcing, but with reasonable amicability. Thus far, things were proceeding nicely. They had been working out the property settlement, and Mary was being more than generous since her husband was attending school and was employed only part-time. She, on the other hand, was employed full-time and was the primary breadwinner of the family. It was only after the property settlement had been agreed upon that Mary was served the divorce papers. John accused her of adultery. Had Mary known that beneath the calm bargaining proposed by her husband an adultery rap had been in the making, she would have been a much tougher adversary. By the time she discovered it, it was too late.

Winter and Hersh[5] have reported tactical advantages which can accrue to careful timing of events. Since conditions tend to deteriorate throughout the process of a contested divorce, they recommend that the husband's lawyer depose the wife as early in the proceedings as possible. At that time, she may have warm feelings toward her husband and may be made to admit, for example, that the husband was a good provider and a good father. Were depositions to be taken at a later date, her opinion might be less favorable. They further indicate that, if the husband intends to seek custody, this fact should not be known to the wife's side until after she has been deposed, for similar reasons. And if the wife is engaged in an affair, and it is the intention of the husband's side to depose her lover, she should not know of this until after she has been deposed, since she would then become hostile and uncommunicative.

Control of time can be useful in other ways. The ability to delay forwarding of alimony checks may reduce the wife's economic resources to a bare subsistence level, or may force her to seek employment. The former may force concessions at the bargaining table as an alternative to starvation; the latter may reduce her ability to demand alimony if she demonstrates her capacity to earn a good income. If the wife is having an affair, she may be impatient to be with her lover and establish a normal living relationship with him (with the side benefit of getting him off of the "available men list" before another woman discovers him). If the husband is aware of this situation, he may deliberately stall the divorce, increasing his wife's anxiety. When the stress gets too much to bear, she may be willing to make inordinate concessions at the bargaining table in order to have the divorce done quickly.

There are even occasional income tax benefits which accrue to delay. If it appears that the divorce could be made final in December, by delaying until January, the husband secures the legal right to file a joint income tax return. Especially if his income is large and his wife's small, the husband will benefit by the delay, even if he has to split the tax return with his wife.

A further advantage to be gained by the manipulation of time is that the party who controls the timing of events induces uncertainty into the life of the other party, and many people find uncertainty stressful; they prefer to know what is going to happen, and when, so that they can prepare for it. By getting keyed up and ready for a hearing, only to have the hearing fall through at the last minute, they experience a wearing emotional crash. And of course, since the hearing did not come off, all this will have to be gone through again at some time in the future. And there are, sometimes, other advantages.

> Jack's wife filed against him, alleging adultery and desertion. Jack had sufficient evidence to lodge a similar complaint against his wife, but intentionally delayed his counterclaim. By law, he had ninety days to file his answer to her claims. He counterclaimed on the eighty-eighth day. He realized that by waiting until just before the ninety-day period had expired, he and his wife would have been separated for eighteen months, the necessary period to qualify for a no-fault divorce in his jurisdiction, and he was able to add this as a counterclaim in his answer. Correctly, he had guessed that his wife would feel obliged to modify her complaint to add no-fault to her claims; this, of course, increased her legal fees. Through this and other actions her legal expenses attained such magnitude that, at one point, her attorney refused to continue with her case until he had been paid $1,000 of his fee. This generated animosity between his wife and her lawyer, and seriously weakened their ability to work as a team to develop their case.

Threats of various kinds are frequently employed, as we have already seen. The prospect of contesting for the custody of a child may so threaten the wife that she will yield an otherwise strong position regarding alimony and property.[6] Where the family owns a number of items of great sentimental value to one of the parties, and when they are in the physical possession of the other party, the other may threaten to sell them off one by one, giving the first party half of the proceeds, or spending the proceeds on legal fees. The first party has no legal recourse and may be willing to trade items of much greater value in return for physical possession of the cherished items. Threat of prosecution for criminal adultery can be applied against an adulterous spouse in some jurisdictions. Where the statutes provide for it, prosecution for interference with the family may be threatened. This is a legal remedy directed against the interloper. Interference with the family is dying away as a statutory remedy, and is available in only a few jurisdictions. However, where it exists, it imposes harsh penalties on the interloper and these may weigh heavily upon the offending spouse.

Even in situations where fair bargaining is seemingly present, underhanded tactics may be employed. An example of such a subtle approach might be termed "snowballing momentum." Suppose the wife's lawyer applies the technique. He begins by giving a few small items to the husband's side, then counters to take a small concession for his own client. He repeats this cycle a few times, gradually working upward in the value of the items under consideration. His objective at this point is not to concern himself with the values of the items being traded, but to produce a spirit of powerful cooperation, to accelerate the bargaining process, and to induce an emotional crest similar to that often found at fast-moving auctions. A momentum develops which increasingly dominates and controls the bargaining. When the momentum is sufficiently high, when the husband is so pleased about the way the bargaining is going that he allows himself to become emotionally wrapped up in the good will projected by the other side, the wife's lawyer moves for the kill—he takes one, two, or three big items for his client, then shuts down the bargaining. The husband is stunned, expecting that the bargaining would continue, and that he would recoup his latest losses. Not so. The issue is closed, the momentum is gone, and so are the last possessions which were likely the sole goals of the wife and her lawyer.

A related technique consists of "forcing beyond the agenda." The basics of the method consist of spelling out, for the other side, the topics to be dealt with in discussion, but with sufficient generality to avoid an explicit definition of what will and what will not be discussed. The topics directly alluded to are relatively minor, requiring little preparation on either side to effect a fair bargaining. Unknown to the other side, however, intensive preparation has been devoted to one or two topics which can be construed to lie within the agenda and which are of considerable importance. Since the vagueness of the agenda seemingly allows these topics to be discussed, and since the other side has had ample opportunity to prepare for the discussion, their unwillingness to discuss the important issues can be made to appear as if they are unreasonable, or as if they have reneged on an obligation to bargain fairly.

A third variation is the "calculated disruption." One of the more subtle approaches consists of seeming to bargain fairly with the other side, but on one's own premises where the meeting can be disrupted by signal or prearrangement. To illustrate the effect, suppose your wife's lawyer presents a well-reasoned argument suggesting that your wife should receive a particular item. Upon his conclusion, your lawyer presents an equally compelling argument suggesting that you should have it. But just before your lawyer gets to the "punch line" of his argument, a secretary opens the door to call your wife's lawyer from the room. The discussion stops. In two or three minutes, he returns, and once again your lawyer tries to argue that you should have the item; this time he completes his presentation, but now it lacks conviction and seems flat and somehow artificial. A counterargument may now be overwhelming. When the "bargaining" of the day is actually concluded, many of your points may have been disrupted and either yielded to her side or set aside for later bargaining, and many of her arguments will have been granted. And of course, when the agenda of the next meeting is prepared, the items to be discussed will consist almost entirely of items you are reluctant to lose, and she can be expected to receive her fair share of them.

Calculated disruption also exists in a violently different form. Bargaining begins with discussion of items which (unbeknownst to you) are of little value to the wife, but which are of some value to you. In many or most cases, her lawyer (or she) makes an argument designed to win these items. However, through careful advance preparation, their arguments are possessed of flaws which enable you to win the arguments rather handily. She allows this to continue as long as she wishes. Then, just before an item of considerable value is brought under discussion, she literally explodes. Livid with rage, she jumps up, slams her palm down on the table, shrieking invectives. "This is no bargaining session, you bastards, this is a calculated rape!" Turning to her lawyer, "You, you son of a bitch, you're selling me down the river, and I'll be damned if I'll pay you one red cent!" She hurls her chair out of the way, storms from the room, nearly tearing the door from its hinges when she slams it shut. Her lawyer is visibly upset. "I'd better go talk to her. Excuse me for a moment." He leaves the room for a few mintues, returning with your wife who is still steaming with anger. At this point, negotiations are seemingly about to break down. Things seem perilously close to moving into a contested divorce. With very little argument, your wife gets the next item on the list, the valuable one she was planning on all along. If she loses the item, she again goes into a tirade and storms from the room, breaking up the meeting for the day. Later, your lawyer is informed that your wife has now become utterly unreasonable—either some concessions are going to have to be made or she has sworn to take the whole thing to court to let the judge adjudicate the matter. Because this form of planned disruption is so sudden and violent in its intensity, you will find yourself disposed toward leniency, especially since you will have received nearly every item discussed up to this point. Because of this, and because of the risk of a bad result in trial, she will probably get the item she wanted.

"Bait-and switch" bargaining also can be found. The technique is nearly identical to the confidence game of the same name. The principle is to offer a substantial bargain to the other side, but when they try to accept it, the initial offer is denied; a misunderstanding has occurred, it is alleged. What is really offered is a lesser bargain (or one of very little worth), and you concede it to them. Grumbling, they accept the lesser bargain, and time is allowed to pass. Eventually, however, the original item again comes under discussion. But this time, your side refuses to hear any argument regarding it. After all, don't they remember that earlier concession? Hasn't your side bent over backwards to be equitable? No sir, there will be no discussion on *this* item. After all, fair is fair, and they have already gotten their share. Consequently, this issue, by foregone conclusion, is yours. When it works, they go away mad, but they go away, leaving you with the prize.

To avoid giving away your case or damaging it in any way, the general rule is to deal with your wife's lawyer only through your own. Always remember, if you have to talk to him, that you must not make threatening gestures toward him or use threatening language. It goes without saying that you must not touch him physically. All such things can be taken as assault or assault-and-battery. Even "telling him off," if it involves foul language, can get you in trouble. Many states have statutes prohibiting the use of foul language; if yours is one of them, remember that his costs of initiating a lawsuit are negligible compared to your own.

PROPERTY AND MONEY IN CONTESTED DIVORCE. A list of assets

compiled earlier can be a very powerful aid to you in bargaining for the spoils in a contested divorce. *You* will have exhaustive knowledge of the family's assets and possessions; your wife may not. She will be aware of the more obvious things (house, car, checking account), but she may have only a vague idea of your sources of income, your holdings in bonds, and even your gross income.

In contested divorce, you will almost certainly be questioned under oath ("deposed") as to your assets by the other side. You will be required to complete interrogatories (sworn affidavits) which will ask detailed questions about your finances and holdings. Thus, you are under serious obligation to answer truthfully. The courts will deal harshly with any attempt to conceal assets. However, you need not provide to the other side any information you are not directly asked through interrogatories or depositions. To keep the *list of possessions* secret from the other side is not concealing assets. If you are wise, the other side will never know about the list. If they suspect its existence they will ask for it and you will be required to release it.

The list of possessions is not intended as a ploy for concealing your assets; rather, its value lies in the power it gives you to bargain with knowledge of all of the possessions which are at risk. Your trading will take into account not merely the value these items have for you but also the value they have for your wife. She often will be surprised at the concessions you require before you will release to her some item that she particularly cherishes.

Your next greatest weapon is possession. The legal truism is that "possession is nine points of the law." This is less true in domestic law than in other areas, but it helps, nonetheless. Supposing you and your wife have separated and are living in different residences. The possessions you have in your residence are not readily examined by your wife, just as those in her residence are not readily examined by you. The locked apartment door represents a formidable barrier. Monthly statements from the bank for the checking and/or savings accounts, paycheck stubs, cancelled checks, personal correspondence, receipts for purchases, loveletters, etc., are not easy to obtain when they are in another's possession.

Possession of money is an advantage. The courts and the other side will take a dim view of you if you close out the joint bank accounts and open new accounts in your own name, excluding your wife. But they have a much harder time arguing against such actions if you withdraw all such cash resources, pay off as many debts as possible (including your legal fees, perhaps to the extent of an overpayment in anticipation of later legal expenses), and then, if there is any money left over, sending your wife a check for precisely half of it, and either keeping the balance in your pocket or in a new account in your name alone. By doing so, you make it harder for your wife to expend the joint resources of the family in ways that are to her particular advantage.

Credit cards and other kinds of charge accounts represent special threats; they are avenues through which your wife can directly attack your financial resources. As early as possible, try to convince your wife that all such accounts should be held separately, not jointly. If you can obtain her credit card, send it with your own card to the issuing agency, enclosing a check for the entire balance with instructions that the account is to be closed. Then, in a few days, start an account in your name alone if you really must have such an account.

If your wife refuses to yield her cards, then follow the advice in Chapter 2; notify the issuing agencies that you have lost your card and that you want a new account number. They will block the old card from being used and will issue new cards (to *your* address, not your wife's, as you will have instructed them). This will effectively prevent your wife from using her old cards and will block use of the "old" account, even if there remains an unpaid balance.

> Things had been somewhat distant between John and Elga, but there had been no serious arguments. One day, while John was doing some work on the house, Elga told him that she wanted to go visit her mother for a few days. John did not object, so she took their three children and left. Two days later, John was astounded to receive a summons and complaint for divorce. Obviously, Elga had been busy behind John's back for some time. John was particularly angered by her unilateral action, and a series of hostile telephone calls took place between his home and his mother-in-law's where Elga was staying. In one such call John indicated that, if there was to be a divorce, he felt it best to split things right down the middle—to sell the house and divide the proceeds, etc. She failed to agree and hung up. Within a week, John received a

> court order evicting him from his house and forbidding him from disposing of any assets. He was later cited for contempt for expending some of the savings account money to defray his expenses.

Elga may have had the legal wheels working for some time to get John evicted, and to tie down his assets. A likelier explanation is that John's telephone call made her realize that John could sell the house out from under her and deny her the security of the family's other financial resources. Faced with such worries, she contacted her lawyer who took care of the matter deftly. We also suspect that John did not properly question the court's order in this matter.

In most jurisdictions, the rights of the court to evict a man from his home, or to secure his assets, are controlled by legal guidelines; for example, the court may be required to have probable cause to believe that the husband intends actually to dispose of such assets, and the court may be required to indicate, *in the order,* what such grounds were. A defective order can be appealed, and any order may be suspect where the husband was not notified of the action to be taken against him. Because men so frequently do not resist the courts' orders in these matters, the courts in many locales have grown lax and have deviated from legal standards and guidelines. Never accept any order at face value if it is not to your liking. Explore the matter with your lawyer, to see whether there may be avenues of counterattack. Chances are, of course, that the counterattack will fail, but to risk $400 for a challenge against the otherwise certain loss of a $50,000 home seems reasonable.

In arguing against the loss of assets, make full use of the two sets of figures which you have assigned to each item (cost if purchased new, and current market value). If your wife or her lawyer argues that she needs the $350 freezer, counterargue that the machine is now half-way through its probable life span and has lost considerable value, and give her $175 to purchase a used one for herself. Whenever she is awarded an item, staunchly maintain that the value she has received is the value of the item purchased new at current market prices. If they argue that you have received $400 of assets in the microwave oven, counterargue that you have received only its current market value—what it would sell for in its current condition. Your ability to argue from both sets of figures can complicate the other side's ability to bargain. Lawyers, of course, are old hands at such bargaining; yours is, and so is hers. She is *not,* but you, because of your preparation, will be. This is an advantage to you.

Be alert for the slightest move on the part of the other side to talk in terms of gross income. Especially if your wife is not employed, they may try to talk about the few dollars she receives, in comparison to how much you earn. But out of this seemingly huge gross income, you will face mandatory withholdings as a result of your job (retirement plan, medical insurance, state and Federal income tax, Social Security, workmen's compensation, and so forth). If you work in the professions, there may be other expenses which you necessarily incur: dues to professional societies, union dues, tools, trips to professional meetings and workshops, professional journals, reference works, special uniforms or protective clothing; if you work in sales, add on expensive clothing, and perhaps a new car every year.

Before allowing any consideration of how much money she deserves, or you deserve, as a result of your earned income, reduce the discussion to your expendable income—your income after all deductions and job-related expenses have been taken into account. Even if the other side doesn't like this approach, the judge may be willing to listen even if he tends to favor the woman. He will be unwilling to hamper your capability of earning an income. To do so is to kill the goose that lays the golden egg. If you can't earn, she can't receive.

Disallow any attempt at a sweeping, blanket transfer of possessions; resist this to the utmost. It is all too easy to agree to the wife receiving "all the household effects," which may include thousands of dollars of items you may need for your own survival. If they attempt this, modify it to read, "all household effects except the following: . . ." and then list every item in the house. Make them bargain for each and every item, all the while insisting to your wife that bargaining would best be accomplished directly between the two of you, leaving the lawyers out of it because all they accomplish is running up the fees.

As assets are divided between you during the bargaining process, be wary of the "meet me half-way" rip-off. The method is employed by the other side in what seems to be a fair bargaining (generally early in the divorce process). Each side agrees that the spoils and debts will be divided fairly between them and that any remaining debts will be the responsibility of the party who incurs them. The technique is enabled by the absence of a dated and signed agreement to that effect.

As a result of bargaining, the assets have been divided, many debts cancelled, and you, through penurious living, have made great strides to reduce your remaining debt load. Then, during trial, the other side asks that the family obligations be fairly divided, and that you "meet them half-way." To the judge this seems fair, but to you it is a rip-off, since you have already paid half (or more) of the family's obligations and are now being asked to assume *half of what remains*. This will result in you accepting at least three-quarters of the obligations, rather than the half earlier understood as a basis. If you try to resist this seemingly generous offer in front of the judge, the other side will ask to see the agreement you allude to and, of course, it does not exist. They will claim a misunderstanding on your part, and that it was never their position that the matter had been settled. All of these arguments and counterarguments, unless huge sums are involved, will bore the judge; chances are he will order you to "meet them half-way."

You can prevent the "meet me half-way" game from being played by insisting on a signed agreement between yourself and your wife. Even if it is sketchily drawn up, even if it is in longhand, it should incorporate all statements of intent and list the items awarded to each side. This agreement is not the "separation agreement." It is a memorandum of understanding regarding what has been agreed upon regarding the disposition of assets in consequence of a particular meeting. In such a signed memorandum a statement that all assets have been fairly divided, and that all remaining debts are, from this date forward, accepted by each party as being their separate and personal responsibility without recourse through the other party, can go far toward protecting you against the "meet me half-way" game. If the other side refuses to sign, even if they beg off on the grounds that such a signature is premature, then indicate that all items discussed during the session have been similarly discussed only in a preliminary way, and that no possessions are physically to be transferred and no action as to debts or other responsibilities is to be taken until a more complete understanding has been reached. If they are willing to agree, they should be willing to sign. If they are not willing to sign, be on your guard.

We have discussed two of the strongest weapons you have in

dealing with the other side: the list of assets, and the actual physical possession of assets. The first and most powerful weapon the husband has, however, is *the right to say no*. This power is far greater than the husband usually believes it to be. He has the right to object, strenuously object, to anything he does not like. He does not have to sign a separation agreement unless each and every word in it is acceptable to him. He does not have to accept the terms of a court order. In many cases it is possible for him to demand that certain phrases or responsibilities presented in the order be modified, especially if he feels that the party which drafted the order (generally the plaintiff's lawyer) misinterpreted the judge's verbal order. If the judge has already signed the court order, it is effective, and the husband must obey the terms of the order; but even while obeying the order he can simultaneously be taking legal action against it. The husband's lawyer can urge him to give up the house to his wife and children; the husband can refuse, saying that there is an approach which is better for him, even if he does not yet know what it is.

No matter how much the other side presses, the husband has the right to say no, no, no, and no. If they feel so strongly about their position, let them prove it to the judge. Let them move the case into a full-blown contest and let the judge decide who is right. Even if the husband has been a real rat, provided he has not lied about his assets, the chances are that the judge will not make an award greater than half of his assets and income, including all alimony, child support, and property awards. Since this is likely the worst that can happen, and since your careful and exhaustive preparation of your case should reduce even this possibility, should they be too antagonistic, you can always say *no*.

9

Trial Preparation—Evidence

WHEN A case goes to trial evidence must be presented. The other side will have little work to do, and will probably do little work, because the standards of proof applied by the judge tend to be less demanding of the woman than of the man. But make no mistake, the evidence your side brings into the courtroom must be real evidence, capable of standing up in court. But what is evidence? Do you really know? Your lawyer knows, but he doesn't have the time to play detective, chasing after clues; neither has he the time to train you. By default, the responsibility for your education, and the responsibility for gathering the evidence needed for the trial, becomes yours.

What Is Evidence?

Evidence is any fact that is brought into the courtroom and presented during trial. Evidence establishes that things which are alleged to have happened did happen in reality, or it proves that alleged events did not happen. In jurisdictions where "dissolution of marriage" or similar no-fault bases for divorce are available, you may hear that evidence of marital fault is of no importance. This is true only in part: evidence regarding marital fault is not important as a determinant of whether you (or your wife) can get a divorce. However, evidence of marital fault can still be a persuasive determinant of how much alimony, if any, the wife will receive, and what rights she has regarding property of the marriage, even if you are divorcing on no-fault grounds. A preponderance of evidence against you can correspondingly increase the financial benefits awarded to your wife. Evidence of marital fault has similar implications in the award of child custody and visitation rights, whether the grounds for divorce are no-fault or not.

What Is a Fact?

A fact is anything the judge believes to be true. You may present to the judge a string of witnesses and filmed evidence to prove your point and still hear him proclaim later that you have failed to support your case, and that the facts point to the opposite conclusion. The facts of a case are precisely what the judge believes them to be; no more and no less.

Case histories, discussions with lawyers, and discussions with those who are involved in or have been involved in matrimonial litigation suggest a certain pattern of judicial behavior: that the judge will believe the evidence presented if it comes from a woman, especially if she is pretty, feminine, nicely dressed in pastels (not mod, revealing, or flashy), if she appears demure, and if the judge does not catch her in a flagrant lie during the proceedings. Giving the judge his due, he will anticipate perjury in the presentations of both sides, but will tend to give the woman the benefit of the doubt. He is, after all, a man (in most cases), and his appreciation of such womanly virtues as your wife will project on the stand is as great as your own.

The judge will also tend to believe the evidence if it is not too strongly objected to by either side. If a fact is presented by one side and is not refuted by the other, the judge will likely consider the fact to be a fact.

The judge will also tend to believe a statement to be true if he wants to. For example, a man won custody of his children from his wife and she appealed. In that state, recently enacted legislation required the tender-years doctrine to be applied in custody issues. Notwithstanding this, and without finding the mother unfit to have custody, the judge had ruled directly against the statute. The case was affirmed on appeal; the father kept the kids. Apparently, in this case, the judge wanted to believe the father's case, despite the statutory requirement that he give the weight of favor to the mother. And the appellate court backed him up. No matter what evidence the mother presented, the judge did not seem to feel her case to be especially moving.

The judge will also tend to believe your facts if he likes you. This is simple human nature, and explains why you should present a good appearance in court, why you should dress neatly and well, have your hair neatly trimmed, etc. Certainly, don't give a conservative judge the idea that you are a weirdo. (Related matters are discussed in Chapter 10.)

Finally, the judge will tend to believe your story and your evidence if he suspects no collusion between you and your wife, if your corroboration is strong, and if you have not been caught up in a lie. Judges believe themselves to be excellent lie detectors and, indeed, many of them are. Sitting under oath, with the threat of a perjury rap looking you in the eye, and with the awesome power of the law surrounding you, the pressure to tell the truth is compelling. Attempts to do otherwise frequently come across fumblingly.

Corroboration

Corroboration refers to the way the facts in your case fit together. If a stranger can swear to the same facts as do you, the stranger's testimony corroborates your own. A variety of sources of evidence, all of which say the same thing, tend to build a story which is irrefutable. Especially for the man, strong corroboration is necessary. We have already seen that the man can sometimes be jailed, or evicted from his home, on the uncorroborated statement of his wife. We have never heard of a similar situation affecting a woman.

The kind of case which the husband ideally should build is one in which every major point is backed up by powerful, irrefutable corroboration. A fact in isolation is often no fact at all.

What Kinds of Things Are Evidence?

Papers. Notes, letters (especially in handwriting), questionnaires completed by one of the parties, financial and other records, medical reports, newspaper clippings, affidavits, court orders, court records, and other kinds of paper are evidence.

> One morning as Jim left for work, his wife asked him to drop some letters into the mail. Later, as he dropped the letters into the mailbox, he noticed that one was addressed to a magazine. Thinking his wife might have paid for an extension of their subscription, Jim withheld this letter for he had, himself, extended the subscription a few days earlier. Later in the day he opened the letter and found a questionnaire completed by his wife regarding her sexual attitudes, and indicating that she had had two affairs since their marriage.

On the basis of this revelation, discovered innocently, Jim moved for a divorce. The value of the questionnaire was not so much in its contents, as in the threatening power it had for the wife. Her handwriting on the questionnaire could readily be identified as her own, by an expert, should she deny she had completed it. The threatening power could be exercised by confronting her with the questionnaire during trial. The questionnaire contained a personal admission of her adultery, and she did not suspect that her husband had such evidence. If she were to admit to the completion of the questionnaire, but maintain that her answers to it were false, she would have had a hard time explaining such behavior to the court.

OBJECTS. Physical objects are also evidence. The belt with which she whipped the children, the butcher knife with which she threatened your life, the cast-iron skillet she used to raise a lump on your head—all such objects are evidence.

PHOTOGRAPHS, MOTION PICTURES, AND TAPE RECORDINGS. These are also evidence, except that surreptitiously obtained tape recordings are not admissible in court in some jurisdictions.

All evidence that the husband attempts to introduce to the court may be challenged by the other side. Your first line of defense is *identification*. Someone at the trial *must* be able to identify each piece of evidence. Suppose, for example, that you have a typed letter from your wife to her lover which contains statements damaging to her case. With your wife on the witness stand being questioned by your lawyer, the scene may go something like this:

> LAWYER: Now, Mrs. Jones, I hand you this letter.
>
> HER LAWYER: Just a minute. I want to look at that. (*He looks, then hands it to your wife.*)

LAWYER: Now tell me. Mrs. Jones, have you ever seen this letter before?

WIFE: No.

LAWYER: No? Isn't that your signature at the bottom?

WIFE: Well, it looks like mine, but I never saw it before, so it must be a forgery.

At this point, your wife has failed to identify the document. The next step may be an attempt to locate a handwriting expert to obtain testimony that the signature is genuine, presuming that the court will allow sufficient time for such an expert to be found. Failing to establish the authenticity of the letter, your wife may not be questioned about it.

As a rule, one may expect the other side to do everything possible to prevent your evidence from being admitted. Where you try to introduce an affidavit, they may respond that it could have been prepared by anyone; where you try to introduce photocopies of hospital records, they may contend that they are not authentic. Even if their arguments are not persuasive and the evidence is finally admitted, they may have so severely challenged its authenticity or import that its value will have been sorely damaged. In one case, a man's evidence was so successfully challenged that he was unable to introduce any germane evidence against his wife at all; he suffered a serious defeat at trial in consequence.

The problem of identifying and authenticating evidence is overcome by a back-door solution. This is through the testimony of witnesses which is corroborated by the evidence. To illustrate how this works, suppose your private investigator is on the stand, being questioned by your lawyer:

LAWYER: Now, Mr. Smith, where were you on the night of January 28?

MR. SMITH: I was at the Park Road motel, outside cabin 16.

LAWYER: And just what did you see there?

MR. SMITH: I saw Mrs. Jones inside, embracing another man.

LAWYER: Now, Mr. Smith, I hand you this photograph and ask you if you recognize it.

HER LAWYER: Just a minute. I'd like to look at that. (*He looks, then hands it to the witness.*)

MR. SMITH: Yes. I took this photograph through the window of cabin 16.

LAWYER: Now, Mr. Smith, would you describe for the record what the photograph shows?

MR. SMITH: Yes. The photograph shows Mrs. Jones and another man embracing.

Notice, in the example, that it was not the photographic evidence which was compelling, but rather the testimony of the witness. The photograph served to authenticate his testimony. Also notice how the lawyer caused the witness to identify the photograph. In each example, the wife's lawyer interrupted the proceedings to examine the evidence. He asks to see the evidence before it is handed to the witness, and he does so for two reasons. First, unless he sees the photograph or letter (or whatever the evidence is), he will have no understanding of where the questioning may be going; without such knowledge he would be unable to anticipate (and subsequently, to prevent) an improper line of questions. Second, some evidence, such as letters, may contain hearsay evidence, unsubstantiated statements, or prejudicial information which might predispose the judge against the lawyer's client, even if he successfully prevents the evidence from being admitted. Better to prevent the line of questions from being started than to allow the prejudicial information to be talked about and then rejected.

The second-best method of authenticating or identifying evidence is applied in situations where a witness exists but cannot be brought into court. Such witnesses are deposed, their depositions transcribed, and a certified copy of the transcript submitted to the court. While this is an expensive process, the depositions of witnesses arrive in court with great credibility, since the witness was questioned in the presence of two lawyers, one representing each side of the case. In effect, the witness has been examined by both sides, just as if he were in court.

Sometimes, such witnesses are reluctant to "get involved" in the divorce, and may be unwilling to testify or to be deposed. At the risk of arousing the ire of such witnesses, they may be subpoenaed. Under subpoena, they are required to cooperate and come to court, or to participate in depositions. Theoretically, failure to respond to the subpoena is punishable in law; in reality, however, if a witness does not show up in court there is little to be gained for one's own case by bringing action against the violator, and lawyers are reluctant to undertake such action.

If a witness appears likely to fail to appear in court, it may be tactically advantageous to depose him in advance of trial.

Some classes of witnesses rely on professional ethics as a basis for refusing to give testimony or to take depositions. Medical doctors are examples. Their ethics prevent them from giving out information that might be harmful to their clients, especially if it is information they received in their professional capacity. Technically, the law does not recognize the "privilege" of the medical profession; in reality, the court is consistently unwilling to press the point, and evidentiary testimony can be obtained from doctors only if they are willing to participate. Similar principles hold for psychologists, but the courts accord them less "privileged" status in their relations with their clients than they accord members of the medical profession.

Jurisdictional problems sometimes make it difficult to obtain testimony, depositions, affidavits, etc., for production in court. For example, a subpoena issued in Missouri cannot compel an Alabama resident to appear in court; neither can it compel him to participate in depositions. Exactly this problem occurred in a case involving both Maryland and Pennsylvania. Custody actions were filed by the husband in Pennsylvania and (illegally) by the wife in Maryland. All the husband's evidence and witnesses were in Pennsylvania and, unfortunately, the Maryland case came to trial first. The courts of both states were technically entitled to hear the case, which meant that if the husband did not fight the custody battle in Maryland, he would legally lose custody and the Maryland decision would be binding. Under such pressure, the husband made a serious error. He submitted himself to the jurisdiction of the Maryland court, which, in effect, closed his rights to prosecute the matter in Pennsylvania. Had he stalled for a brief period he would have been able to rely on the Pennsylvania action as a means of issuing subpoenas for the deposition of key witnesses. Failing to do so, he had no basis for compelling Pennsylvania witnesses to take depositions other than through unenforceable Maryland subpoenas. In consequence, most of his valuable evidence never entered the courtroom, and he lost badly. Apparently it did not occur to him that he might have opened a hearing in Pennsylvania on some different but closely related matter, solely for the purpose of having legal cause in action against his wife which would involve deposing unwilling witnesses.

The third-ranking method for identification of evidence is for the husband to identify it himself, assuming that he can do so.

This is a weak method, owing to the fact that the court and the other side have a tendency to believe that the husband must have dummied up the evidence. By all means, if possible, important evidence should be identified by someone other than the husband.

Some kinds of evidence tend to be authentic in and of themselves. Letters written in the wife's handwriting tend to be so compelling that identification is nearly a foregone conclusion. Business papers which are kept in the conduct of everyday business (cancelled checks, check registers, earnings records, receipts of purchase, formally prepared business agreements, deeds, titles, etc.) typically are entered as evidence without too much fuss. But the principle remains: if the evidence is important, the husband must be prepared to identify the evidence and to certify its authenticity, and the best way to do so is through witnesses.

The manner in which evidence is collected can be important. We have indicated that surreptitiously obtained tape recordings are illegal in some jurisdictions. Evidence obtained illegally cannot be used in the courtroom, and may be a basis for criminal action against the party who gathered it. In some jurisdictions it is illegal to record conversations of people on the telephone; in other jurisdictions it is legal to record them from your own telephone conversations. Wiretapping someone else's telephone is illegal in all jurisdictions in the absence of a court order, and court orders are authorized only in criminal and national defense cases.

Similarly, bugging someone else's car or apartment to tape-record their conversations without their knowledge may be illegal in your jurisdiction and, furthermore, it can be quite risky. For example, entering an apartment to bug it might be considered breaking and entering with subsequent criminal prosecution. Such activities are probably best left to the experts—private investigators licensed in the jurisdiction—who know the ropes.

However, there are differences, under the law, regarding what one can do and what can be used as evidence. The rules of evidence for civil procedure are different from those of criminal procedure. In some circumstances these differences might allow bugging, although the resulting tapes are not admissible as evidence. In some cases this can be of great benefit, even if the recordings are not used in court.

In a California case, a father hired a private investigator to bug his wife's conversations with his eight-year-old daughter. The mother had spent many months in a mental institution, so that the father had temporary custody. For these and other reasons, visitations between the mother and child took place at the home of a mutual friend. Often, after the weekly visits, the child seemed disturbed and withdrawn. The father suspected brainwashing activities in which the wife was attempting to influence the child to produce testimony favoring her custody during trial.

The only place where mother and daughter were alone was in the back yard of the friend's home; consequently, the entire back yard had to be covered with concealed microphones. The tapes did, indeed, provide evidence of brainwashing, but more important, they revealed such abrupt mood changes in the child that the investigator felt the mother might be drugging the little girl to facilitate the brainwashing process. Urinalysis proved out the point. Definite traces of drugs were found. The tapes were not used at the trial. The urinalysis was. The father won his child in custody.

But consider how serious it could have been to the father's case if the concealed microphones had been discovered! Probably best left to the experts.

MORE ABOUT WITNESSES. The words spoken by people in the courtroom while being questioned under oath are referred to as testimony. Testimony is the single most believed-in source of information used in the courtroom. The quality of the witness is that he directly knows or has perceived something. His personal experience enables him to relate his perceptions to the court.

Unfortunately, time does damaging things to memory; a three-car pile-up on the freeway can become a five-car pile-up in a year's time. Witnesses tend to remember not what they saw, but what they think they saw. There is a mental process which works over the memory until the events seem to fit together in the witness's mind. Even witnesses who are attempting to be truthful on the witness stand, because they feel that every drop of information they possess must be made available to the court, sometimes go too far; they push their stories over the line that separates truth from imagination. Despite these shortcomings, witnesses are the most credible source of information you can get into the courtroom. Also, unfortunately, if you ask a witness to appear for you, or if you subpoena a witness to appear, you are liable for his travel expenses, meals, and loss of wages during his appearance. Since many witnesses do not know this, many are frequently not reimbursed for their expenses.

There are a number of different kinds of witnesses to be found in divorce cases. Most frequently encountered is the type who can provide testimony relating to the rights and wrongs of the case, to the things someone did (or did not do), or to conditions of things or people which the witness observed. Such witnesses are those who say that they saw the wife in an embrace with her lover; who saw that the house was little better than a dung heap; who saw the husband drunk and passed-out after a party; who saw the husband beat the wife with a broomstick; who saw the bruises on the wife's arm where the husband grabbed her; who saw the wife pin four diapers on the baby and leave him to lie in his own feces in the crib for hours.

Witnesses are those who have important contributions to the case you (and the other side) are trying to build. But witnesses are restricted in terms of the testimony they are allowed to give. They cannot venture beyond what they have seen and heard; and more, they cannot talk about what someone else said to someone else (such testimony is hearsay). They can, however, be asked (and can answer) questions about what the parties did or said in their presence. Thus, a next-door neighbor can testify that she heard you using foul language to your wife. The greatest weakness of the witness is his inability to stick to the facts of what he saw; he has a tendency to wander into the realm of speculation or to venture opinions. If he speculates or ventures opinions, he will be brought up short by the opposing lawyer. Too many such objections will make it seem that the testimony is all opinion and no fact, discrediting the witness.

The *character witness* is probably the second-most frequent witness found in the divorce trial. The function of the character witness is to prove that someone is a good person or a bad person. Your character witnesses are there to say that you are likeable, honest, straightforward, dutiful, God-fearing, brave, friendly, etc., etc.—in their opinion. Her character witnesses will say the same things about her. If there has been some impugning of the overall reputation of one party or the other, such statements are counteracted by character witnesses. The testimony of character witnesses is generally confined to the personalities of the parties in the action.

Expert witnesses are frequently professionals, such as medical doctors, psychologists, psychiatrists, social workers, nurses, and accountants. "Expert witness" is a title given to the witness only after an examination on the witness stand characterizes this person as expert in some body of learning. The process of examination is referred to as "qualifying" the witness as an expert, and includes questioning him about his educational background, his job experience, his publications in professional journals, etc.

After the witness has been placed on the stand and questioned by the lawyer who has called the witness, the other lawyer will have a crack at him. Especially if they see the expert doing damage to their case, they will try to discredit him by pointing out weaknesses in his background, experience, etc.; they may go to the trouble of obtaining textbooks in the expert's field to see if he is as familiar with the subject matter as an expert should be (attempting, of course, to prove that he does not know his stuff). Finally, it is the judge who will decide whether the witness will be considered expert.

The value of an expert witness is that, once qualified, he can be asked questions which call for his *professional opinion,* not necessarily based on facts he has observed in the case before the court. A pediatrician expert witness can give his *opinion* that sores observed by others on the baby's bottom were due to lack of proper hygiene; a witness can only state his *observation* that the child, in the care of the mother, was wearing a soiled diaper for over three hours before it was changed. A pattern of child care may be observed by a witness; an expert witness can give his *opinion* that such a pattern bodes ill for the child's future growth and development.

The expert witness need not be a trained professional, and a rarely used source of expert witnesses can be found in parents. In cases involving custody, it is sometimes possible to qualify other parents as expert witnesses; to do so requires, as a minimum, that they be parents and that they are provably doing a good job. Their kids are healthy, happy, have no police records, do well in school; preferably their kids range from late teenage down to the age of the child over whom custody is being contested. If qualified as experts, parents can provide their opinions regarding how well and how properly the father, for example, manages and cares for the children, or alternatively, how poorly the mother performs her parenting functions.

The *parties* to the action are also witnesses (of the common variety). During their testimony, they are allowed to make allegations against each other, provided they come up with some shred of evidence (something they saw, for example) to support the allegation, and they are entitled to deny accusations made against them. In other respects, they are treated as witnesses and are not allowed to venture their opinions regarding why other persons performed certain acts or what the probable sequelae will be. Usually, the courts afford the parties considerable leniency in their testimony, as do the lawyers, in an attempt to give each side a full opportunity to present its case, but the strength of their cases depends on the corroborative evidence they can introduce through witnesses and other sources to support their allegations and to refute the allegations of the other side.

The *children of the parties* can be witnesses; there is no law against it. But the testimony of children can be prevented by the judge in many jurisdictions, and the judge is likely to prevent it if the child is young. Children are generally not placed on the stand, because both parties and the judge find it abhorrent and damaging to the children. Still, the courts will sometimes listen to the opinions of children regarding which parent they prefer, especially if the child is "intellectually mature" enough to make the decision.

Court officials are sometimes witnesses. Most frequently the officials are social workers from a state-controlled social welfare agency or a child welfare bureau. The court in many jurisdictions can order that a social worker conduct an investigation into the two homes of the disputing parents in a custody case and recommend to the court his or her findings. A guardian *ad litem* also may be appointed by the judge to represent to the court the legal interests and welfare of the children apart from the interests of the parents. The guardian *ad litem* is usually a lawyer, frequently an older one of outstanding professional reputation. Just how this qualifies him to speak about children and their needs somehow eludes us. When so appointed by the court, the guardian *ad litem* is an officer of the court. He will conduct his own investigation, and render his own findings to the court. The husband will generally have to pay the (very high) fees of the guardian *ad litem*. In some cases, the children are awarded to the guardian *ad litem* as a temporary custodian. The testimony of court officers is treated as expert testimony, although some attempts may be made to discredit it, and their testimony, together with any reports they may submit to the court, arrives with a presumption of correctness which, in many cases, it definitely does not deserve.

Collusion is frequently suspect in divorce cases; the courts are suspicious of testimony delivered by the husband's best friend, or the wife's best friend. It is almost assumed that such people will stretch the truth or lie (commit perjury) to protect their friends. In the few states that still retain fault-only grounds for divorce, collusion is suspect if the testimony of husband and wife dovetails closely. This may have a bearing on the selection of witnesses. That witness is believed who causes the wife to faint when he walks into the courtroom; he is believed if, during his testimony against the wife, she jumps up from her seat and screams, "How could you do this to me, you rat!" The stranger, or the disinterested party, is usually more credible than a close associate. If the case is contested, the reliance on witness testimony will be strong; see that you locate witnesses who span the requirements.

Assembling Your Evidence

If your case against your wife is one of adultery, in trial you will be questioned by your lawyer in such a way as to bring out the aspects of your marital situation which demonstrate your contention of adultery, and other witnesses and evidence will be introduced to prove your claim. This approach, seen superficially, allows you to "tell your story" to the court. Seen more carefully, it will be noticed that the lawyer asks particular questions designed to draw out your testimony along particular lines. To prove adultery it is necessary that intent be demonstrated. His questioning will develop your testimony to show such intent on the part of your wife. Where other witnesses can corroborate your testimony vis-à-vis intent, he will draw out from them the needed corroboration. Each point that must be proved to establish adultery will, one at a time, be drawn out from each witness. Although there may have been many screaming, hair-tearing fights between you and your wife, these will receive only passing notice (to show that things were not good between you and your wife); aside from such perfunctory treatment, the lawyer will ignore fights and arguments. These would be germane to claims of extreme cruelty but not to claims of adultery.

If her affair with her lover was but a passing fling, and if he was a one-time associate of yours, she may try to defend against your adultery complaint by arguing that the whole thing was a setup. You and her lover were old buddies from your army days, and you paid him to seduce her. Her lawyer will try to obtain from his witnesses, and from her, evidence that her defense of connivance is well founded. If she has no counterclaims against you, and if you have no other claim against her, her lawyer will not dwell on testimony which might establish or defend against desertion, extreme cruelty, failure to support, etc.

As lawyers will develop their respective cases according to the available grounds and defenses, so must you be guided in your collection of evidence. The rule which should be burned into one's brain is: *what kind of evidence will be needed for my case?* Don't waste time gathering evidence you will not need. Your lawyer, and many books,[1] may suggest the kinds of things that can represent proof of your claim (or hers). The development of evidence, considered simplistically, involves: finding proof that what you say about her is true; finding proof that the likely things she will say in rebuttal are false; and finding proof that the likely things she will say about you are false. Evidence also should be gathered to demonstrate that many of the bad things you have done were caused by your wife, or that there were benign, rational reasons underlying your actions. Against her statement that you were never home, you might be able to show that you were frequently absent as a result of your job which requires you to travel extensively—and while she always complained about your absence, she didn't seem to have any difficulty spending your money. Predictably, your wife will have similar rationales to explain her behavior, and your evidence should be designed to find loopholes in her arguments. All evidence gathered should be definitely related to the particular grounds and the likely defenses which will be used in the case.

At the same time, one's field of view should be a broad one. Evidence of marital fault, of whatever kind, should be collected routinely if it comes readily to hand. If you have committed a marital fault that she has not been aware of, evidence to counteract a claim on that fault also should be gathered. These are secondary considerations to the development of evidence associated with the claims and counterclaims actually used in the filing and the answer. Their importance can be seen in the fact that the claim and the counterclaim can be modified to incorporate new grounds, or to drop old ones, right up to the point of trial. Just imagine your surprise two weeks before trial when she drops her claim of adultery against you (which she *knew* she could not prove) and inserts in its place a complaint of extreme cruelty against which you have absolutely no evidence in rebuttal!

In addition to the attack/defense of claims and counterclaims, a great deal of energy must be devoted to gathering financial evidence regarding your wife, your children, and yourself. Such evidence will be needed for any divorce or custody action, regardless of whether the action is to proceed on fault or no-fault grounds.

EVIDENCE AGAINST YOUR WIFE. The evidence gathered for use against your wife must show, as conclusively as possible, that the things you are charging her with are true. You must have examples of *specific* things she has done, and these must be tied down by time, date, location, other people present, and the social circumstances. The evidence gathered should demonstrate a pattern in her behavior which has persisted over some period of time. An exception to this could be some cases of adultery. In many states, demonstration of a single act of adultery on the part of your wife is sufficient grounds for a divorce; in other states, the court will forgive a single act which results from a moment of irrationality. More generally, however, the pattern concept is important. A single argument in which she clouts you on the head with a skillet is not sufficient for extreme cruelty; it takes a persistent pattern of acts which are dangerous to life and limb.

Building the pattern requires that you go back in time, to the earliest acts which she committed that are part of the pattern you wish to show. In exercising your memory, begin with present events, and work back in time (this is the "anchoring technique" used by psychological and sociological researchers to obtain complete and accurate recollections of past events). With a piece of paper and a pencil in front of you, take notes on your recollections of events, first listing only the events (the party at the Smiths where she blew up, the time the Joneses were at your house, etc.), and list such events as far back in time as you can. Then come back to the most recent events and elaborate on your notes (what happened? who witnessed it? what was the social setting? what was the date? the time of day? where did it take place? what caused what to happen? what happened as a result? how did others react? how did you feel about the thing that happened, both when it happened and later? were there direct, but long-range things which happened as a result?).

Keep these notes, and keep exercising your memory regarding them. You should be able to produce very complete notes for these events, even those that happened long ago, if you keep working at it. Carry a small pad of paper in your pocket and keep a pad and pencil by your bedside, to jot notes down as things occur to you, then work them over later. Keep part of your mind constantly tuned to the problem of recalling things that she did (and you did) which are related to the case. Each time you work on your notes, begin with the most recent events for which you have something more to add, then work back to earlier and earlier times.

Dates are important; they provide a temporal flow to events. Try to assign exact dates to events if you can, otherwise approximate dates, or even guesses as to when things took place. In the notes you keep, distinguish exact dates from approximate dates from guessed dates. You may find that some dates are seemingly in conflict. Excellent. That is one reason you are performing this exercise, to locate conflicts in your recollections so that they can be resolved. Sometimes you will have the distinct feeling that something is missing from an event, or that some bridge which should be present between two events is lacking; this may be nothing more than a feeling, a nudge in the back of your brain which suggests that a piece of the puzzle is not there. Dig a little. It is there in your brain if you can just retrieve it from storage; try to remember, to think about the events surrounding the missing piece. If this is not fruitful, drop the quest for a while and let your subconscious deal with it. It may awaken you in the middle of the night with the answer.

Such activities will enable you systematically to recall massive amounts of material regarding your wife's past actions. Next, deal with the present. What is your wife doing now? How does she spend her time? Don't assume you know, unless you have made the effort to find out. Verify your suspicions and expectations. Keep your ears open to things she says she does and begin making lists of them by date and time. How much time does she spend in each of these activities? Do any of her current behaviors provide fuel for your evidentiary fire? Does she work? How many hours per week? How much paid vacation? What other fringe benefits? What salary or wage rate? Do her work hours interfere with caring for children? with housekeeping? What does her work consist of? With whom does she associate, on the job and off? Does she come straight home after work, or are there periods of time unaccounted for? What are her spending patterns? Does she spend money extravagantly? How has this spending pattern changed over time? Any possibility that funds are being siphoned off for other purposes? How far is she traveling in her car? Are there periodic unexplained trips? Try to build a rounded picture of how she spends her time in the here and now, and be curious about blank spots.

Be equally curious about her future. Her plans are frequently significant. If she now plans to move to a different state after the divorce, this can complicate access to your children if she wins custody. The courts do not like totally to deny the father access (because he loses interest in paying for them), and will consider the fact of the wife's planned relocation when deciding custody. Does she plan to accept a job which will demand long hours away from the children when they are out of school? This suggests that she may not be in a good position to take care of the children. Does her job show promise of generating a good income in the years to come? Perhaps this means her needs for your money are lessened. Is she planning to go to school? Such schooling may qualify her for work which would enable her to be self-supporting; perhaps you should offer to pay for two years' schooling in lieu of alimony. Does she plan to marry her lover? If so, she may fight for a lump-sum settlement in lieu of alimony. Does she plan to continue seeing him between now and the trial? This provides opportunity for you to continue gathering evidence. Her plans for her immediate and distant future are of great importance to you; they should not be neglected in your search for evidence.

Events which have taken place in the past have a way of leaving traces which persist in the present. These traces consist of two things: people's memories and physical evidence. Physical evidence abounds, but you must find it. The short dark hair you discover on the collar of her coat is of interest, especially since your hair is gray and hers is long and blonde. About that trip she took three months ago; what did she wear on the trip? Check the pockets of the coat she wore. Hmmm, a spent train ticket between City A and City B, dated and punched to show that it was used. Into an envelope with it, together with a note regarding where and on what date you found it. Did she take any luggage? Oh, yes. The small overnight bag. Look through it. Search through the pockets inside the liner. Hmmmm. Vaginal jelly and a diaphragm. Why would she need contraceptives on a trip away from you? Put them back as you found them. She might miss them if she takes another trip. Make a note as to the date and location of the discovery and move on. How about the bottom drawer of her jewelry box. You never look in there. But you do now. How about that! A letter. "My darling Mary . . ." Read it, then put it back for the moment, but plan to photocopy it as soon as possible. The photocopy goes into an envelope with a note as to the date and location of the discovery. Check her lingerie drawer—you may find some interesting things beneath her undies. Does she have boxes of old letters, and papers stored on the closet shelves? Review their contents. When she sleeps, go through her purse, taking care not to disturb the way in which things are stored in the pockets. Any strange photographs? List the credit cards she carries by account number. If things go bad enough between you, remove the cards in order to close the charge accounts. What else do you find? If it would not be missed, take the snippet of evidence and place it in an envelope, with an explanatory note as to where and when it was found and why it may be significant.

If you can, take over the family finances and do the check writing for all the bills. This will give you an opportunity to examine the cancelled checks. Does everything seem in order? Any unnecessary expenditures she is making? Are all of her expenses explainable? Go back in time through the checks, and through the records of earnings of the family. Have either payments or incomes jumped or dropped in the past two or three years? If so, home in on the period of time when the change occurred and seek an explanation for the phenomenon.

Systematically begin going through all the drawers, cabinets, closets, and storage places throughout the house. Don't forget the undersides or back faces of drawers where valued papers may be taped in concealment. Try to project yourself into her mind. If you were she, where would you try to conceal things? How about the kitchen, the food storage areas? Her crochet basket and sewing box? Aha! The clothes hamper, in back of the clothes dryer, behind the boxes of detergents and bleaches? Would she be clever enough to conceal her treasures using reverse psychology? One wise man said that if you want to hide a present to your wife, put it at the bottom of her pile of unmended socks. Would your wife have concealed something in that pile of spare parts and pieces of junk you have accumulated in your shop? You haven't touched that pile of junk for years. Look for anything that does not seem to fit, anything new and out of place which might have a bearing on your case. Devote attention to her car. Monitor the distances she drives and the dates on which she drives such distances. Give the car a good going over. Search under and between the seats, look in the trunk and glove box.

Don't overlook the obvious: letters left lying on the coffee table from sources unknown to you or from old college boyfriends; notes, photographs, ticket stubs dropped into the wastebasket. It is not at all uncommon that some perverse part of our subconscious causes us to leave clues to our illicit behavior in the open where they can readily be found; it is almost as if we wished to be found out. The husband who comes home with lipstick on his collar is one example, the wife who leaves a love letter lying in plain sight is another. He (or she) may even take a certain perverse pleasure in the fact that the other has not noticed the evidence, even though it was in plain sight. This is followed by the presentation of even more evidence, more overtly displayed, until finally the message is clear. The wise man continues not to notice such things; he merely records them, documents them, and adds them to his file of evidence. Thus the evidence continues to be forthcoming, more, and more, and more.

Much physical evidence does not exist in terms of pieces of paper. Photographs, tape recordings, motion pictures, etc., may have to be brought to bear on the problem. Since you cannot take the courtroom to the scene, perhaps you can record the scene for the courtroom.

> Jim's wife maintained that her job was a lowly clerical job, while Jim earned much more as a professional. She also claimed a serious disability which prevented her from walking with safety on anything but the best walking surfaces. Without her knowledge, and while she lived nearly 2,000 miles away from Jim, photographs were taken of her office, showing it to be rather prestigious. Photographs of her car showed it to be nearly brand new, compared to photographs of Jim's car which was a wreck. Motion pictures were taken of her walking on ice, cleaning snow off her car, and driving off to work, actions which belied her statements regarding her disability.

FINDING WITNESSES. Almost all of the kinds of evidence discussed above are circumstantial evidence, and as such, the courts tend to accept them with a grain of salt, since circumstances are not always what they seem. And, with few exceptions, the kinds of evidence discussed require identification; unless strongly substantiated, they will not be admitted. The best corroboration comes from witnesses, but where do you find them?

You will have named a large number of potential witnesses in the list of events developed earlier in this chapter. You named the people present, remember? These are sources of information for you and should be followed up. The reason men do not tend to have good witnesses at trial is that they do not go out and get them. There are a number of reasons for this. The man feels a deep sense of guilt at the breakup of his marriage, whether it is his fault or not. He feels that, somehow, he should have been able to hold it together. Somehow, it was his responsibility, perhaps the greatest responsibility ever given to him, the formation and holding together of a family, and he failed, failed, failed. A second reason is that he still has strong emotional feelings about his wife. The fact that she has filed against him augments his feelings that he is the wrongdoer; he didn't want to be, but he is. In many cases he loves, or at least respects, his wife. He doesn't want to do things which are deliberately harmful to her, and the business of signing up witnesses to say bad things about her is simply too much to bear.

These psychological difficulties are endemic to men who are undergoing serious divorce, and they can reduce a man to total inactivity, even in his own defense. If your divorce is headed for contest, and if you find yourself unable to interview potential witnesses, get help! By contacting a men's rights organization you may encounter kindred spirits who know full and well what is happening to you, for they have been there before you. They may be able to show you how to do what you have to do, and help you to get a feel for it. Alternatively, if the emotional pressures are severe, you may wish to seek both medical and psychological intervention; medical in the form of stress-relieving drugs which can restore much of your capability to function even when you feel overwhelmed by the pressures against you; psychological in helping you explore the truth of the emotions and your own degree of culpability in the failure of the marriage. Don't wallow in indecision and guilt. Do something about it. Take some step, however small, but make sure it is in the right direction, and do it quickly.

Despite such efforts, you may find the initial contact problem—in the personal difficulty of meeting friends and neighbors to ask them why your marriage went wrong, what you did wrong, what she did wrong—you may find this unpalatable. Many, if not most, men do. Then get someone else to do it. There may be one advantage to having someone other than yourself make the initial contact. If you ask a question of a next-door neighbor who is a personal friend of yours, do you think you will get an accurate answer from him as to what he has seen about you and about your wife that might be relevant to the divorce? Perhaps not; he may feel like protecting you from what he has seen, or may dislike your wife to the extent that his responses are obviously biased in your favor, regardless of what he has seen.

There are at least three reasonable alternatives to doing the job yourself. First, there is your lawyer. Because of his verbal capacity and knowledge of the law, he would make a pretty good interviewer to screen the witnesses initially, but his fees are high. Unless you are very well situated, you probably cannot afford the expense of such an approach.

Second, there are social workers, psychologists, and sociologists. Such people frequently have interviewing skills and a sensitivity for the way people respond. They are less expensive than lawyers, but would have to be coached regarding the kinds of questions to be asked. The job market for these professions is currently depressed, and it may be possible to locate a well-qualified person at a very reasonable rate.

The third alternative has not, to our knowledge, ever been tried. This surprises us, since it seems so obviously a good notion. There are people who are trained, professional interviewers! They are employed by marketing research organizations, public-opinion research organizations, and survey research organizations, and their wage rates are lower than those of people mentioned above. By telephoning such an agency it might be possible to locate an interviewer in your immediate vicinity, for many organizations have interviewers spotted throughout the nation. You would tell the organization that you are seeking an individual skilled at obtaining "sensitive" or "psychological" data. If you expect the initial interviews to be conducted with housewives during the daytime, a female interviewer may be preferred; women have less difficulty opening doors than do men.

Other than a lawyer, whoever is to do the interviewing must have some guidelines regarding the kinds of questions to ask. If you are familiar with the law and the kinds of information that will be required, you can work out a set of questions that will cover the issues; otherwise, ask your lawyer to devote an hour or two to the task. As a result of such considerations, you should have a list of questions to be asked of everyone who will be interviewed. If your interviewer is a survey research interviewer, she may be able to point out and correct any overt biases in the way the questions are asked. Once the questions have been prepared the way you want them, type them up and run off enough photocopies to get the job done.

The outside interviewer should be provided with the names and addresses of the potential witnesses and should have some inkling of how each person fits into the picture (that is, the person's relationship to you and/or your wife). The interviewer also should be provided with a letter of introduction to the potential witnesses. The letter should say that you have asked the interviewer to talk to people regarding the issues associated with the breakup of your marriage, and that you hope for their sincere cooperation in a matter that is of great importance to you. Also, the letter should provide one or more telephone numbers where you can be reached should there be any question regarding the interviewer's credentials.

There are several goals to be attained through the initial contact with a potential witness. The first is to break the ice, to establish friendly feelings with him or her. This accomplishes two things. It facilitates access to sensitive and personal information held by the witness, and it tends to ally the witness with your side of the case. The second goal is to "feel out" the witness with regard to whose side he or she may be on—yours or your wife's; a witness who is initially hostile to your side need not be rejected from consideration, especially if he or she possesses information that is very valuable to you. The third goal is to get a general idea of the things the witness might be able to say that would be beneficial or damaging to your case—an overview of probable testimony. Such information gives some idea of how valuable or weak or damaging the witness might be to your side. The fourth goal is to obtain the right to return for additional discussion if such should be needed. If the witness is likely to be a good one, you will want to return, perhaps several times, to obtain more complete and detailed information. The fifth and final goal is to establish the need for silence, to suggest to the potential witness that he or she should not discuss the case with others. There are two reasons why the witness should not talk about the case to others. First, of course, is the fact that your domestic problems should not be bantered about the neighborhood, the office, or the clubhouse. Second, it would be preferable if this witness did not talk with the other side. Understand that the other side has a clear legal right to talk to this witness, and that they can demand this witness's presence in the courtroom by subpoena. No man has the right to refuse his knowledge to the courts. But if the initial interview is handled properly, you should end up with a witness on your side who will be reluctant to talk to the other side, and even become hostile to them if they should press the issue.

Contact should be maintained with possible friendly witnesses. This is not as easy to do as might be imagined. About 5 percent of all families move each year. If your most treasured witness moves 500 miles away, you may need to keep in touch. Despite the expense of bringing him to your trial, he may be the best witness you've got. To keep in touch, make sure you have the telephone number and a proper mailing address for the witness. Even if he moves, he will probably leave a forwarding address and first class mail will be forwarded automatically if sent to the old address. If the witness is college age or younger, ask him to provide you with the name, address, and telephone number of "someone who will always know where he can be reached," generally a parent or relative. This is one of the best methods of keeping tabs on people. It is even used by the U.S. Bureau of the Census.

The initial interview with a witness should take between thirty minutes and an hour to accomplish if you stick to the issues and do not engage in chit chat. After the initial interviews have been completed, the notes that have been taken should be reviewed carefully. It will be obvious that many potential witnesses will have little, if anything, to say of importance to your case. Others will be obviously hostile and dangerous to your case. Set these two types aside temporarily. Of those remaining, try to arrange them into some form of priority list for additional interviews. These interviews will be attempts to go deeper into the things they have witnessed relating to your case. They should establish clearly what each witness can say in support of your case. Some witnesses may be character witnesses who can provide nothing more than their perceptions of you as a gentleman. Others may have seen the slovenly way your wife kept house, or observed her entertaining men while you were out of town. Establish what they can say and what they cannot say. Evidence which they cannot say, but which you need for your case, means that you have additional work to do. In many cases, the witnesses will remember the names of other people who may be potential witnesses; perhaps some of these people can fill in the gaps. If so, obtain an initial interview with them and find out.

Do not discount the people who appeared hostile to you at the initial interview. Their interviews can give you some idea of what they might say against you if they are called by the other side. You can be prepared to resist their testimony by producing the conflicting testimony of others, or by briefing your lawyer as to the strengths and weaknesses of the witness.

Do not be surprised to have your wife telephone to let you know she is aware of what you are up to. Indeed, if one of the potential witnesses you interviewed is a friend of your wife, you can expect her to pick up the phone to warn your wife as soon as you leave. Of greater concern is to discover a call to your wife from a potential witness whom you believed friendly to your side. Check this out with the person in question to be sure it really happened. It may be that your wife is afraid of one or more of your witnesses and is seeking to make you doubt the power and integrity of your witnesses.

At least during the initial interview with a witness, your dealings should be quite one-sided. You ask the questions and they provide the answers. Enough is revealed in the simple act of asking certain questions and not others; such information can be of value to the other side. Try to operate on a "need to know" basis. If a potential witness does not need to know something in order to help you, then don't tell him. If he asks for information, try to sidestep. Say that you don't want to bias his viewpoint by giving your own or by repeating what others have said, and that, although you would like to tell him, it might appear as an attempt to influence him if he were ever asked about it on the witness stand. To another you may say that, while you need information which he has, you don't want to involve him any more than you have to, and the less he knows about what is going on, the better it will be.

If much time passes between the final interviews of the selected witnesses and the time of trial, some review of their testimony may be needed. This requires meeting with them and going over their previous statements as recorded in your notes. This will refresh their memory regarding what they have witnessed. If the witness seems frightened of appearing on the witness stand, get your lawyer to do a short simulation of trial for all key witnesses. He can demonstrate the kinds of questions that might be asked by the two lawyers and how the witnesses should respond. It is nice to have dovetailing testimony, testimony that comes together nicely to prove a case; however, if you drill your witnesses, practice them in the primary questions they will be asked and the answers they are supposed to give, you will produce a bad courtroom performance. If they have been coached, they may get stage fright and jam up when they forget their lines, or they may rattle off their well-memorized lines like the machines they have become. Either outcome is undesirable. You know what they can say; see to it that your lawyer also knows and he will develop their testimony.[2] Your witnesses will then have the normal fumbles, fear of doing wrong, and hesitancy of voice to be expected of honest witnesses in the courtroom. Some additional pointers on the management of witnesses can be found in Cannavale and Falcon.[3]

As potential witnesses, look to neighbors, friends, acquaintances, business associates, school teachers (regarding the children's academic performance), guidance counselors (regarding any special problems the children may have and results of psychological and educational tests they may have received), special education teachers (regarding any kind of handicap the children may seem to have, or may be alleged to have by your wife), her friends, her acquaintances, her business associates, other parents. Be guided at first by the list of events you have drawn up as examples of her misbehavior, but then expand into other areas to establish different aspects of the case. Don't ignore babysitters as potential witnesses. They are frequently in the home when it is at its worst, just as mom and dad are leaving a messy house and tired kids in someone else's hands. Parents may be in a rush to get going, and tempers may flare. The babysitter is often impartial, unlike many neighbors, and is in a unique position to observe family interactions under stressful conditions.

School teachers, special education teachers, and guidance counselors, if they testify, will generally testify in the role of expert witnesses. Other expert witnesses may include your family doctor, one or more medical specialists, psychiatrists, psychologists, accountants, pharmacists—in short, just about any specialty you can think of. Your lawyer can advise you on the need for, and capabilities of, certain kinds of expert witnesses; he may also know of experts in various disciplines who perform well on the stand and who might have favorable predispositions toward cases such as yours. If there are men's rights organizations in your area, they may have dossiers on various experts who have testified in trials for their members.

Preparation of Financial Evidence

In all contested divorces, custody cases, and motions to modify alimony, support, or custody, financial evidence must be prepared. There are two aspects to this problem: first, to document the income and assets of the parties; and second, to document the financial needs of the parties.

The problem is frequently quite complex. If you and your wife have several properties, incomes from partnerships or proprietorships, holdings of stocks or bonds, and incomes from wages, the assistance of a bookkeeper or accountant may be useful in untangling the financial picture. The intention of such an untangling is to make clear to the court, in terms the judge can understand (and he will not be willing to listen to sophisticated doubletalk), just what the family's resources and needs are. This, in itself, is a difficult problem. It is further complicated by the facts that (1) the judge may well suspect you of trying to conceal your assets (especially if your income is greater than your wife's), and (2) that your wife may be doing her level best to demonstrate to the court that her financial needs are much greater than they actually are.

Your incomes, assets, and expenses must be documented clearly, unambiguously, completely, and irrefutably. It is a fact that the typical American family cannot document more than 50 percent of its expenditures; a family which has an income of $16,000 is hard-pressed to produce receipts and cancelled checks which total more than $8,000. Most families cannot even provide an accurate statement of how much they spend on food. Of the three primary categories of necessaries (food, clothing, and shelter), only the cost of shelter is readily documented. This may seem strange, but clothing is purchased today in supermarkets, drugstores, and department stores where checks and receipts frequently do not show precisely what was purchased. Checks written to a supermarket cover, in addition to food, paper products (paper towels, toilet tissue, paper plates, etc.), cleaning products (mops, detergents, scouring pads, etc.), pet foods, automotive motor oil, and rock salt for icy driveways.

As an experiment, one man attempted to keep complete and exact records of every penny earned and every penny spent over a one-year period. The results were as follows: 100 percent of all income was accounted for, as accurately as possible; receipts or cancelled checks for expenditures were available, but only about 80 percent of these could be accurately assigned (to such things as food, clothing, shelter, cleaning products, medical costs, recreation, insurance, utilities, sanitation, etc.). The "miscellaneous" category, that hodge-podge of unknown and unclassifiable expenditures, represented about 20 percent of all known expenses. Considering that an intensified effort to document all expenditures produced such a poor showing, it is easy to understand the inability of many to do better than 50 percent.

There are a number of explanations for this phenomenon. At the supermarket people often cash checks in excess of the cost of goods they buy. Much of the pocket money that results is spent on purchases that are not easily documented, for example, a pack of cigarettes and a newspaper at a newsstand, or lunch at a fast food restaurant.

It is not necessary to dwell on the reasons for the shrinkage between the money you spend and the money you can account for spending. What is important is that your inability to explain your expenses can be made to appear as if you are unable to establish the need for your income. Suppose you are able to document 45 percent of all expenditures. Where did the other 55 percent go? You are unable to answer. Well, did you *need* that missing 55 percent? Of course. Then just what did you need it for? Your embarrassed answer is, "Well, uh, ah, you know, uh (*pause*) . . . . . things!" Not very satisfying to the judge, is it?

Given that it is virtually impossible to document 100 percent of all expenditures, but that something of the sort must be attempted, here is one approach which may be helpful. Every day, for a solid month, keep track of each and every penny you spend. Carry a small notebook for the purpose. When you pick up a bag of groceries (and other items), pay for them by check. When you get home, separate the purchases into categories (food, paper products, medicine, etc.) and total the cost of the items in each category (the task goes quickly with a pocket calculator). When you purchase tools and supplies at a hardware store, unless the receipt is already itemized, write on the receipt the check number and the cost and identity of each item. When you use pocket change to pick up a magazine in a drugstore, either get a receipt and write on it "magazine" or enter the item and its cost in your notebook.

If you make a number of purchases at a department store and pay for the items with a single check, treat them as you did the groceries; separate them into categories when you get home, and total the expenses in each category. During this month, every tip, every cab fare, every penny is to be accounted for. To the extent possible, pay by check for all purchases and get a receipt. Record the item either on the check or the receipt, at the time of purchase if possible, or later during the same day. Do not put it off until tomorrow or you'll never do it; you won't be able to recall exactly what the item was.

You may find, after a week or so, that the categories developed to classify items are not as refined as they should be, or that you should add additional categories to those now in use. Make the needed changes in your record-keeping scheme and set aside the first week's records. Begin afresh with the second week and continue for four consecutive weeks. When you have completed a four-week record-keeping period, total the expenses in each category you have developed, and add up the category totals to get the grand total of all expenses for all categories. Then divide the total expense of each category by the grand total, multiply the answer by 100, and the result will be the percent of all expenses that belong to each category.

The categories to be developed for expenses should, to the degree possible, parallel the guidelines of the Internal Revenue Service. Classifications should be established, for example, to cover all job-related expenses. The divorce courts are somewhat more lenient than the IRS, however, and all of your job-related expenses should be aggregated for presentation at trial. This would include, for example, the cost of travel to and from work, which is not deductible under IRS rules. It would also include, in many cases, business lunches with co-workers, which would not qualify for deductions under IRS regulations. The court is interested in the man's money-making, both in the present and in the future. As such, all expenses that are incurred in the pursuit of his profession tend to be considered reasonable by the courts, including expenses required to maintain professional status with professional peers, provided it is not overdone.

In addition to the categories used for income tax reporting, classifications should be established for personal expenses (food, medical expenses, shelter, clothing, insurance, household supplies, household equipment, telephone, other utilities, recreation, legal fees, alimony, etc.). Use as many categories as you feel you need.

Adjust your expenses to cover a full year. Where receipts are not available to allow these to be computed, estimate them on any reasonable basis. In dealing with many personal expenses, the one-month record-keeping will provide an improper estimate unless special care is taken. For example, if you performed the one-month record-keeping experiment during July, the cost of electricity may have been high owing to the use of the air conditioner; the cost of heating oil may have been nil. Had you conducted your experiment in January, quite a different result would have been obtained. Some adjustment of expenses can be based on checks written to utility companies throughout the previous year.

In assembling the summary picture of your finances, start with gross income from all sources (itemized as to source) over a one-year period. Set out all payroll deductions over the same period of time, classified into two categories: those deductions that are mandated by law or corporate policy, and those deductions that you can control voluntarily (such as withdrawable annuities voluntarily purchased through a corporate retirement program). Itemize payroll deductions within each of these categories (FICA, Federal income tax, state income tax, corporate retirement, etc.). Funds withheld from the paycheck as loan payments to a credit union are classified as payments against debts.

Credit card and other revolving charge accounts represent expenses in categories you already have established. For bank loans, mortgages, credit union loans, and other fixed-payment obligations, a separate category should be created. Itemize such debts by type or purpose (for example, "home improvement loan"), and write down the original amount of the loan, the balance outstanding as of today's date, the month and year of the last payment required to satisfy the note, and the amount of the monthly payment. Total the monthly payments for all such loans and multiply by 12 to obtain the annual cost of debt payments. Adjust this figure accordingly if any of these debts will be paid off within the next twelve months.

At this point, you will have set forth your annual income, against which you will have applied all nonvoluntary payroll deductions, all fixed debt expenses, and all job-related expenses.

The balance of your income is what you should refer to as your spendable income; only here do you have some latitude to apply money as you wish. Against this spendable income, apply your personal expenses, category by category.

The completion of this exercise results in a reasonably clear picture of income and expenses for yourself. Unfortunately, in this form it is unsubstantiated. You will need proof that the figures you set forth are true reflections of your income and expenses; proof that you are not padding the figures to make your income seem less, or your expenses seem more, than they actually are. Copies of your income tax return for the past five years or so should show the trend of your income and deductions over time[4] and can demonstrate that current incomes are not appreciably below earlier ones (especially if your income tends to fluctuate up and down). Cancelled checks for major expenses, photocopies of mortgage notes, earnings records (the stubs of your paychecks), etc., can all be used to demonstrate the authenticity of your stated figures. If you are currently experiencing a sharp rise in expenses or a sharp drop in income, anticipate attack by the other side and have justification and proof of these facts ready at hand.

Assets such as real property, partnerships, proprietary interests, stocks, bonds, debentures, annuities, etc., should be segregated into categories according to ownership. Suggested categories are: (1) items you owned prior to the marriage; (2) items held in your name alone but purchased after the marriage; (3) items held jointly by you and your wife that were purchased after marriage; (4) items owned by your wife before marriage; and (5) items held solely in your wife's name and purchased after marriage. For each item, list the current fair market value of the item if sold now as is, adjusting the current value for any brokerage or agents' fees and fixup costs prior to sale. For categories (1) and (4) also obtain the fair market values of the items at the time of marriage.

Having accomplished all of the above, your finances will be in relatively good order. Next, devote some attention to your wife's finances. The considerations are quite similar to those that apply to yourself, but the data are harder to come by, since frequently she will be unwilling to provide proof of her expenses and incomes in any detail.

The court will be interested in seeing how the standards of living of the contending parties compare, since it will try to establish more or less equal standards for the parties. The judge will not, however, spend much time being concerned for your welfare unless you provide data which are right on target. The problem becomes one of establishing an historic baseline for her incomes, assets, and expenses, and establishing it so well that if she claims lowered incomes or elevated expenses, you will be able to show how and to what degree she has falsified her finances. This difficulty is compounded by the court's willingness to overlook sloppy accounting in a woman, but to punish a man for the same error. With diligent effort and a lot of cagey thinking, many of the inherent problems can be overcome.

> Jim's wife, as we earlier reported, had moved about 2,000 miles away. She claimed that her living expenses were incredibly high owing to the unusually high cost of living in her region. To counter this attempt to inflate her expenses, Jim subscribed to a newspaper in the town she lived in, located, via telephone, the addresses of the utility companies in her town, and wrote letters inquiring about rates and average costs of various utilities. By comparing all newspaper advertisements for apartments over a one-month period, both in her region and his own, and through the responses of the utility companies, Jim discovered that:
>
> 1. One-bedroom apartments cost 94 percent more in Jim's area than his wife's area; two-bedroom apartments cost 73 percent more; and three-bedroom units cost 86 percent more. Augmenting this difference was the fact that, where she lived, practically all apartments were rented furnished; in Jim's area, furnished apartments were nearly impossible to find.
>
> 2. The average "asking price" for a house in Jim's area was $55,000. The corresponding figure in his wife's area was $22,000.
>
> 3. The overall average cost for utilities in his wife's area was less than 80 percent of the cost for the same utilities in Jim's area.
>
> Presented to the judge during a pretrial conference, the summary data, accompanied by the letters Jim had written, the

responses he had obtained, and a written overview regarding how the data had been obtained, these facts successfully demonstrated that Jim's wife was trying to inflate her expenses.

In one case, a woman swore in her interrogatory that she spent $60 a month on cosmetics and $20 a week at the beauty parlor. While the court allows women to spend money on such things, the husband was able to demonstrate that she had spent less than $20 a month in total for such items before they separated. The data came from reference to cancelled checks and credit card receipts.

In another case, a woman included $20 a month for liquor in her expenses. But part of her defense against her husband's counterclaims was that she was a reformed alcoholic and was currently attending meetings of Alcoholics Anonymous. Why, then, would she need booze?

Although the husband's ability to get an accurate accounting of his wife's expenses is limited, it should be pressed. If the slightest evidence can be found to indicate that the wife is attempting to inflate her expenses or minimize her incomes, and especially if falsification can be shown in her sworn documents (depositions, interrogatories, or affidavits), the argument can be made that her word cannot be trusted (or that her accounting cannot be trusted), and therefore your side will not countenance any statements as to incomes or expenses which are not backed up by financial records. If she claims her rent is $275 per month, make her produce cancelled checks to support her claim. Before you accept her claim for $480 in medical expenses per year, demand to see all the receipts which add up to that figure. Before she is caught up in a lie, such demands on your part may be considered excessive and harassing; after she is caught, they are your just due.

In evaluating the incomes and expenses of your wife, good baseline data can be obtained from the receipts, cancelled checks, and income tax records which you have retained over the years. Just as the opposition will inspect your financial data with a jaundiced eye, you may exercise a similar circumspection. Look for sharp deviations in her expense patterns. The balance of her checking account on each monthly statement since the two of you separated can be demanded in interrogatories. If, five months after the separation, you note a sudden drop in her checking account balance, be wary of an attempt to squirrel away assets.

To the degree possible, be alert for attempts to inflate the costs of day-to-day living; these may be reflected in such things as a steady, month-to-month increase in clothing costs or other expenses compared to your own, or to the monthly consumer price index. In one case, a wife received several thousand dollars from her wealthy mother. She placed this money in a trust fund held by her lawyer. As she needed money, he could dole it out to her. In this fashion she had access to all the money she needed and was able to display such low checking and savings account balances as to suggest she was starving. If these things can be detected, prepare to demonstrate to the judge the undue growth of her expenses in comparison to the growth of your own. This may reveal a clear attempt to boost her expenses prior to trial.

We earlier noted that judges respond punitively to men who attempt to conceal their assets from the court. To a lesser degree, judges tend to react similarly against women. If your case involves flagrant and dramatic attempts by your wife to lie her way to greater and greater alimony, and if you have strong proof of her lies and attempts, you may wish to sit quietly, refusing your wife's demands until you can demonstrate her greedy deceitfulness to the judge. Especially if she lies on the stand to further her unjust demands, your careful preparation may cause her to lose more than she ever bargained for.

10

Trial Preparation—Assembling the Case

FROM EARLIER chapters it will be obvious that the preparation of a case for trial consists of bringing together two kinds of things: (1) the relevant points of law in the jurisdiction which advance one's arguments before the court, and which deny arguments advanced by the other side; and (2) the actual events which are the causes for the divorce and which comprise the issues brought to the court for decision. In this chapter, we consider how these two components of the case can be brought together.

In very large part, especially if yours is a complicated case, the responsibility for achieving the vital integration of law and events must be your own. That this is so stems from the fact that you undoubtedly know the facts and circumstances of your case better than your lawyer, and from the fact that the properly prepared case requires so much time that either you will be unable to afford to have your lawyer do it, or your lawyer will be unable to invest the needed amounts of time.

Where to Begin

Chapters 4, 5, and 6, dealing with the law of divorce and custody, are the touchstone. Begin there to get a sense of the legal issues and considerations involved in domestic contests. Discuss with your lawyer a reasonable overall strategy, and give some thought to the grounds and defenses which currently seem reasonable. Having done this much, you are ready to take the first independent steps.

Make up a list of all the things you feel your wife did which were wrong, and which are related to the "marital faults" which will (if your evidence is strong) prove your grounds or your defenses. These behaviors of your wife should include things she has done which may bear on the custody of your children. Beside each event, list the evidences you can present in the courtroom to prove that the faults and misbehaviors are true. If you made up the list of events discussed in Chapter 9 on evidence, you have already accomplished this step. Keep this list in a place that is absolutely secure; if the other side sees it, your entire case may be destroyed. Similarly, any evidence you may have collected to prove the listed allegations should be held secure at all times.

Next make up a corresponding list of your own marital misbehaviors and faults, including those related to custody, together with the evidence you think she can produce against you. Distinguish three kinds of evidence: evidence you *know* she now has in her possession, evidence she *may* have, and evidence you know she does *not* now have. This list also goes into safekeeping.

Next, make up another list about yourself, a list of your good points. The points should illustrate: (1) that you are a nice guy; (2) that you are a superior husband, no matter what they say about you; and (3) that you are a superior parent/father, no matter what they say about you. The list should be only a list of positive points. Ignore anything bad about yourself which may come to mind. Did you carry out the trash regularly? That is a good point. Did you keep the home well repaired? Or, if you didn't do it yourself, did you see to it that repairmen were called when necessary? More good points. Are you a likeable guy? Do your friends think well of you? Are you patient? Did you ever stay home from work to take care of your sick wife or sick children? Did you ever stay up at night when a member of the family was sick? Are you a good neighbor? Do you help those around you when they are in trouble? List as many positive points as you can, then put the list away with the rest of your papers. From time to time, take it out and enlarge upon it. Add new points to it, elaborate on those earlier mentioned. Two things are accomplished by creating this list. First, by focusing on positive aspects, the list will help you to see that you are, in fact, an OK sort of guy. This can be helpful if your wife and her friends are badmouthing you. The second thing the list does is to prepare you to resist the derogations of the other side during trial. They will say as many nasty things about you as possible; you will refute them by illustrating how the opposite is true. No one is perfect, you will have made mistakes and will be forced to admit to some of them. The list of good points prepares your counterattack by readying examples which contradict their claims.

Keep all these papers under lock and key, and operate on a "need to know" basis; no one who does not need to know of the existence of any of these papers has a right to know anything about them. Should these papers fall into unfriendly hands, you will face disaster.

The Principles of Preparation

The principles of preparation are simple. First, prepare your case to counter every bad thing your wife can say about you. You will probably fail (unless you are a saint). This proof of your humanity is no great cause for alarm. Your job is to do the best you can to refute everything you think she might throw at you. Second, prepare your case to prove that every good thing you say about yourself is true. Line up character and material witnesses who will provide confirming evidence. Third, prepare your case to prove that every bad thing your wife did is something that really happened, and that it happened just as you said it did. The list of events regarding your wife, together with the details of social setting, persons present, etc., will guide you in establishing the needed proofs. Fourth and last, prepare your case so as to include citations of statute and case law which demonstrate that your arguments and allegations are valid from a legal viewpoint, that your proofs are legally acceptable, and that, taken as a whole, your arguments and proofs are both relevant and dispositive. Locating the relevant statutes and cases involving getting one's feet wet in legal research, a topic that we discuss at length in Appendix A. If your case shows the slightest signs of contest, we suggest that you read Appendix A now before continuing.

Packaging Your Case—Organization

No matter how much information you have gathered, no matter how many cases you have read, no matter how many witnesses you have lined up, your case can still be an accident looking for a place to happen, and that place may be the courtroom. The missing element is organization.

Before diving into the topic of organization, let us briefly consider the role of your lawyer at trial. It is in the courtroom that the experienced trial lawyer comes into his element. Fortunately, some people thrive in that environment; it is challenging. Throughout most of this book we have pressed home the point that *you* are the one who must be prepared, *you* are the one who must become familiar with the law, *you* are the one who must gather the evidence. But in the courtroom, it is *the lawyer* who must perform. Certainly, you must be prepared to deliver your testimony on the witness stand, and to withstand cross-examination. But the responsibility for the conduct of the case at trial belongs to your lawyer. If he muffs it, all is lost; it is that simple. Everything up to this point has been directed toward this moment. Now it is up to him.

While you are on the stand delivering testimony, or while you sit at the table at the front of the courtroom, your lawyer has a number of ongoing activities which simultaneously place serious demands on his attention. Some of the things he is attempting to do are: (1) monitor the responses of your wife as he questions witnesses (if he sees her stiffen up as he enters a line of questioning, he knows he's on the right track); (2) monitor the responses of the judge, to gauge how he is receiving the points being made by either side; (3) memorize everything every witness says on the witness stand, in order to detect contradictions, points which must be refuted, points which must be conceded, etc.; (4) skillfully attack the other side's witnesses, convince the judge of their incompetence as witnesses, draw forth contradictions, and also evoke as much good testimony from the witnesses of both sides as he can; (5) keep the examination of witnesses and presentation of proofs moving smoothly towards the legal proofs he wishes to establish in terms of points of law; and (6) do all this while maintaining a standard of decorum in presentation and examination, even if he is burning with anger about some of the things he has seen, or if he is dreadfully concerned about the way things are going (he does this to prevent the other side from perceiving how well or poorly they are doing, and to lend dignity to the proceedings). Your lawyer in the courtroom is a busy, busy man —the key man. In earlier stages of the divorce, he had a strong and supportive role in assisting you to shape your case; now it is your turn to bear the supportive responsibility.

In the operating room of a hospital the surgeon is the key man, a vital member of a well-rehearsed team. When he reaches a certain point in the surgery he will toss one instrument into a pan and hold out his rubber-gloved hand. Instantly, without a word, his skilled assistant will slap the newly needed instrument into the surgeon's palm.

Now you are the assistant, and your lawyer is the surgeon. Unlike the surgeon, however, the lawyer will often not know what tools (information) he will need until the moment arises. Then it is your responsibility to be able to produce the needed instrument instantly. Trials move quickly, and there is no time to look for lost papers. Now you begin to understand the need for organization. By all means, discuss with your lawyer the best way to assemble your materials to allow instant access. Here is one possible approach.

Package the materials in two separate sections. Label the first, "Arguments on the Merits." In this section go all materials related to fault, custody, points of law regarding divorce and/or custody, the witnesses, etc. Label the second section, "Arguments on Finances." In this section go all materials relating to money. Now let us explore the contents of each section in greater detail.

Arguments on the merits. The first materials which will be needed during the trial are those that relate to the plaintiff, since the plaintiff's case is presented first. Plaintiff's material and defendant/counterclaimant's material thus form two subsections within the arguments on the merits. No matter whether you are the plaintiff or the defendant, the contents of arguments on the merits really consist of two batches of material, one which is against her claims and one which is in favor of your claims.

Against her claims. Within this section are a number of file folders. For each witness she might call, there should be (as a result of your preparation) a dossier. You should know in advance, either as a result of interrogatories and depositions, or as a result of your own thinking and sleuthing, who her witnesses will be, and you should have prepared a dossier on each. Label each dossier with the witness's name, and staple a summary of neatly typed information to the inside cover of the folder. The summary for a given witness should consist of three parts: (1) your best guess as to the nature of the information this witness might be able to give, especially if it is damaging evidence; (2) if this is one of your wife's witnesses, the second component of the summary should relate to proofs (via testimony and other evidence) which can be used to refute the witness's testimony; and (3) the summary should contain in précis form whatever information you have on ways to destroy the credibility of this witness. If the witness is related to your wife by blood, marriage, or friendship, this should be stated; if the witness owes a favor or money to your wife, this might be mentioned; if you have evidence that the witness has made a bad showing in court before, or if you have been able to uncover evidence of perjury or criminal activities—whatever you have should be mentioned in the summary.

Within the folder, perhaps neatly clipped to the folder and indexed, are more complete statements than were provided in the summary, and (perhaps) references to numbered envelopes wherein you have placed evidence which can be used against the witness. Everything which relates to a given witness should be in the folder for that witness, or else the folder should contain a note saying where the evidence is stored among the materials you have brought with you. Such cross-referencing will allow you to produce quickly any testimony from your witnesses that contradicts the testimony of your wife's witness. In the event that the same evidence relates to two or more of her witnesses, obain separate photocopies of these materials so that complete sets can be placed within each folder. In short, each dossier should stand alone; its contents should be as complete as possible, and should not rely on the contents of other folders.

In consequence of the claims and counterclaims, of the communications with your wife both before and after the breakup, and as a result of your preparations, you will undoubtedly have a pretty good idea of the other forms of evidence your wife may bring into court. If these are documents, you may have copies of them. Otherwise, you may have merely an understanding of the arguments she will present and the proofs she will offer. The second set of folders against her claims are topical in nature; for each topic you feel she might forward, a separate folder should be set up.

Such folders should be labeled as to the topic contained within, and stapled to the inside cover should be a summary of points she might try to make. The main contents of the folder should consist of possible counters, through your proofs, to each possible thing she might attempt. As with other witness dossiers, the summary and the main contents of the folders should be cross-referenced to facilitate working from the summary to the more lengthy description of how her approach might be thwarted.

The third and final component of the "against her claims" section is one or more folders relating to statute and case law which can be used to deny her evidence and arguments. Separate headings (or folders) should be prepared for each major argument she might make. If she is suing you on adultery, she must show intention and opportunity. If she has shown opportunity, has she also shown intention? You may have a case in which a complaint in adultery was dismissed because, while opportunity was present, the showing of intent was inadequate. You should have a brief summary of that case in a folder labeled "Adultery," and a reference to where the case may be found in the lawbooks.

To summarize, the "against her claims" files consist of three sets of folders: (1) dossiers regarding her potential witnesses; (2) folders dealing with her probable arguments; and (3) folders dealing with statute and case law. To the extent possible, each folder should be self-contained and should not rely upon material contained within other folders. The three sets of folders should be easily distinguishable (perhaps by using different-colored file-folder index labels); however it is accomplished, the folders should be ordered so that you can locate any needed folder without hesitation.

YOUR CLAIMS. Just as for the materials you have assembled against your wife's claims, there are three sets of folders which comprise your side of the case. As before, the first set consists of dossiers concerning each of your witnesses. Each dossier contains a summary of (1) the points the witness might be able to contribute through testimony, (2) how the opposition might attempt to counter the witness's testimony or destroy his credibility, and (3) what other information you have, through the testimony of other witnesses, or through other evidence, which would support the testimony of the witness.

The second set of folders is topical, just as for your wife, and consists of the points you can make in your own behalf, the arguments you can produce against your wife, and the evidences you have to back up your statements. Also included are points regarding how the opposition might counter your statements, and what evidence you have to support your claims against their counterattack.

The third set of folders consists of statutes and cases which support your views, or which can be used to overturn their opposition to your views. In style and content, these folders are similar to the legal folders in the "against her claims" set.

ARGUMENTS ON FINANCES. This is the second major set of materials to be developed for trial. During the trial, information from Arguments on the Merits folders and Arguments on Finances folders will be concurrently in use. When your wife takes the stand, she will be asked to tell her whole story. Unless financial issues have been completely settled, her story will include a description of her financial plight as well as her presentations on the merits of her case. The same will be true for you; you will tell the entire story, finances plus merits, all at one shot, under the skilled questioning of your lawyer. Of course, if all financial details have been settled prior to trial, you will have no Arguments on Finances folders in your case.

There are five folders in the Arguments on Finances section. All of these spring from the preparations suggested in earlier chapters. The first folder, labeled "Assets and Liabilities," contains what might be termed a balance sheet, except it need not actually produce an accounting balance. Instead, it is a listing of the family's assets and liabilities. Where assets and liabilities are separately assignable to you or to her, these should be listed apart from jointly held assets and liabilities.

The second folder, labeled "Financial Needs," contains two basic kinds of information: (1) information related to spending patterns and recent changes in spending patterns, and (2) individual financial needs, separated by category. The two kinds of information are separately set forth for you and for your wife. If you have information regarding your wife's tendencies to deliberately inflate her expenses or conceal her assets, here is where it will be found.

The third folder, labeled "Incomes," contains a simple enumeration of the sources and amounts of income derived from each source. As before, sources and amounts are separately listed for you and for your wife.

The fourth folder, labeled "Wife's Potential," contains whatever you have been able to assemble regarding the money-making potential of your wife. The income produced by her current job would be found here, as would information regarding career ladders and future income potential with this or other employers. Here are to be found your evidences regarding her probable future income levels, predicted as well as you can and discussed in terms of her probable future were she to benefit from selected forms of special training. The fifth folder is a legal folder which contains statute and case law that might be applicable to your views regarding the disposition of property, assets, etc., and regarding the amounts and terms of alimony, child support, etc.

As with arguments on the merits each of these folders should stand independently of the others. If two or more folders need some of the same materials, place photocopies of the materials in each. The contents of each folder should be indexed by a summary sheet and cross-referenced as to the location within the folder where more information may be found. The arrangement of the folders, and their physical location within the sets of files, should be such as to allow immediate access to needed data.

You and your lawyer will enter the courtroom with the set of files (the lawyer will also have a set of his own, containing briefs, transcripts of depositions, etc.—all copies of materials in your own files), a box containing evidence too bulky to fit within the file folders, but placed in envelopes or small containers and numbered for identification, and a string of witnesses. You are then as ready as you can be.

Your Lawyer and Integrating Your Material

Just as children have a hard time "growing up" their parents, clients have a hard time educating their lawyers. You will have prepared a massive pile of information regarding your case and the case the other side may bring against you. These materials must not be developed in a vacuum. Continuing dialogue between your lawyer and yourself is an absolute must. He must be made aware of your activities, your discoveries (good *and* bad), and your thoughts regarding the case and how it should proceed. He may not always agree. Listen to him; he is your legal advisor. As with any advisor, you may feel free to disregard his advice. It is your life. If that is understood between you, disagreements will cause few problems.

On the other hand, the lawyer too should be doing things for the case, and in your discussions he should bring you up to date regarding progress of the case, actions of the opposition, and so forth.

The relationship should be a relatively independent partnership where each of you has things to do, and when these have been accomplished you again meet to exchange notes and plan the next steps. If this is the type of relationship you have, your lawyer will probably have a good understanding of how your material is coming together, of what material you have, and how he might use it during trial.

Alternatively, if the lawyer doesn't seem able or willing to grasp or consider the things you are doing, then something is amiss. We have seen it recommended to lawyers that they threaten to withdraw from a case when their client becomes reluctant to go along with their recommendations. If your lawyer threatens to withdraw, then the relationship between you is a terrible one; encourage him to withdraw and pay him off. Because you have copies of all materials in his files, he cannot hold you back. Go to another lawyer, one who is willing to be more reasonable.

Do not fear to change lawyers, even up to the last minute. The depth of understanding the typical lawyer has as to the complications of a particular matrimonial action is generally so shallow that little harm can result from changing, and if you and your lawyer cannot work together, retaining him may risk your case at trial.

It is unlikely that serious disagreements between you and your lawyer will occur if you have applied the procedures recommended for choosing him in the first place, and if each of you has worked for the other in the development of the case. Continuing dialogue between you is the key to understanding the directions the case must take, and to agreeing on how it should be prepared and presented at trial. Succeeding in this, your case will certainly contain some unpleasant surprises for the opposition.

11

Psychological Preparation

PSYCHOLOGICAL PREPARATION is necessary to maintain operating efficiency at a high level in the face of stresses which, in divorce, may reach incredible levels. It has been said that the stress of a nasty divorce is exceeded only by the death of someone beloved; men have died in consequence of the stresses placed upon them by divorce.

Psychological preparation will help you gain a better understanding of what is happening to both yourself and your wife. It will help you cope with the emotional complications incident to divorce, such as planlessness and loneliness, and can increase your capacity for fighting the good fight. In this chapter we discuss these and related matters.

What Is Happening to You?

We are not talking about the legal process of divorce here; we are talking about the inner workings and hidden mechanisms that make up You—the mysterious combination of blood, bowels, and brains that feels, thinks, acts, reacts, and emotes. Our concern is for how you feel, and for how well you understand why such feelings occur. We hope to provide a few suggestions for dealing with some of these feelings when they get out of hand, as they predictably will.

Being a typical man, you have probably prided yourself on how well you can control your emotions, even in crisis situations. But now, with your wife gone, with divorce imminent, you sometimes find yourself afflicted with a sudden sadness, and perhaps tears come. That is all right. No one can see you. It is kind of funny, sad-funny, how the sadness does not seem to be a sadness *about* anything; it is just a sadness which settles on your shoulders like a dark mantle, quietly, and without warning.

Your thoughts may return to the marriage, maybe just thoughts about the whole marriage, not any particular thing about it. If you are still in the house, it seems awfully empty. Quiet. The atmosphere within may be gloomy, even if the day outside is bright and cheerful. You feel that you should do something, not anything in particular, just something. But somehow you don't want to. Kind of like wanting to pace the floor, and not wanting to. Another wave of sadness. You try to shake off the mood.

You recall that things really hadn't been very good between you and your wife for a long time, anyway. The sadness is not as if you were in love with her and she had left you, but the sadness seems similar to this. Another thing is that the sadness sometimes takes you unawares. Like yesterday, at work at your desk, when suddenly you almost cried. Funny.

These and related emotions are part of a natural phenomenon experienced by practically everyone who undergoes divorce. Psychologists refer to it as the "death of a relationship." It has little to do with love, but may involve love. For several years, you and your wife had developed a closely integrated, mutually dependent lifestyle. The things you did were dependent on the things she did. When you were first married, you probably tried to spend a lot of time with her. As the newness wore off the marriage, the two of you began living a "married singles" lifestyle in which she did her thing and you did yours. The home became a place where you took your meals, spent your nights, and got your sex. While this may seem a way of living independently of your wife, there is a sense in which the two of you are still highly dependent on each other. When she went bowling with her friends on Tuesday nights, leaving you home with the kids, you learned how to fill this time with a hobby, or reading, or playing with the kids. Gradually this became a routine.

Eventually, if your wife did *not* go bowling on some particular Tuesday night, you may have felt annoyed; your private time for your hobby was interrupted by her presence. Do you see how, in this situation, your actions depended on hers? You depended on her absence.

In other ways you depended on her presence. When you came home to find her unexpectedly gone, a note on the refrigerator telling you to toss a TV dinner into the oven, you were angered at her lack of consideration, or at the inconvenience she caused you.

Even though the two of you drifted more and more apart, even in the separation there was a dependency between you. Even in quarreling, there is an interactive dependence. If you had a bad day at the office and came home spoiling for a fight, you needed your wife to play the game or there would be no fight. A fight takes at least two people.

If you think back through the last days of your marriage, you will begin to see literally hundreds of things which you did, or did not do, in response to her mood or to what she said, did, did not do. If you look deeper you can see that the same thing was true for her.

Consider each of these tiny, innumerable dependencies as fine strands of spider's silk spun between yourself and your wife. Thousands of little dependencies which relate to the things you do, the things she does in response, the things you do in response to that, and so on. These silken strands defined the relationship between you and your wife.

With the divorce, an invisible sword has slashed apart most, or all, of those dependencies. The relationship is dead. Death of a relationship occurs when a loved one dies. All the old dependencies are severed. We feel sadness, and we weep. But these same feelings can occur, and recur, without anyone dying. It is this sadness which you are feeling. Does it disturb you? Do you feel foolish when you nearly weep in public about the loss of a wife you haven't loved for years? Doesn't seem logical does it? But the logic is there, and the sadness will continue to recur, even long after the divorce is over.

What do you do about this phenomenon? Recognize it for what it is. Recognize your feelings as your honest feelings of the moment. When the sadness hits it will pass in a few minutes. Especially if you are alone and cannot embarrass yourself by crying in the presence of others, allow yourself to appreciate the emotion of sadness; not to enjoy it, but to appreciate it. Reach down inside yourself and help the sadness float to the surface. The emotion will probably intensify and you may weep. Good.

Let yourself cry. Your weeping may take the lid off of a lot of suppressed emotion, and may do much to alleviate the great stresses you have been living with. You may then be able to get the best night's sleep you have had in months.

A second phenomenon has probably already been experienced, or it will be experienced immediately after the divorce. The phenomenon can be described as a combination of wanting to do something, but not knowing what, and also not really wanting to do anything. Depression may be present, and you may feel really "down." A sense of brooding inactivity, of having an itch but not knowing where to scratch. The inactivity is bothersome, but nothing seems right to do about it. Especially if this emotion occurs right after the divorce, you may experience a feeling of all things having come to an end, there is nothing more to do, and what will happen now?

The name applied to such feelings is *planlessness.* It can occur in relation to the death of the marital relationship because the emotional dependencies between you and your wife used to provide unspoken guidelines to your behavior. You knew what to do to occupy your time as a result of what your wife was doing. What you did affected what she did, and this fed back to affect what more you did. With the death of the relationship, the feedback is missing. The cues—frequently so subtle as to pass unnoticed—which used to provide direction for your actions while living with your wife are no longer there, leaving you with an impression of not quite knowing what to do next.

Planlessness seems to affect men more frequently than women, possibly because the woman's world is so tied up in the home and related activities. After the divorce, although she may have to get a job to help make ends meet, when she returns home she can easily slip back into the old familiar role of homemaker; she can cook a meal, clean a floor, or change a bed. By contrast, the man, after the divorce, returns to a new set of tasks: fixing his own supper, cleaning his own home, doing his own laundry. His male development has prepared him for the role of wage earner, but not for this new role, and it fits like a poor suit—too tight here and too loose there. Nonetheless, these activities are performed minimally but adequately, and then what? Nothing. The empty evening. Wanting to do something, but nothing to do. Planlessness.

While planlessness is common and is generally benign, for some it can bring on serious depression requiring medical or psychological countermeasures. For others, planlessness can be so serious as to disable activities and thoughts which could overcome the problem; in consequence, the period of planlessness becomes protracted.

Planlessness and loneliness are frequent companions, and many men try to alleviate these sensations by throwing themselves into exhausting socializing parties, singles bars, night clubs and go-go dancers. If one returns home sufficiently late and sufficiently exhausted, sleep can be immediate and one can avoid having to feel.

For others, planlessness and loneliness can combine with the severe blow to the male ego that often accompanies a divorce. Such men often feel that their inability to make the marriage work, plus the fact that the wife has filed against them, plus the fact that they are older, plus the fact that they feel sexually less attractive to women—these factors in concert produce a need to reestablish one's sexual prowess while simultaneously avoiding the painful feelings of planlessness and loneliness. Sexual adventuring begins in an atmosphere of parties and singles bars. The name of the game is to find 'em and bed 'em. Most men soon discover that the women they are getting are as neurotic as they themselves are acting, and they drift away from the sex scene.

Such activities are not likely to provide a solution to the problems of planlessness and loneliness. Planlessness is exactly that; being without plans. Under these circumstances, it is perfectly natural to be without plans, but it is not natural to stay that way. The way one overcomes planlessness is to begin making plans. Not grandiose illusions, but common, everyday plans regarding current and immediate future activities. The plans that are missing are not the life-goal plans; you still have those, although they may have been redirected by the divorce process. The missing plans are the little ones, the plans for everyday living, the minute-to-minute "next I'll do this, and tomorrow evening I'll be doing that" which lead toward some personal goal.

One way to start the planning process is by planning to learn about domestic matters, and planning to learn them so well that you become an accomplished homemaker. These skills are survival skills anyway, and they make life more pleasant, they save money, they improve the quality of life, and they provide confidence in the knowledge that you can do what needs be done. We know of one man who was so pleased at having learned how to sew on a button, that he declared a personal holiday and

took his downstairs neighbor (who happened to be a comely lass) to the beach the following day. Don't laugh. There are a lot of people who do not know how to sew on a button. If your means are small, this simple skill can make the difference between having a pair of pants to wear or not.

But no matter how much you know about homemaking, your skills can be polished. You can learn to accomplish more in less time, gaining you more time to spend in more pleasant surroundings, to do other planning, and to act on those plans. Naturally, social life should be a part of those plans, but social plans should be undertaken with a sense of balance; no longer will you exhaust yourself in meaningless encounters with women.

Anxiety, guilt, and untoward emotionalism frequently are experienced by men going through divorce. Even if yours is a simple divorce, you may expect these feelings to be visited upon you. With anxiety, one feels that something bad is about to happen; there is some fear involved and a definite feeling of tension. Sometimes the anxiety has a known, definite cause (for example, you fear the judge's decision at the end of a *pendente lite* support hearing), but at other times, for no apparent reason, you may simply feel anxious. This is termed "free-floating anxiety" and almost always has a large number of causes, none of which is immediate. It can produce cold hands and feet, and a desire to curl up into a little ball, or huddle in a corner, or go to bed and turn the electric blanket on high. Some people get so tense that one can actually see their rigidly tightened muscles.

Countermeasures against anxiety depend on the source or sources of it. Anxiety which feels like an impending sense of doom, which results from not knowing what is happening to your case in divorce, sometimes can be alleviated by finding out just exactly what is going on. Call your lawyer, or do some legal research. If the anxiety level is so severe that you cannot work or think, then seek medical support, especially if the feelings are chronic.

Guilt feelings are almost always present at the breakup of a marriage. Both you and your wife will have them, but *please* do not talk about them with your wife. Admitting guilty feelings to her may be taken as an admission of wrongdoing which she could use against you on the witness stand. The guilt feelings stem from the fact that you did not do all that you should have done or could have done to be a better husband or a better father. That the marriage is on the rocks is all, or mostly, your fault.

While you may feel this way, the guilt is simply not justified. It takes two to make a marriage, not one, and even if your wife was willing to go to marriage counseling to save the marriage, and you were not willing, the chances are that marriage counseling would have done little, if any, good anyway. It's a fact—most people who go to marriage counseling to save a marriage do so too late. By the time they go, they are really looking for an excuse to break up the marriage. What about all the slights and shortcomings of your wife over the years? Weren't they influential in weakening the relationship between you? You bet they were. Of course, you were no angel, either. Half of the fault of the breakup is yours, but only half. Go ahead and feel guilty about your half of the responsibility and let her feel bad about her half. You are *not* entirely to blame for the breakup of your marriage.

Moreover, there are a number of powerful social forces which tend to push people apart, and often, we are relatively powerless to counteract them. A frequent complaint of wives is that their husbands spend too much time on the job, that they married their jobs rather than their wives. Their complaint is justified. Men frequently do spend too much time selling their lives to their corporations, while investing too little of themselves in their wives and families. But consider the alternative: how happy would she be if you were to resign your position and take up one that would allow you to spend much more time at home? Your income would drop appreciably. You might not be able to afford the current home. Would she accept the drop in standard of living, or would she merely use it as something else to blame you for? Would she take the view that you are *capable* of earning more than you are, and that you have no right to sit around the house when other men are bringing in the bucks?

Guilt is a dangerous emotion, because in our childhood we learned to expiate our guilt through punishment. Many a little boy, on having done something wrong, felt so guilty that he would ask his parents to spank him so he could feel better. Guilt causes us to feel deserving of punishment. It causes us to feel that we have no right to defend ourselves against our accusers. The divorce court is one of the worst places to let oneself be hag-ridden with guilt. If we cannot defend ourselves before the judge against our equally guilty wives, we are lost. If your guilt feelings are strong enough to prevent you from acting, contact a psychologist, psychiatrist, priest, or pastor. Talking to him may materially reduce these emotions and restore your capability to function.

Untoward emotional states often are symptoms of heavy mental stress. Anger is one modality in which such states are manifested. If you find yourself exploding into a rage over some trivial thing, you will know that you have been under severe stress for some period of time.

You may be enjoying yourself at a quiet social gathering and, very suddenly, feel a compulsion to get out and away from there; perhaps you may feel that the whole scene has suddenly turned odious and that you are repelled by the people around you. You may experience similar feelings while you are at work.

You may find yourself suddenly slipping into near-hysterical buffoonery, giggling over every moderately funny crack, giggling uncontrollably until tears come to your eyes. This is another symptom of stress.

Rapidly shifting emotional states are yet another manifestation. You feel like laughing one minute, crying the next; you feel content one minute, deeply sad the next. These are often stress reactions.

It is important that you understand these reactions, for stress can be harmful, both physically and mentally. Stress can grow gradually, imperceptibly, and can reach monstrous proportions without notice. In cases of divorce, one is generally aware of when stressful situations occur, but frequently we are unaware that these stressful situations leave behind an invisible residue which persists long afterward. What we experience is a stressful event, and we get over it, then another stressful event, and we get over it, and so on. But what actually happens is that we do not quite get over it before the next one hits. The residues of successive stress loadings accumulate within us until our bodies must throw them off through violent emotional reactions. However, if we know that we are under stress, there are steps which can be taken to minimize its effect, methods of alleviating stress.

Monitoring and Controlling Stress

The thought that occurs to many is that whenever stress gets too much to bear, then it is time to see a psychologist or psychiatrist. This is not necessarily so. If the opposition learns you have been seeing a mental health professional they will do their level best to make it appear that you are mentally unstable. This can add evidence to your wife's ground of extreme mental cruelty (your uncontrollable rages, the verbal and physical abuse you inflicted on her during the marriage are but other manifestations of your mental instability); it can also aid their preparation of a custody case (who wants to give the kids to a mentally unstable father?).

Do not consider going to a mental health professional unless you find your emotions simply getting out of hand, or unless you notice a perceptible reduction in your ability to intelligently and energetically deal with the problems confronting you. Even then, defer counseling until you have tried some of the suggestions below.

Gaining a better understanding of your own particular sources of stress should strengthen your ability to cope with it. Transactional Analysis may represent one avenue through which your understanding of yourself and the nature of stress as it acts on you can be improved. The language of Transactional Analysis is comparatively simple, and many of its concepts are easily grasped. The Notes for this chapter provide a couple of references.[1]

Transcendental meditation (TM) is an approach which some claim relieves stress. It is not a method of meditating on the problems of the world, or of contemplating your navel. It is a method of relaxing the mind and body. During the meditation process, researchers have documented significant physiological indicators of deep relaxation, and those who routinely practice meditation report being better able to handle stress in their lives, in addition to other benefits. Courses in transcendental meditation are now available in many community colleges and high school-sponsored adult education programs. If such offerings are not available, try reading the book *The Relaxation Response,* which spells out one approach to the method.[2] If you take courses to learn the technique, please do not advertise the fact to outsiders. Many people consider transcendental meditation a form of far-out religious cult. It is not. But if the judge is one of the ignorant ones, the other side may use such information to their advantage. (If you have a history of mental illness, especially schizophrenia or delusional disorders, TM should be avoided.)

Tai chi is an oriental dance form consisting of studied, flow-ing, rhythmical body movements. It is a form of mild exercise which, for some, results in an improved sense of well-being and improved ability to handle stress.

Exercise, in and of itself, can be stress-relieving. If you are a jogger, keep it up. If you are sedentary in habit, a little exercise, even a leisurely daily walk around the block, can help to relieve stress. Unless you are in good physical condition, please do not try to perform like a high school athlete. Don't see how many push-ups you can do, or try to do ten laps around the block. This will merely discourage you. You can make it a habit to treat yourself to thirty minutes of relaxation each day by walking down to the store to get a newspaper. The Royal Canadian Air Force exercise program is excellent for toning up your body, and can be used indoors in foul weather.[3]

Relaxation training is a collection of methods which can be applied to achieve greater relaxation and to help overcome the tension which results from stress. There are a number of approaches available, and your library may aid your exploration. Without special recommendation, we mention one approach in the chapter notes.[4]

Dietary and other habit patterns can be influential in controlling stress. If you eat on the run or find yourself dashing about to get things done, it may help to force a slowdown. Sit down to eat, and take your time. Deliberately try to enjoy the taste of your food and resist the urge to jump up and get on to the next activity. If you eat at irregular periods from one day to the next, you may benefit by introducing a bit more regularity. Eat at more or less the same times from day to day. Shifting the quantities you eat also can be beneficial. Nutritionists have long argued that breakfast should be the largest meal of the day, lunch the second largest, and supper the smallest. This does not mean that breakfast food (the traditional cereal or bacon and eggs) should be eaten in larger quantities, but that you might start including in breakfast some of the things you probably eat at dinner. A large breakfast may take a little adjustment on your part, but it pays a dividend by setting up your day on firm footing.

Especially if you have recently been on a diet of restaurant food, TV dinners, and sandwiches from the local delicatessen, you may benefit by doing more of your own cooking to better balance your diet[5] and by taking a good multivitamin supplement.

If you sleep poorly, exercise may help. A cup of hot milk to which you have added a teaspoon of sugar, drunk before retiring, can induce a nice drowsiness to aid sleep. Proper rest is an absolute necessity if you are under stress. But if you find you are suddenly needing more than eight hours of sleep each night, you may be burying yourself in bed in order to avoid the pressures of the day. Avoid this trap by facing the day squarely. Get the sleep you need, but no more than you need.

Actively planning the day can introduce some order into what might otherwise be chaos; take a few minutes before retiring or after breakfast to plan out the major activities of the day. These are non-job plans. Job planning can be accomplished on the job. The plans we mention here include the things you want to do off the job: before going to work, during coffee break or lunch hour, and after work. Plan for the activities you must accomplish, but also plan for complete living. Among other things, you need recreation, and you should plan for it, even if recreation is no more than an hour spent watching television. Television, in case you hadn't noticed, is a marvelous, mindless time-waster. If you have things to accomplish, restrict your TV watching to reasonable limits, and plan fruitful activities to fill time normally lost watching the tube.

Planning is a means to an end, not an end in itself. Plan accurately, schedule well, and be realistic. Do not plan for more than you can accomplish, and do not insist on a life of achievement-achievement-achievement. Such a life is slavery. There may be times during the process of your divorce when you will be putting in twenty hours a day. To meet such demands, your body should be a pampered tool: properly exercised (both physically and mentally), properly nourished, properly re-created, and properly rested. Your planning should be planning for whole-life living, rounded and fulfilling, not exhausting.

Psychology and the Opposition

In your history of living with your wife you have learned how to interpret her moods from fragmented sentences and gestures. You know when she is angry even if others would never guess it. You know her preferences in food, clothing, and recreation. You know a *lot* about her. Your knowledge of her personality and habits is undoubtedly of great value in the divorce process.

It is this knowledge which tells you how far you can push in a bargaining before she will say no and bring bargaining to a close. It is this knowledge which allows you to understand what she wants from the property settlement, and what she is willing to pay to get it. Yes, this knowledge is valuable.

But if you know her so well, why were you so surprised when she walked out? Why were you surprised when papers suddenly were served on you? If you know her so well, why did communications between you get so bad that a divorce is now in progress?

It is almost certain that you do not understand your wife as well as you should. While it is probably too late to save the marriage, there are still some gains to be made by learning a bit more about her. We mentioned Transactional Analysis earlier in the context of improving your understanding of yourself. Now we mention it again as a means of improving your ability to understand your wife. Even a small understanding of the technique may go far in providing some capability for interpreting her moods, wants, desires, and behaviors more accurately. Such knowledge can pay dividends in two different ways. First, the things she says she wants from the settlement may not be the things she really wants. She may be demanding all sorts of possessions which she doesn't really need; perhaps what she really needs is a personal sense of security. If you can respond to her real needs, much of her opposition and unwillingness to bargain may vanish. Even if such happy results are not forthcoming, your knowledge should improve your understanding of the bases from which she is bargaining and should correspondingly improve your ability to maneuver.

DEALING WITH THE FEAR OF TRIAL. For many, the courtroom is a fearful place. If you find yourself worried about what may happen to you there, the best education you can possibly get comes simply from going down to the courthouse and sitting in on a few trials. Divorce trials in most jurisdictions are "open" trials; anyone can walk in, sit down, and observe the proceedings. If your case is moving toward a contest, try to find out where the contested cases are tried, go there, and sit in for a while. You will get from this experience a good sense of how a trial operates. What you will not get is an understanding of how your guts can crawl with fear when you are on the witness stand. We once heard of a trial lawyer of many years' experience who took the stand for the first time at his own divorce trial. He later said that he had never been so frightened in his life. The fear is very real. It will happen to you. The best weapon against it is a superbly prepared case.

If you have been concerned about having your case spread all over the newspaper or all around town, a visit to the courtroom will quickly remove that source of concern. You will discover that the courtroom is virtually empty of observers; only the parties, their witnesses and lawyers, and the court officials are there. There may be one or two observers, but they are probably there simply because they have nothing better to do with their time.

Fear of public disclosure is generally unfounded; only if you are extremely wealthy or nationally prominent in politics, in short, only if you are a "public figure" can you expect anyone to be particularly interested in your case. The chances are that you simply aren't that important.

The visit to the courtroom may not prepare you for two other emotional problems attendant to trial. The first is a natural embarrassment caused by having to describe to strangers intimate or personal things relating to yourself and your wife. Your lawyer should be made aware of your embarrassment prior to trial, for he can modify the method of questioning to make the burden of self-disclosure easier. Rehearsing the production of embarrassing statements to a friend or to your lawyer also can be helpful. The other emotional difficulty stems from the fact that your wife will be in the courtroom with you. When you say something nasty about her, she is going to be right there to see you, looking you right in the eye. In this society, we tend to look down on tattletales and we attempt to avoid accusatory confrontations. The business of calmly describing to others the bad things someone else has done runs counter to these societal views. You may expect your wife to glare at you in utter contempt and hatred while you sit on the stand saying what you have to say; you will probably find it difficult to say bad things about her; you will be embarrassed. Expect these sensations to occur. When they do, ignore your wife to the degree possible. Do not look at her. Instead, focus your attention on your lawyer when he is questioning you, and divide your attention between her lawyer and your own when you are being cross-examined by the other side.

Role-playing and rehearsal also can be useful, both in familiarizing you with the process, and in helping you to get a feel for what happens. Your lawyer can set you up in a chair and play out the roles of himself and the other side's lawyer, asking questions of the sort you are likely to encounter. If your lawyer is not available, friends who have been through nasty divorces may be able to provide a reasonable facsimile. If role-playing and rehearsal are used, be careful *not* to rehearse your witnesses in their testimony. Their testimony should be left alone to be presented naturally on the witness stand. Your lawyer can role-play the witnesses to give them a feel for things if it seems necessary, and he can do so without damaging their testimony.

Your lawyer will probably brief you regarding manners and dress in the courtroom. He will advise you to present a neat and clean appearance. The length of your hair, or the presence of a beard, is not so important as it used to be, but both should be neatly trimmed and obviously well combed and clean. A suit is proper dress. The variety of men's fashions now available provides considerable latitude in dress, but as a rule the suit, tie, and shirt should not be flashy. A picture of restrained good dress is preferable.

The briefing should also include suggestions as to your demeanor. The wife's lawyer will sometimes try to arouse the husband to display temper before the judge. If he succeeds, he will have made great progress towards proving his case by convincing the judge that you have a vile temper. When being cross-examined, be sure to take a little time before answering each question from the opposing lawyer. This helps to keep your temper under control. Before you answer, glance at your own lawyer. He may have a signal for you, a warning, perhaps. Take a little time to formulate your answer, then keep it very brief and to the point. Don't hedge, and don't give lengthy explanations. The more you say, the more the other side will have to work on and to turn against you.

More frequent than attempts to arouse your temper are approaches by your wife's lawyer to set you at your ease. His demeanor may be relaxing, reassuring, and polite. You may find that his understanding approach helps you to relax. He may even make a joke, causing the court to laugh, breaking the tensions that have been generated. If you sense this kind of thing happening, *beware!* Never lose sight of the fact that this man is *her* lawyer, not yours; he is there for one and only one purpose—to make sure that his client wins a total victory. If you fall for his approach, you will develop a sense of security which is absolutely unfounded; feeling secure, you will volunteer information that the other side should not be able to get without a struggle.

You may also find it difficult to listen to the things your wife says about you. She may tell lies of astounding magnitude. Little events may be blown out of all proportion. If you came home mildly tipsy after a party, she may describe you as falling-down drunk; you vomited all over the children's beds, couldn't get your pants down in the bathroom and defecated all over yourself and your clothing. While such things are shocking, you must sit on your temper. The judge may be watching your reaction carefully. One of your tasks in the courtroom is to take careful note[6] of the things said by witnesses and claims made by the lawyers, and to be in a position to discuss these with your lawyer at lunch or at the end of a day of trial. If your wife blows things out of proportion, and if she goes too far, you may be able later to demonstrate to the judge the magnitude of her lies. Your job in the courtroom is not to produce an emotional display; instead, spend your energies making notes of what she has said and figuring how you might be able to counter her statements.

If you are addressed by the judge, lace your response with the words "Sir" and "Your Honor." Judges expect deference, they want deference, and they get angry if they don't receive deference. Always be nice to the judge, even if you would like to cram a fist down his throat. There is absolutely nothing to be gained by making an enemy of this man, and there is everything to be lost. Keep a cool head on your shoulders and a civil tongue in your mouth.

12

Beyond Divorce

For most people, the issues of divorce and custody are concluded at the time of trial. Others experience continuing legal activities. Such activities include (1) enforcement of court orders, (2) modification of court orders, and (3) appeal. As with the basic issues of divorce and custody, each of these activities is surrounded by a substantial body of law, statutory and case, which directs the courses of action.

Enforcement of a court order refers to the process of forcing someone to live up to the terms of a court order. Modification of a court order refers to the process of changing the contents of a court order. Appeal refers to the process of submitting a decision from a lower court to review by a higher court with the hope of forcing the lower court to modify its decision. Issues of enforcement and modification sometimes arise during the pendency of the divorce trial. Appeal, of course, cannot arise until after the trial decision has been rendered.

Enforcement of Orders

The three most commonly encountered enforcement problems attendant to divorce and custody are enforcement of orders for support, enforcement of orders for custody, and enforcement of visitation rights.

Enforcement of orders for support. When an ex-husband/father fails to pay the alimony or child support ordered by the court, the former wife may undertake legal action to force his compliance. In some jurisdictions, the male pays his support to a probation department or to a family service agency of the state or county government. In such situations, the former wife merely notifies the agency that the ex-husband is in arrears, and the agency is empowered to hold a legal hearing or to institute proceedings against the husband in court. In other situations, the former wife initiates activities by having her lawyer file for a hearing.

When the agency or lawyer files for the hearing, the ex-husband is notified that the hearing has been filed; the nature of the charges against him is included in the service. Usually, the nature of the hearing requires the former husband to "show cause why he should not be held in contempt of court" for failing to obey the court order. Because the contempt power of the court can result in fines, jail sentences, and other penalties, the husband usually prefers to pay up his arrearage well before the hearing. If he does so, the hearing is usually cancelled. The husband generally will be required to pay all of the legal expenses the wife incurred in the process of causing the husband to comply with the order.

In situations where the husband and wife live in different states, a "long arm" statute is available to force the husband's compliance. The statute is the Uniform Reciprocal Enforcement of Support Act. To bring the act to bear on the problem, the agency or lawyer files suit in the wife's state and demonstrates to the court that the husband is in arrears. The court then notifies the court where the husband lives that action is being taken against the husband under the URESA. A summons is sent to the husband in his jurisdiction, ordering him to appear before the court. If the husband pays his arrearage, generally the action will be dropped. If, for some reason, he does not pay up, the URESA empowers the court to compel his compliance and to extradite him to the wife's state for trial. As before, the husband usually will be required to pay the legal expenses of both sides.

Historically, the effectiveness of the URESA has been sorely curtailed by the need to establish service on the husband. Clever men have avoided this by disappearing—changing their names, jobs, and locations. If the husband cannot be found, he cannot be served and cannot be brought before the court. Recently, steps have been taken to remedy this. Information retained by the Federal government now can be accessed to help locate the missing father in child support problems. The computerized Parent Locator Service (PLS) traces fathers through their Social Security numbers and other identificational data, and reports the information back to the state that requested it, generally within six days. The Federal government is enabled also to employ the Internal Revenue Service as a means of collecting support payments. Since the IRS collection machinery is spread over the entire nation, jurisdictional problems do not encumber its activities.

ENFORCEMENT OF ORDERS FOR CUSTODY. Sometimes the noncustodial parent refuses to return the child to the legal custodial parent. In some cases, one parent may receive the child during a routine visitation period and immediately scram into another state. In such situations the procedures are almost identical to those discussed above, except that one additional remedy may be available. The parent who has legal custody may seek a writ of *habeas corpus* against the other parent. *Habeas corpus* is a summary procedure; the offending parent is hauled into court, the authenticity of the writ is examined and, if the writ is genuine, the child is delivered to the proper parent without more ado. In some cases where children have been ill-treated by their mothers, the fathers have sometimes snatched the children and gone to another state, hoping to gain legal custody there, or at least to have the issue of custody heard anew, so that the court can hear the miserable way in which the mother was treating the children. When hit with a writ of *habeas corpus,* the father has lost before he has started. Once the writ is seen to be genuine, the child is returned without any consideration of the merits of the existing custody situation.

ENFORCEMENT OF VISITATION RIGHTS. Denial of a father's visitation rights is a frequent problem. Where the former wife harbors ill will for the father, she can find a thousand excuses why the father cannot see his children. Johnny is sick, or tired, or nervous, or he has to go to the doctor's office, or he is out of town, and so forth. The father has two remedies. The first is to quit paying child support. The courts realize that this is the only effective means the father has for forcing the mother to comply with the legally-mandated visitation, but they also realize that without child support it is the children who are affected most adversely. Decisions vary widely and suggest the seriousness of the conflict which the court experiences. Generally, however, the court ends up by ordering the father to pay the child support, whether he sees his children or not.

The father's second remedy is to file for a hearing to hold the wife in contempt for refusing to obey the order. Her response is usually to allow visitation rights until the hearing is dropped, then again to prevent visitation. This game can be played indefinitely. Even if the wife goes to the hearing, about the only thing the court can do is bawl her out. If the wife were to be fined, the children would suffer from the loss of money, and indirectly the husband would be the one paying the fine. If the mother is jailed, the children would have to be kept by the inferior custodian (the father) or by a state agency or guardian during her confinement, which would obviously not be to the benefit of the children. As well, having a jailbird mother might, in itself, be psychologically harmful to the children. The court is reluctant to jail mothers.

In sum, there seem to be no effective means for compelling the wife to let the father see his children, even where her acts are clearly illegal.

Modification of Court Orders

Agreements between the parties that are not incorporated within court orders technically fall within the law of contracts and usually can be modified by the parties as they wish, provided only that they both agree upon the nature of the modification. An agreement that has been incorporated in a court order, such as a consent order, requires the participation of the court in the modification.

In the case of a consent order, if both parties are willing to make the changes in the order, the court frequently will allow the modification unless it feels that the modification is against the interests of the parties or of the children. Again in the case of a consent order, where one party wants to modify its terms and the other does not, the court generally will not allow the modification unless it feels that the change is absolutely necessary.

Speaking more generally, modification of a court order is obtained by going to court for a hearing. During the hearing, the party who requested the modification must generally show a "change of circumstance." A change in circumstance is as difficult to demonstrate, or as easy, as the court wishes it to be. If the nature of the modification is for a father to have his alimony reduced, generally he must show dramatically adverse financial conditions in comparison to those at the time of trial. In the case of a mother seeking to obtain custody away from the father, even trivial excuses have been recognized by the courts as showing a change of circumstance. Because of the diversity of things which do and do not demonstrate a change of circumstance, we leave the exploration of this problem to the reader with the recommendation that before seeking a modification, he spend some time in the law library.

Before considering a motion for modification, one should obtain a copy of the court order and the part of the trial transcript that relates to it. It sometimes happens that the wording of the order and the surrounding transcript allows sufficient leeway for the party to do as he wishes anyway. In particular, one should not depend upon the interpretation of the order as advanced by the other side; he should feel free to interpret it for himself and to act accordingly. If the other side objects, let them carry the burden of modifying or enforcing the order.

Appeal

Within a statutory period of time after the final decree of divorce, either party may move to appeal the case to a higher court. The function of the higher court will be to examine the transcript, the related orders and decisions, and sometimes the evidence that was available to the trial judge. The appellant (the one who files for the appeal) in a divorce or custody matter most frequently bases his appeal on abuse of discretion, claiming that the judge did not fairly hear the evidence, that he ruled against the evidence, or that he handled the case with improper judicial procedures. On appeal, the trial judge's decision is presumed to be proper; it is up to the appellant to show, without introducing new evidence or testimony, that the judge was wrong. The odds against success are about 50 to 1. The first hurdle to overcome is that of *certiorari*. One must petition the higher court to hear the appeal. If the higher court sees little legal principle involved, it will deny *certiorari*—in effect, it will refuse to hear the case. If *certiorari* is granted, the case will be heard on appeal. Preparations for the hearing are highly technical in nature, and require scrupulous adherence to procedure. Since crack legal talent is needed, the expenses are considerable. Moreover, the husband may be required to pay the legal expenses of both sides. Thus, appeal may not be advisable unless the likelihood of success is very, very good. Before moving for appeal, one should carefully examine the likelihood of proving, or creating and then proving, a change in circumstance sufficient to warrant a modification of the lower court's order.

APPENDIX A

How to Do Your Own Legal Research

THIS APPENDIX is included for those readers who feel that their cases warrant the utmost degree of activity on their part—that is, they are unwilling to accept the painful deprivations that result from societal and judicial biases against the American male in matters of divorce and custody. For such readers, the necessary commitment of time and energy is not too much to ask if it improves the possibility of future happiness. The legal research outlined here could require perhaps a hundred hours or more of the father/husband's time as well as a considerable financial investment—in materials, in typing and transcribing services used in compiling your notes, in hours taken from income-producing work. Still, in a difficult case, and where the stakes are high, the effort and expense may be more than justified.

We hope that your case is not so difficult, and that your own research—however deep—may be done from the motive of intelligent participation, rather than sheer survival. We do not attempt to give the reader a complete exposition of all aspects of legal research. Instead, we attempt to equip him with sufficient information to allow him to get started. As his experience increases, so also will his grasp of methods, procedures, and resources.

When you look up statutes and cases in lawbooks, you are doing "legal research." This is actually a simple matter, but there are two hurdles to overcome in the beginning. The first is your unfamiliarity with the books wherein such information is to be found; the second is your unfamiliarity with "legalese," that strange, high-falutin', five-syllabled dialect that lawyers use. Your lawyer can be of great help in overcoming the first hurdle by showing you the books in his library. Ask him to show you the statutes that relate to divorce in your jurisdiction. He will probably also have a set of books called "annotated statutes" for your state. Ask him to show you the sections of these volumes that might relate to your case.

Annotated statutes are statements of statutes (the law that underlies judicial action) paired with a sequence of annotations, or comments, usually presented through selected cases which have been tried, appealed, and as a result have become case law. In the volumes of annotated statutes one can read a section of statute, and then see how this statute has been applied in cases tried in the jurisdiction; also, it can be seen how the cases have *interpreted* the statute. Interpretation is a necessity, since the statutes are almost always written in highly generalized language. For example, in one jurisdiction, a statute reads that the "court may hear matters regarding alimony and may modify alimony from time to time as circumstances may require." In the cases that follow, one reads that the remarriage of the husband is not a circumstance of such a nature as to allow a modification of alimony. This is an interpretation of the statute. The exact wording of the statutes and the sequences of cases which apply and interpret the statutes vary from jurisdiction to jurisdiction, which is why the law must be studied in one's own state.

Ask your lawyer to allow you access to his library from time to time, so that you can spend some time reading the annotated statutes. Ignore the initial strain of trying to make sense of what the statutes and cases are saying. After the initial exposure to legalese, the ability to comprehend it grows without particular effort.

As you become familiar with the annotated statutes, you will notice that many lawbooks have a pocket built into the back cover. Inside this pocket should be a pamphlet, the "pocket part" (assuming your lawyer has kept his library current). The pamphlet is rewritten from time to time and issued (for a price) to those who have the main book. When a new pamphlet is issued the old pamphlet is discarded and the new one takes its place. This allows the main volume to be kept up to date without having to rewrite the whole thing. Sections of the book will be keyed to the pamphlet, generally through paragraph numbers.

The cases and statutes presented in volumes of annotated statutes are but the tip of the iceberg. They serve as a starting point to familiarize you with the basic legal doctrines in your jurisdiction. When you have become familiar with the annotated statutes you will have learned a lot and will have spent a lot of time reading. You will then be in a position to take the next step.

The Law Library

Of all kinds of libraries, the law library is unique in its degree of indexing and cross-referencing. It is so magnificently organized that even a novice will be able to select from the mountain of books the ones that are of primary interest to his case.

The approach we suggest is a four-step process which systematically increases the depth of exploration until all needed information is obtained. Put briefly, the four steps are (1) familiarizing oneself with the library, (2) familiarizing oneself with law, (3) defining the search pattern, and (4) researching in depth.

THE LIBRARIAN OR AIDE. All law libraries have one or more librarians and/or aides whose duties include helping others locate needed materials. Avail yourself of the services of these people and allow them to help you find the materials you need. As you become familiar with the locations and contents of primary reference works, you will discover that you are automatically learning the locations of other works that may be of interest. Even if your familiarity with the library is good, you may occasionally need a book from an unknown location. Don't waste your time—ask.

THE PRIMARY LEGAL REFERENCE WORKS. There are ten primary legal reference works, or sets of works, that you are likely to need. The first task will be to locate them.

1. There are two encyclopedias that deal solely with various areas of the law. They are *American Jurisprudence* (abbreviated "Am Jur") and *Corpus Juris* (abbreviated CJ). There is also a more recent version of each (*American Jurisprudence Second* and *Corpus Juris Secondum*), abbreviated Am Jur 2nd and CJS. (Abbreviations are important, since practically all legal references use abbreviations rather than the full titles of the works.) For practice, locate these important works, and find either the index or the contents of particular volumes as shown on the spines of the books. Locate the topic of "divorce" or that of "custody," and do a little reading. The first thing likely to impress you is the extensive index that precedes each major topic. Literally hundreds of subtopics may be listed by page or paragraph number where the discussion appears.

2. The United States has been divided into geographic regions. For

each region there is a different version of West's regional digest. The library may shelve all digests together or may keep each digest next to the "regional reporters" (discussed below) to which they relate. If you live in Iowa, the appropriate digest is the *Northwest Digest;* for Pennsylvania, the *Atlantic Digest,* etc. Ask the librarian to show you the West regional digest for your state. The digests are similar to encyclopedias, but they deal more heavily with particular cases which have been tried in the geographic regions covered by the digest. Each digest consists of over a hundred volumes. The materials are, as always, beautifully indexed, and you should experience no difficulty locating material related to your particular areas of interest.

3. You may already have become familiar with the annotated statutes for your jurisdiction in your lawyer's office. They should be located in the library as well. If you haven't reviewed them earlier, do so now.

4. For each of the geographic regions of the nation, there are, in addition to the regional digests, a set of books referred to as West's regional reporters. Separately within each region, these volumes are produced chronologically, each new volume containing the verbatim texts of judges' decisions. When there are enough new decisions to fill a volume, a new volume is produced. In busier geographic regions four or more volumes may be published each year. A special set of *key numbers* identifies cases according to their primary legal significance; key numbers also appear in the West digests, and serve to link materials in the digests to those in the reporters. If you locate a case of particular interest in one of the digests, chances are that similarly interesting cases will be found in the regional reporters under the same key number. The regional reporters are always referred to by abbreviated names rather than their full titles. The Northwest Reporters are abbreviated "N.W.," etc. It is standard practice in legal work to refer to particular cases or articles by the volume number (if there is more than one volume in the particular collection), followed by an abbreviated name or title, followed by the page number on which the article begins. For example, the judges' decision in the case of Vendepo versus Vendepo can be found in volume 37 of the second series of the Northwest reporters, beginning on page 916. In abbreviated form, the reference would be found as: Vendepo v. Vendepo, 37 N.W. 2d 916.

5. In your state may also be found a set of *state reports* or *reporters* for the *state supreme court,* or for the *courts of equity,* or for *chancery courts.* Exactly which of these reporters will exist for your state, and their exact titles, will vary from one state to another. These volumes are similar to the West regional reporters, except they are published only for one state. To discover which of these may be of interest to you,

ask the librarian to help you locate them, then do a little reading. If you are interested particularly in divorce (or in some other specific topic), the librarian may even know which of the state reporters carry such decisions. The decision for the case of Vendepo v. Vendepo can be found in volume 240 of the Iowa reporter, beginning on page 895. The abbreviation would be: Vendepo v. Vendepo, 240 Iowa 895.

6. Special scholarly reports regarding selected areas, or topics, of law are frequently written and collected into a set of massive tomes called the *American Law Reports*. There are currently three series of these reports, abbreviated ALR, ALR 2d, and ALR 3d. Each report summarizes the author's intensive study of some question of law. The ALR covers the wide domain of American law, so that only a relative few of the reports deal with divorce and custody matters; however, those that do generally present a high quality of research and reasoning. Articles can be located through the *ALR Quick Index*.

7. The kinds of things that must be proved to the court before the judge can decide the issues before him, can be found in a set of volumes, *American Jurisprudence Proof of Facts Annotated,* abbreviated Am Jur Proof of Facts. It is there, under the heading of adultery, that one will find that proof of adultery requires proof of intent and opportunity, together with examples of what has been considered sufficient proof of each. These volumes are not the same as *Am Jur Trials,* which is a set of discursive articles of value in their own right.

8. The starting point for any reader of domestic relations law should be a good text. We have found nothing to compare with Homer Clark's *Law of Domestic Relations,* published by West. It may be on the library shelves. If the library doesn't have it, buy it.

9. The business of "bringing a case down to date," or of exploring the history of a case, is made possible by the publications of Shepard's Citations, Inc. There are about seventy sets of these publications, one for each state, several for the Federal government, and one for each of the regional reporters. For work in your state, two of these publications will be immediately useful: Shepard's Citations for your state and Shepard's Citations for the West regional reporter covering your state. Each Shepard publication actually has three parts to it: a hardbound volume, a paperbound supplement, and advance sheets which update the supplement. Other sets of Shepard's Citations may be useful later; for example, citations from a different geographic region which has laws similar to those in your own state. But for now, it is sufficient to locate those that relate to your own jurisdiction.

10. To better understand "legalese," two publications are helpful. The first is *Black's Law Dictionary,* which tends to be the standard

legal dictionary, even though others are available. The second is *Words and Phrases,* a several-volume set which presents words and phrases, some discussion of their meaning(s), and illustrations of how the words and phrases have been used in cases.

There are, of course, a great many other publications which are useful. Those described above are important because they give the novice entrée to a difficult field of knowledge. The first chore facing the reader is simply to locate these materials in the law library.

Familiarization with Law

Law depends on both statute law and case law. Of the greatest importance are the statutes and cases in your own state. These, in the sense of legal theory, are *compelling* upon the court. The judge has no option but to rule according to the law as statutes and cases present the law to him. This is a statement of the legal principle of *stare decisis,* that the decision given a particular case is to be in accord with the decisions given earlier cases where the facts are substantially the same. The judge has no right to make up special laws or considerations in the judgment of your case—he has to use the same law that applies to everybody else.

Of course, the principle applies only to the laws of each particular jurisdiction. Maryland statutes and cases cannot be made to apply to a case being tried in Michigan. For a case being tried in Michigan, the statutes and cases in Michigan are compelling upon the judge. Statutes from other states are utterly inapplicable in Michigan, but where the statutes of two states are similar, their cases may develop along similar lines. In such circumstances, the decision of a case in a different state may be persuasive on the judge. Such a decision may represent a link in a logical argument, a link which is missing in the cases of the state where the trial is taking place. Effectively argued, an out-of-state case can, therefore, have *persuasive* influence, but the judge is not bound to apply its principles as he is the cases decided in his own state.

In searching for cases, then, one seeks to find cases which are similar to the situation in one's own case as a means of "enabling" the principle of *stare decisis,* to force the judge's decision in the desired direction. Bearing this in mind, the study of domestic law begins with reading a text. We have recommended Clark for this purpose. It need not be read cover to cover; one may read just those chapters of personal importance, but we suspect that several chapters will be found of interest. Such reading will provide an understanding of the dimensions of domestic law, and will illustrate something of the disparity in the laws of the different jurisdictions. Numerous footnotes throughout the work refer to particular cases; those of interest may be noted for later reading in the law library. (Remember, you can buy a copy of Clark's for less than you'd pay a lawyer for an hour of his time. The investment is well worth it.)

After reading relevant sections of Clark, understanding some of it and misunderstanding the rest, you will have gained enough knowledge to take the next step: to explore one or both of the legal encyclopedias. There you will find text which explains the same kinds of legal issues in different words, thereby rendering clear materials earlier found obscure. During the first attempt to read the legal encyclopedias, you may feel yourself literally buried by the great mass of material. To avoid this problem, carefully examine the table of contents which precedes each major topic, and pick out only one or two to read. During the reading, take notes on things of interest, recording the volume and page number where the information is found. Also, if the reading suggests other topics to be explored, take notes on the suggestions so that you can go to them later. This will prevent you from "splintering" your effort—hopping aimlessly from one topic to another.

It may be useful to avoid reading too much during the familiarization phase. Read only enough to fill your head, not so much as to confuse you. Having reached the saturation point in the encyclopedias, return to Clark for a rereading of the same materials examined in the encyclopedia. By this time, most of the issues will be clear.

Continue in this way, working back and forth between Clark and the encyclopedias, until all topics of interest have been covered. Notes taken on the readings will, when the endpoint has been reached, be fairly voluminous. It may be instructive to go back to the earliest notes you took; progress will be seen in the increasing sophistication of the notes. Where once there was confusion regarding the distinction of residence and domicile, now there are notes clearly dealing with one or the other in a meaningful way. Reviewing the notes also helps to put the subjects in perspective. Certain matters will have grown in apparent importance, others will have lessened. Before increasing the depth of exploration, it may be wise to set priorities as to what issues are most deserving of attention.

Defining the Search Pattern

Earlier readings were directed toward the law of divorce and custody in general. Through them you will have gained a pretty clear idea of what the issues are and how they are variously dealt with by the jurisdictions. In the next stage of operation you will narrow the search pattern and increase the depth of the research.

The readings will have given you some idea of what to expect as the legal contest develops. The kinds of grounds and defenses which might be employed are becoming more clear. The kinds of evidence which may bear upon the issues of trial are becoming understood. New avenues of attack and defense may have been discovered.

Before jumping immediately to cases to prove a point, however, more must be learned. One needs to focus attention on the necessary things and to avoid interesting distractions. One way to avoid needless activity is to determine what will be required to prove the grounds for divorce that have been advanced by you or your wife. For this, go to the volumes of Am Jur Proof of Facts. Each of the needed proofs must be supported by testimony and other evidence if the judge is to grant the divorce on a particular ground. One approach to preventing a divorce is through denying proof. For example, if your wife is trying to divorce you on the ground of adultery, you may be able to prevent her by demonstrating to the court that you had neither the inclination nor the opportunity to commit adultery wtih the named co-respondent. The wife, in presenting her case, must have testimony and other evidence to make out her case. You may be in a position to render her proofs harmless by contradictory evidence, or by preventing evidence useful to her case from falling into her hands. The examination of Am Jur Proof of Facts will spell out what must be demonstrated to win a case; since these are the things that must be shown, restrict your energies to them, and to things related to them. When you have dealt with the central concerns, you can go on to related concerns. Such an approach tends to assure that the most important bases are covered.

Now that you have some idea of what both sides will do in order to make out their respective cases, your exploration goes deeper, this time into the study of the relevant annotated statutes for your state. Each issue considered in Am Jur Proof of Facts should now be studied in light of the statutes and cases of your own jurisdiction. How are the courts interpreting and applying the statutes to the cases they try? Are there threads of logic which seem to tie cases together? Are the courts consistent in their decisions? Can you locate a number of cases which help you to understand how much evidence of what type seems to predispose the court to a particular decision? Can you find statements of "rules of thumb" which the judges apply in setting alimony, in deciding child custody, in allocating property to one party or the other?

The annotated statutes are worthy of careful study, and the notes you take should be reasonably full. On completing this study, it's good to review all research work to date. Go back to the first notes you took and see if the earlier questions have now been answered. You may find that many earlier questions were not truly germane to your case. Should you reorder your priorities? What new topics seem to warrant exploration? What new legal terms have you learned? Are there words or phrases you need to look up in *Black's Law Dictionary,* or in *Words and Phrases?* Have you referred to the pocket parts of the volumes you have been reading? Are you gathering a number of potentially useful case references, both to support your case and to refute that of the opposition?

When your review of progress has been completed, your thinking should have been consolidated somewhat; earlier feelings of formlessness should be disappearing and the case should begin to appear more organized, more definite in direction and scope. If such is your feeling, you are ready for the next step.

Next direct your attention to the West regional digest for your area, including the pocket parts, to firm up your understanding of legal principles and to obtain additional references to cases that may be useful. At this time, the direction of research should begin to shift toward the gathering of good cases, those which are closely similar to your own situation and which either bode good or ill for your own case. One goal of this research is to establish the "preponderance of cases" regarding each issue involved in your case, to see whether the thrust of the law is in favor of a given issue, or against it. The dates of relevant cases can become important here, since recent decisions may be suggestive of changing judicial attitudes. A second goal of the research will be to establish the "intent" of the statutes that apply to your case; in some cases, intent will be specifically cited in decisions. Proof of legislative intent can be important, since it can argue for or against the way certain cases were decided, strengthening or weakening their impact on the court. In gathering such materials, cases from one's own state should be given most attention; out-of-state cases carry much less impact. Nonetheless, your lawyer may feel that the cases in certain other states are influential in your jurisdiction. If so, you may wish to review the regional digests for such states as part of your research.

Now settle back to do some lengthy reading. Beginning with the most important cases for which you have references, locate the cases either in the West regional reporter or in your state reporter. Especially in the West regional reporters, skim the keynotes and abstract of the decision, since these will provide some understanding of the case and the legal issues that were seen by the appellate court as underlying the case. Keynotes and abstract may be missing from the state reporter, but if present, take the time to skim them before reading the case itself.

In reading a case, several notes should be taken. These include: (a) the degree of similarity of the case to your own; (b) whether the case was decided by the appellate court in a way favorable to your own case; (c) whether the case contains language that could reflect adversely on your own situation if the entire text were to be placed before the court; (d) whether the decision contains language that favors your own case; and (e) whether there are specific words that seem so well put together for your purposes that you might want them incorporated in a trial brief (if so, you may wish to extract a verbatim section of the text, or to photocopy part or all of the decision).

After you have read a case through, make a value judgment regarding the value of the case for your purposes; a scale from −5 (minus five) to +5 (plus five) might be used to "grade" each case. A score of −5 means a case which is strongly opposed to your position, a score of +5 means a case which is strongly in favor of your position, and a score of 0 (zero) means a case which is inapplicable to your situation. Many, if not most, of the cases you read will be scored zero. The objective of the procedure is to separate those cases of greatest importance from those of less importance as far as your own situation is concerned. A case scored as −5 is a serious threat to your case, while a +5 case is a powerful aid.

After *all* cases on your list have been examined in the reporters, you are ready for the next step, that of Shepardization.

Shepardization

Shepardization is the process by which one discovers how the law has dealt with a particular case since that case was first decided at the appellate level. An old case may have been revisited many times by the courts; sometimes in a succession of retrials of the case by the original parties, sometimes in a sequence of citations to that case in other cases later coming to appeal. When you have discovered a case which seems to be strongly related to your own situation, you still cannot count on that case being current law until you have assured yourself that later cases have not involved the history of that case in such a way as to have modified its applicability to your own situation.

The key is in the Shepard's Citation series. As mentioned earlier, there are about seventy of these publications, one for each state and one for each of the geographic regions covered by the West digests and reporters; each Shepard Citation publication consists of a hardbound book, a paperbound supplement, and a series of advance sheets which update the supplement. You have by now located two such sets, at least: the set dealing with your state and the set dealing with the geographic region containing your state.

Now, suppose you are interested in a particular case within your own state. You want to discover all the later cases which may have used or modified the meaning of this case (call it X v X). First go to the Shepard's Citation book for your state. If you live in Michigan, the particular volume will deal with the Michigan Reports. What was the reference to this case? Suppose it was 338 Mich 487. Scanning the tops of the pages of the Shepard's Citations, look for the page or pages dealing with volume 338. Having located them, look down the columns of boldface numbers to find the page number. Having located page 487, you will note that the first entry below the selected page number (within parentheses) is a reference to the West regional digest that contains this case (even though the same case is reproduced in the Michigan Reports). Below that entry there is a series of references. Each reference is to some case, or to some article, which has cited the case you are interested in. Your next task is to run these "referrals" down, to check out the subsequent cases and to see whether any substantial change has been made in the interpretation of X v X. There also will be references to articles, such as law review articles (the journals published by law schools), which have used X v X in some capacity. Not all references to X v X will be included within the Shepard's Citation books for your state; you must also check the Shepard's Citation book for the West regional digest area to pick up the additional references. Through this process you will be assured of picking off all the situations in which X v X has been talked about.

You should Shepardize all cases which you have scored −5 or +5. If time permits, continue the Shepardization process down to the +4 or −4 cases, the +3 or −3 cases, and so on until you have worked through all the relevant literature.

The business of reading cases and Shepardizing them is lengthy, and time-consuming. You can expect to spend between ten minutes and two and one half hours on a relevant case. If you explore fifty cases or more, the time investment will be considerable. Moreover, as your sensitivity to the law and its concepts improves, there may be a number of topics that you feel warrant special scrutiny. Before researching these for yourself, take the time to explore the topics already discussed by the authors of the American Law Review. Look in the ALR Quick Index for the articles which might be of interest. These articles probably will give you some more case references that will be worth following up in the reporters and Shepard's Citations. Having gone this route, your time expenditure in the law library may well exceed 100 hours, but you are now competent enough in matters relating to your case to be able to work in tandem with your lawyer—perhaps even to educate *him* a bit.

APPENDIX B

Helpful Readings

BEFORE DASHING out to buy a carload of books, consider that the municipal or county library represents one of the few bargains left in America. In return for the taxes you pay, you have free access to thousands of dollars worth of books. A second bargain is the publications list of the U.S. Government Printing Office. The USGPO has a number of free catalogues, or price lists, of publications, many of which are relevant to divorce, custody, and related matters. To get the free price list (catalogues), write:

The Superintendent of Documents
U.S. Government Printing Office
Washington, D.C. 20402

Divorce and Custody

Black, Henry Campbell, *Black's Law Dictionary,* 4th Ed. (rev.), West Publishing Co., St. Paul, Minn., 1968.

The standard law dictionary.

Cannavale, Frank J., Jr., and Falcon, William D. (ed.), *Improving Witness Cooperation,* Stock No. 027-000-00411-3, U.S. Government Printing Office, Washington, D.C., 1976, $1.45.

A short handbook prepared for the U.S. Department of Justice which contains a number of practical suggestions for dealing with witnesses.

Child Support Data and Materials, prepared for the Committee on Finance, United States Senate, November 10, 1975, U.S. Government Printing Office, Washington, D.C., $1.90.

Contains information relating to the Parent Locator Service of the Federal government, the relationship between state locator services and the Federal service, etc.

Clark, Homer H., Jr., *Law of Domestic Relations,* West Publishing Co., St. Paul, Minn., 1968.

Although in need of revision, this is probably the best all-round book on the law of divorce, separation, custody, annulment, and related topics.

Cleary, Edward W. (ed.), *McCormick's Handbook of the Law of Evidence,* West Publishing Co., St. Paul, Minn., 1972.

Discusses what is, and what is not, evidence, as well as the proper methods for questioning witnesses, the privileged relation between client and lawyer, other privileges, etc.

Harvard Law Review Association, *A Uniform System of Citation,* 11th ed., Harvard Law Review Association, Gannett House, Cambridge, Mass., 02138, 1967.

A small pamphlet presenting uniform abbreviations for various legal works, together with preferred methods for citing legal works as references.

Hirsch, Barbara B., *Divorce: What a Woman Needs to Know,* Bantam Books, New York, 1975, $1.50.

Accurate law in most respects, and interesting case histories. Written for women.

Lindey, Alexander, *Separation Agreements and Ante-Nuptial Contracts,* 2 vols., Matthew Bender, New York, 1977.

A massive and expensive two-volume set dealing with the law of divorce and custody in addition to reparation agreements. Contains numerous forms which can be assembled to assure proper wording of a separation agreement. The book is updated periodically through issuance of inserts. Authoritative and valuable.

Roalfe, William R. (ed.), *How to Find the Law,* 6th ed., West Publishing Co., St. Paul, Minn., 1965.

A textbook dealing with the conduct of legal research. Also has some comments on legal writing.

Winter, Edward J., and Hersh, Brian R., "Child Custody Litigation," in *American Jurisprudence Trials,* 22:347–516.

Absolute "must" reading for any father who wants custody. *Am Jur Trials* is to be found in any good law library. It will be noted that the lawyer-client relationship advocated by Winter and Hersh differs from that suggested by your authors. In other respects, the article is of great value.

Money Problems

Callenbach, Ernest, *Living Poor With Style,* Bantam Books, New York, 1972, $1.95

Good ideas for getting the most out of your money while nearly destitute.

Dowd, Merle E., *How to Get Out of Debt and Stay Out of Debt,* Henry Regnery Co., Chicago, 1971, $5.95.

Practical guide to reducing debts. Includes valuable discussion of the Federal government's Wage Earner Plan as well as standard bankruptcy procedures.

Father Absence

Biller, Henry B., "Father Absence, Maternal Encouragement, and Sex Role Development in Kindergarten-Age Boys," in *Child Development,* 40 (969):539–546.

Biller, Henry B., "Father Absence and the Personality Development of the Male Child," in *Developmental Psychology,* 2 (1970):181–201.

Biller, Henry B., "Fathering and Female Sexual Development," in *Medical Aspects of Human Sexuality,* 5 (1971):126–138.

Biller, Henry B., and Weiss, Stephan D., "The Father-Daughter Relationship and the Personality Development of the Female," in *The Journal of Genetic Psychology,* 116:79–93.

Carlsmith, Lyn, "Effect of Early Father Absence on Scholastic Aptitude," in *Harvard Educational Review,* 34 (1964):3–21.

Emmerich, W., "Parental Identification in Young Children," in *Genetic Psychology Monograph,* 60 (1959):257–308.

Hetherington, E. Mavis, "Effects of Father Absence on Personality Development in Adolescent Females," in *Developmental Psychology,* 7 (1972):313–326.

Lessing, Elise E., Zagorin, Susan W., and Nelson, Dorothy, "WISC Subtest and IQ Score Correlates of Father Absence," in *The Journal of Genetic Psychology,* 117 (1970):81–195.

Santrock, John W., "Paternal Absence, Sex Typing, and Identification," in *Developmental Psychology,* 2:264–272.

Fathering

Biller, Henry, and Meredith, Dennis, *Father Power,* David McKay Co., New York, 1974, $9.95.

Dr. Biller is one of the foremost authorities on the father-child relationship and a prominent psychological researcher. 'Must" reading for a father who is interested in his children.

Dodson, Fitzhugh, *How to Father,* New American Library, New York, 1975, $1.95.

Down-to-earth and reasonably sound adivce on parenting. Includes a very useful appendix recommending toys, children's books, children's records, games to play, etc.

Gregg, Elizabeth M., et al., *What To Do When "There's Nothing To Do,"* Dell Publishing Co., New York, 1968 (8th printing 1974), $0.95.

Survival Skills for the Single Male

AUTOMOTIVE MAINTENANCE

Fremon, George, and Fremon, Suzanne, *Why Trade It In?,* Strait and Company, Princeton, N.J. 08540, 1976, $5.00.

The best guide we know of for maintaining a car properly when one knows virtually nothing about the inner workings and hidden mechanisms of cars.

GENERAL REPAIR AND MAINTENANCE

Koff, Richard M., *How Does It Work?* Doubleday & Co., Garden City, N.Y., 1961.

Entertaining and informative book describes how many tools, machines, appliances, musical instruments, chemicals, etc., work. For both kids and grown-ups.

Lemons, Wayne, and Montgomery, Glen, *Small Appliance Repair Guide,* TAB Books, Blueridge Summit, Pa., 1970.

How to troubleshoot, disassemble, and repair many common household appliances.

Wheeler, Gershon J., *Home Repair,* Reston Publishing Co., Reston, Va., 1973.

Deals with tools, preventive maintenance, repair, and home improvements. Including discussions on plumbing, electricity, walls, ceilings, floors, painting, etc.

FOOD PREPARATION

Davis, Adelle, *Let's Eat Right to Keep Fit,* New American Library, New York, 1970, $1.75.

An overall view of nutrition by its most popular advocate.

General Mills, Inc. *Betty Crocker's Cookbook,* Golden Press, New York, 1976.

A new edition of a popular and complete cookbook.

General Mills, Inc., *Cookbook for Boys and Girls,* Golden Press, New York, 1975.

One way for Dad to avoid the sugardaddy approach to visitation is to put the kids to work. Here is an opportunity for father and child to work constructively together.

Rombauer, Irma S., and Becker, Marion Rombauer, *The Joy of Cooking,* Bobbs-Merrill Co., Indianapolis, Ind., 1964.

A deservedly popular, comprehensive book on cooking, with explanatory text providing the underlying "theory" for many kinds of recipes.

Williams, Roger J., *Nutrition in a Nutshell,* Dolphin Books, Garden City, N.Y., 1962, $1.45.

A layman's discussion of the importance of good nutrition; exposes the diet fads preached by some nutritionists.

SEWING

Cunningham, Gladys, *Singer Sewing Book,* Golden Press, New York, 1969.

For those having a sewing machine who wish to exploit the power such a machine gives—all aspects of sewing (clothing, draperies, etc.). Includes a chapter on mending.

Department of the Army, *Repair of Clothing and Textiles,* TM-10-267, U.S. Government Printing Office, Washington, D.C., 1950, $0.25.

Excellent guide to the hand repair of clothing.

HOME MANAGEMENT

Bacharach, Bert, *How to Do Almost Everything,* Simon and Schuster, New York, 1970, $6.95.

Tips on personal and household care.

Greenblatt, Edwin, *Suddenly Single,* Quadrangle Press, New York, 1973.

Designed for the suddenly single male. Deals with setting up house or apartment, stocking and using the kitchen, food storage and cooking (with simple recipes), care of the home, handling and entertaining children, etc.

Miscellaneous Books Relating to Law and Divorce

Bloom, Murray Teigh, *The Trouble With Lawyers,* Simon and Schuster, New York, 1969 (or Pocket Books, New York, 1970).

An interesting commentary on the sorry legal state of the nation, the ineptitude and dishonesty of some lawyers, etc.

Epstein, Joseph, *Divorced in America,* Penguin Books, New York, 1974, $1.95.

A description of the before-during-and-after of going through a divorce, with a lot of interesting commentary.

Framo, James L., "The Friendly Divorce," in *Psychology Today,* Vol. 11, No. 9, Feb. 1978, p. 76.

The author describes "divorce therapy," a psychological approach which attempts to avoid acrimonious divorces.

Krantzler, Mel, *Creative Divorce,* New American Library, New York, 1974, $1.95.

A professional counselor, having gone through a divorce, presents insights into the emotional and other problems faced after the divorce, together with suggestions for avoiding some of the pitfalls.

Rosenblatt, Stanley, *The Divorce Racket,* Nash Publishing Corp., Los Angeles, Calif., 1969.

Rosenblatt presents detailed examination of two cases, the Astor case and the Chaachou case, which dealt with the divorce of a man from a woman he had never married. Worth reading.

Sheresky, Norman, and Mannes, Marya, *Uncoupling: The Art of Coming Apart,* Dell Publishing Co., New York, 1972, $1.50.

A general discussion of divorce with a view toward amicable dissolution.

Sherman, Charles E., *How to Do Your Own Divorce in California,* Nolo Press, P.O. Box 544, Occidental, Calif. 95465.

A do-it-yourself book, including the necessary forms, for obtaining an uncontested divorce in California. It is imperative that the latest version be obtained so that forms and procedures will be up to date. Cost is about $6.00. Of no value to those who are not bound for a California divorce.

Wheeler, Michael, *No-Fault Divorce,* Beacon Press, Boston, Mass., 1974.

A well-reasoned book dealing with divorce and custody, concentrated in the "no-fault" area. Recommended.

APPENDIX C

Men's Rights Organizations

The development of this book was assisted by Mr. George Doppler, a national coordinator of men's rights organization activities. We sent questionnaires to organizations whose names and addresses were furnished by Mr. Doppler. The questionnaire requested information regarding the activities and attitudes of the organizations. What follows is based on the responses of those organizataions that answered our request.

Most organizations have been formed by men who have fared badly before the courts in matters of divorce or custody. Theirs is an uphill fight in which money, supplies, staff, and leadership are all sorely needed.

Some organizations list hundreds of members, some mention only one. In larger organizations it frequently happens that between 10 and 20 percent will be active members; the rest, though inactive, may be dues-paying contributors or supporters. Size is not directly a measure of the value, utility, or effectiveness of an organization; these factors depend upon the goals, resources, and leadership of the group, among other things.

Each organization seems to have certain beliefs perhaps founded on the experiences of early members or founders of the organization. A few discrepancies can be observed in the beliefs held by various organizations. For example, some feel that it is effective to picket courthouses during selected trials; others do not. Some feel that placing observers in the courtroom, who wear large campaign buttons declaring them to be "court watchers," has a sobering influence upon the judge; others feel this is ineffective. Some feel that representing one's self as one's own attorney (*pro se* or *propria personum* representations) causes the judge to accord the male his legal rights; others feel that "going *pro se*" can be terribly dangerous.

To the man in trouble, there can be little doubt that men's rights organizations can be helpful. If the list we present fails to include one in your area, we encourage contacting one or more by telephone. They may know of one in your area which we do not list.

Individual services which men's rights organizations often furnish tend to be of the following kinds: (a) the provision of social and psychological support—organizational members tend to know the score, they have been through the grist mill themselves, and they know what the male goes through; (b) the provision of manpower support—in selected cases some organizations will provide direct aid in the form of human labor (gathering evidence, interviewing witnesses, surveillance activities, etc.); (c) the provision of information regarding the statute and case law, the pitfalls to be avoided, the tactics which seem to be successful, etc.; and (d) the provision of information regarding significant people (judges, social workers, psychiatrists, lawyers, et al.), their qualifications, performances, biases, honesty, etc. Men seeking such assistance will frequently be asked to join the organization as a condition of receiving aid and there is usually a membership fee. There may be other fees or charges which are incurred in return for the provision of special services.

Below we list the names and addresses of those organizations which responded to our survey. Names and telephone numbers of people to contact within the organization are provided where possible. Organizations are listed alphabetically by state rather than by organizational name. The following codes indicate the activities and services of the organizations:

A —helps men with alimony problems
Ap—helps men with appeal problems
C —helps men with custody problems
Ca—collects case decisions at appellate level
Cs—helps men with child support problems
D —helps with divorce problems
Do—dossiers are maintained for significant people
Dt—helps men with divorce trial problems
L —lobbying or political activities
P —picketing, court-watching, or publicity activities
R —makes referrals to lawyers believed to be good

Rf—collects reference materials, either professional or popular
S —helps men who have problems with legal separations
Sa —helps men with separation agreement problems
Sp—undertakes special studies or projects
St —studies factors which influence decisions at the original trial level (in contrast to appellate level)

Mr. Rudy Johnson
(907) 225-6808 Ap,C,Ca,Cs,D,Do,Dt,L,P,R,Rf,Sa,St
Family Law Reform & Justice Council of Alaska
P.O. Box 897
Ward Cove, AL 99928

Mr. Clint Jones
(714) 968-2973 D,Do,L,P,R,Rf,S,Sp,St
Divorce Aid, Inc.
9109 Pelican Avenue
Fountain Valley, CA 92708

Mr. I. Dean Youngman
(415) 848-2323 A,Ap,C,Cs,D,Dt,L,P,R,Rf,S,Sa
Equal Rights for Fathers
P.O. Box 6327
Albany, CA 94706

Mr. Howard P. Jeter
(415) 841-7839 A,Ap,C,Cs,D,Do,Dt,L,P,R,Rf,S,Sa,Sp,St
Family Law Action Council
P.O. Box 3213
Berkeley, CA 94703

Fathers United for Equal Justice
Box 201
Fullerton, CA 92623

Mr. George Partis
(707) 833-2550 Dt,St,L,P,Rf,Ca
United States Divorce Reform, Inc.
Box 243
Kenwood, CA 95452

Mr. Thomas Alexander Jr.
(301) 571-8383 A,Ap,C,Cs,D,Do,Dt,L,P,R,Rf,S,Sa,Sp
Male Parents for Equal Rights, Inc.
One West Sixth Street
Wilmington, DE 19801

Mr. Gerry Mooney
(305) 893-9709 Ap,C,Cs,D,Do,Dt,P,R,Rf,S,Sa,St
Florida Fathers for Equal Rights
1302 North East 118th Street
North Miami, FL 33161

Mr. Edward J. Winter Jr.
(305) 371-5225 A,Ap,C,Ca,Cs,D,Do,Dt,P,Rf,S,Sp,St
National Society of Fathers for Child Custody & Divorce Law Reform
Biscayne Building,
19 West Flagler Street
Miami, FL 33130

Mr. Lee Silen
(812) 477-8538 or (812) 477-8537 C,Cs,D,Do,Dt,L,P,R,Rf,Sp,St
Fathers for Equal Rights, Inc.
P.O. Box 2028
Evansville, IN 47714

Mr. Theodore Gwynn
(301) 664-5819 or (310) 247-5757 C,D,L,P,R
Fathers United for Equal Rights and The Second Wives Coalition
P.O. Box 7585
Baltimore, MD 21207

Mr. John L. Barnes, Sr.
Fathers United for Equal Rights Foundation of Montgomery County, Maryland, Inc.
P.O. Box 3308
Silver Spring, MD 20901

Mr. J. J. Gysling
Council for Family Law Reform in Michigan, Inc.
925 Kirts Road
Troy, MI 48084

Mr. Richard F. Doyle
(612) 464-7887 A,Ap,C,Ca,Cs,D,Do,Dt,L,P,R,Rf,S,Sa,St
Men's Rights Association
P.O. Box 189
Forest Lake, MN 55025

Mr. Charles L. VanDuzee
(612) 224-6298 A,C,Cs,D,Do,L,P,R,Rf
United States Divorce Reform Inc. of Minnesota
1031 Pleasant Avenue
St. Paul, MN 55102

Mr. Eugene Austin
C,Ca,Cs,D,Do,L,P,R,Sp,St
National Council on Family Law
P.O. Box 104
Foley, MS 63347

Mr. Anthony Gil
(201) 696-5156 A,Ap,C,Cs,D,Dt,L,P,Rf,S,Sa,Sp,St
Family Law Council
U.S. Divorce Reform Inc. (N.J.)
P.O. Box 217
Fair Lawn, NJ 07410

Mr. Robert N. Roma
(201) 843-8156 A,Ap,C,Cs,D,Dt,P,R,Rf,S,Sa,St
Fathers United for Equal Rights, N.J. Inc.
P.O. Box 900
Maywood, NJ 07607

Mr. Norman F. Kopp
(315) 452-0905 or (315) 455-1023 A,Ap,C,Cs,D,Do,Dt,L,P,R,Rf,S,Sa,St
Deprived and Discriminated-Against Males of Central New York (DADAM)
P.O. Box 254
Eastwood Station, Syracuse, NY 13206

Mr. William J. Ralston
(716) 372-3416 C,Do,L,R,St
United Parents of Absconded Children
Wolf Run Road, Box 127-A
Cuba, NY 14727

Mr. George F. Doppler
Ap,C,Ca,Cs,D,L,P,R,Rf,S
Family Law Reform and Justice Council of Pennsylvania
P.O. Box 60
Broomall, PA 19008

Conrad and Donna Weniger
(814) 382-2986 A,Ap,C,Ca,Cs,Do,L,P,R,Rf,St
Fathers for Fair Support and Custody & Second Wives Coalition
R.D. No. 2, Box 200
Conneaut Lake, PA 16316

Mr. Jerry Soloman
(714) 343-4551 C,Cs,Do,L,P,R,Rf,Sp
Fathers United for Equal Rights
3 Green Ridge Street
Scranton, PA 18508

Mr. Vernon L. Smith
(214) 692-1492 Rf,Sp,St
Institute of Legal Research and Education, Inc.
P.O. Box 31813
Dallas, TX 75231

Mr. Elliot H. Diamond
(703) 471-5535 or (703) 471-5525 A,Ap,C,Cs,D,Do,Dt,P,R,Rf,S,Sa,St
Fathers United for Equal Rights
P.O. Box 1224
Arlington, VA 22210

Mr. Kenneth Muenzler
(512) 442-5336 Ap,C,Cs,D,Do,Dt,L,P,R,Rf,St
Texas Fathers for Equal Rights, Wives and Grandparents Coalition
P.O. Box 14882
Austin, TX 78761

Mr. Basil Archey
(512) 735-7461 C,D,Do,P,R,St
Texas Fathers for Equal Rights
2514 West Mulberry
San Antonio, TX 78228

Mr. Gerald A. McBreen
(206) 863-5788 A,Ap,C,Cs,D,Do,Dt,L,P,R,Rf,St
Washington Chapter United States Divorce Reform
P.O. Box 11
Auburn, WA 98002

APPENDIX D
Glossary

THE GLOSSARY provides common-sense interpretations of legal words and phrases encountered in divorce. More complete and precise definitions can, and should, be found in Black's Law Dictionary.

Abandonment: Willful nonperformance of a marital duty. *See also* Desertion.

Abuse of discretion: An assertion that a judge ordered things he was not empowered to order, or that he mismanaged the legal procedures of a hearing, or that he significantly ignored the facts of a case.

Adultery: Sexual intercourse between a man and a woman where at least one of the two is married to someone else.

Adversary system: A basic legal procedure in which two parties contend against each other in litigation.

Affidavit: A written statement, signed by the one who made the statement and notarized to attest to its truth.

Affirm: A statement by a court of appeals that a lower court judge was correct in his ruling.

Agreement: An oral or written statement indicating that two or more people are in accord as to their rights, obligations, duties, and/or actions.

Alimony: Money paid by one person for the support of the ex-spouse.

Alternating custody: A mode of custody in which, at certain times or under certain conditions, the mother has custody, while at other times or conditions the father has custody. *See also* Sole custody.

Annullment: The formal recognition that a marriage never existed.

Answer: The response made to a claim by the respondent. *See* Counterclaim.

Ante-nuptial contract (or agreement): An agreement between man and woman regarding terms and conditions to be respected after their marriage.

Appeal: A pleading to a higher court to alter the conclusion of a lower court.

Appellant: One who files for an appeal.

Appellate: The level of a court of appeals, e.g., "appellate level."

Bar: A defense against divorce; a basis for preventing or denying a divorce.

Best interest and welfare test: A criterion by which the court adjudicates custody of children through considering only issues affecting the interests and welfare of the children.

Change of circumstances: A change in the economic, physical or social situation of a party which serves as a basis for the modification of a court order.

Child: *See* Infant.

Claim: A charge made by one party against another. *See also* Counterclaim.

Claimant: One who files a claim against another. *See also* Counterclaimant.

Collateral estoppel: A legal doctrine which prevents a matter from being tried because a related matter was earlier tried; the new matter is "estopped." Also applies to evidence known but not used.

Collusion: An illegal agreement. A bar to divorce when the court discerns that husband and wife have conspired to divorce through such things as manufacturing of false evidence.

Common law: Refers to the old English customs and practices which form the framework for the legal systems of the "common law" countries, which include the U.S., Canada, and all other ex-British colonies.

Community property: Property belonging to a "community," consisting of property and assets acquired after marriage, regardless of whether the title to same is in the name of one or both of the marriage partners.

Comparative rectitude: A legal doctrine which holds that, when both man and wife are guilty of marital fault sufficient to award a divorce, only the least offensive party will be given the divorce.

Complainant: *See* Claimant.

Complaint: *See* Claim.

Condonation: A bar to divorce effected by demonstrating that one's marital faults were known by and acceptable to the spouse.

Connivance: A bar to divorce effected by demonstrating that the spouse has covertly condoned or overtly ignored one's marital fault (as by looking the other way).

Consent agreement: An agreement entered into by two or more parties without intervention by the court.

Consent order: An order of the court to which the parties willingly agree; also, a consent agreement which is later embodied within a court order.

Constructive desertion: A ground for divorce in which one party forces the other to desert; the first party deserts constructively. Example: A husband badgers a wife to the extent that she leaves the home and refuses to return against his entreaties (i.e., she deserts); the husband, however, may have constructively deserted her by forcing her to leave.

Constructive service (or notice): Any kind of service other than service upon the person, such as publishing the summons and complaint in a newspaper.

Contempt of court: A holding by a court that one has violated the court's order; punishable by fines and/or imprisonment.

Contempt power: The power of a judge to find a party in contempt of court for violating a court order, performing with disrespect to the court, etc., and to punish the offender.

Co-respondent: A party other than husband or wife who is enjoined to a suit for divorce; especially, the one who has committed adultery with a spouse charged with adultery.

Counterclaim: The defendant's claim against the plaintiff.

Counterclaimant: The defendant who makes claims against the plaintiff spouse.

Court order: A written command of the court requiring one or both parties to perform in certain ways.

Cross bill: *See* Counterclaim.

Cross-examination: Questioning during a hearing by the adverse lawyer.

Cross file: *See* Counterclaim.

Cruelty: *See* Extreme cruelty.

Custody: The right of one or both parents to have physical possession of minor children.

Decree: A statement of a judicial decision, especially a final order on an issue. *See also* Court order.

Default judgment: A decree of divorce (or other matter) made when the defendant does not resist the claims of the plaintiff.

Defendant: The spouse of the plaintiff; respondent.

Defense: A bar to divorce, such as collusion; or, relating to the defendant and his attempt to resist the claims of the plaintiff.

Depose: To question someone under oath in the presence of the lawyers of both sides and a court reporter.

Deposition: The questions asked and answers given by one who is deposed as reflected in the reporter's transcript.

Desertion: A ground for divorce which is enabled by a spouse who fails to perform his or her marital duties, such as failing to support or leaving the marital home for an undue period of time.

Direct examination: Questioning during a hearing by one's own lawyer.

Discovery: Activities which take place prior to trial to provide the lawyers of both sides with information regarding the facts of a case. In most cases accomplished through the completion of interrogatories and depositions by the parties.

Discretion of the court: The power of the judge to weigh evidence as he sees fit, and to rule accordingly.

Divorce: The legal process of rendering a married couple no longer man and wife.

Divorce *a mensa et thoro:* Literally, divorce from bed and board; a legal separation effected by judicial decision which leaves the parties living separate lives but still man and wife.

Domicile (domicil): The state where one intends to live permanently. The "home" state.

Draft: To draw up a legal paper. The art of drafting proper legal prose is called "draftsmanship."

Due process: A vague term relating to the provision of fair proceedings, legal protections, and sanctioned procedures in the activities of lawyers, judges, et al., in the treatment of any given case.

Estoppel: A legal doctrine which prevents one, in consequence of accepting or admitting earlier actions, from pleading for relief on the basis of previously known (and possibly suppressed) facts. An ex-wife who is attempting to inherit her husband's estate by admitting that the divorce was obtained through collusion is estopped from reinstating her marriage.

Evidence: Documents, photographs, testimony, and other things introduced in trial to prove or disprove claims or counterclaims.

Ex parte: Relating to a hearing in which one party to the action does not appear, either in person or through a lawyer.

Extreme cruelty: A ground for divorce enabled by a spouse who persistently inflicts and threatens serious physical harm upon the other party.

Extreme mental cruelty: A ground for divorce enabled by a spouse who persistently subjects the other party to psychological pressures resulting in nervousness, loss of appetite and sleep, etc.

Facts: Evidence conjectured by lawyers or judges to be true.

Final decree of divorce: A decree holding that a marriage no longer exists generally as of the time the decree is issued.

Foreign divorce: Divorce in a state or nation other than that of present residence or jurisdiction.

Grounds for divorce: The legal bases upon which divorces may be granted, provided sufficient proof and other legal requirements are met.

Hearing: A court proceeding, but often restricted to a single matter, such as the adjudication of a request for temporary alimony. Sometimes subject to relatively informal procedures.

Improper notification: A defective method of serving notice of a legal action upon a party. Where the defect exists, the results of such legal action may also be defective and may be quashed on rehearing or appealed to a higher court.

Indignities: A ground for divorce similar to extreme mental cruelty.

Infant: An unemancipated child.

Interlocutory decree of divorce: A decree of divorce which, upon proper petition by one or both parties, may be dismissed by the court. In the absence of such petition, after a specified period of time (the interlocutory period) during which the parties remain man and wife, the decree becomes a final decree of divorce (q.v.), may not be set aside by the court, and the marriage is dissolved.

Interrogatory: A questionnaire to be completed by a party to a legal action as one component of discovery (q.v.). In divorce cases the questionnaire demands information regarding incomes, assets, expenditures, witnesses, facts relating to claims, counterclaims, etc.

Irreconcilable differences: A ground for divorce in a few states in which the parties claim that differences between them are so great as to warrant a divorce.

Judicial discretion: *See* Discretion of the court.

Jurisdiction: Refers to whether the court is empowered to hear or decide a particular matter.

Jurisdiction over the person: Power of the court to hear and decide an issue in consequence of the residency or domiciliary of a party, or upon the party's submission of his person to the power of the court.

Jurisdiction over the subject matter: Power of the court to hear and decide an issue in consequence of the topic of the issue. A traffic court does not have jurisdiction over the subject matter of divorce.

Lack of evidence: A defense against claims or counterclaims which is effected by demonstrating that the opposite side failed to prove his or her allegations.

Latches: A bar to legal relief and, specifically, a bar to divorce exercised by judicial discretion in which the judge holds that, after grounds for divorce became available, the party waited too long to bring suit for divorce.

Litigation: Refers to legal contest in the courtroom.

Lump-sum alimony: A payment of a fixed amount of money by one spouse to the other for settlement of the spouse's property or financial interest in the marriage. Payment may be in one or several installments. Not tax deductible.

Mental cruelty: *See* Extreme mental cruelty.

Migratory divorce: A foreign divorce obtained by moving from one's normal state of residency into a state where residency requirements are short and/or grounds are readily available in comparison to those in the home state.

Motion: A pleading before the court to adjudicate a matter or to modify or quash an earlier court order.

No-fault: A generic term referring to grounds for divorce such as having lived separate and apart for a statutory period of time, or nonadversarial grounds such as irreconcilable differences.

Notice: The provision of information to a person to inform him that he is a party to a lawsuit; service of process.

Notification: The process of giving notice.

Oral agreement: An unwritten agreement between parties made manifest through speech or actions.

Oral decision: A judicial decision spoken by a judge, usually at the conclusion of trial or hearing. The decision may later be transcribed.

Parens patriae: The legal concept that the state is the parent and protector of its citizens who cannot secure their rights for themselves, especially infants and incompetents.

Party: Someone entering into an agreement or contract, or someone being sued, suing someone else, or enjoined in a lawsuit.

Pendente lite: Pending litigation. In divorce, *pendente lite* hearings deal with support and custody and intervene between the filing of the lawsuit and the later trial.

Permanent order: A court order issued at the conclusion of litigation. Such orders may be subject to later modification.

Plaintiff: One who files suit; a claimant.

Pleading: A statement of allegations brought to the court for adjudication; a complaint.

Prayer for relief: That portion of a pleading which specifies what the court is requested to do if the pleading party proves his allegations.

Pre-trial examination: *See* Discovery.

Process: The papers of a summons and complaint which are served on parties involved in a lawsuit. *See* Notice.

Process server: One who delivers process to a party.

Provocation: A bar to divorce effected by a spouse who induces or causes the other to commit a marital fault.

Quash: To cancel or overthrow.

Reconciliation: A defense against divorce effected by demonstrating that the parties have resumed marital relations.

Recrimination. A bar to divorce effected by demonstrating that both parties are sufficiently at fault to warrant a divorce.

Re-cross examination: A second round of questioning by the adverse lawyer.

Re-direct examination: A second round of questioning by one's own lawyer.

Relief: What the court orders, or what is asked of the court to order, so that a burdened party is made unburdened. Burdened by a bad marriage, divorce is the relief sought.

Remand: An order from a higher court that some or all aspects of a case should be reheard by the lower court.

Residence: A practical interpretation of domicile (q.v.) based on living in a particular state and/or county for a specific and continuous period of time.

Res judicata: The legal doctrine that a matter once tried will not be retried on the same facts.

Respondent: One who answers to the charges of the plaintiff; a defendant.

Reverse: An alteration of the conclusions of a lower court by a court of appeals so as to mandate the opposite decision.

Separation: A basis of no-fault divorce (q.v.); also divorce *a mensa et thoro* (q.v.).

Separation agreement: An agreement between husband and wife which sets forth the distribution of property and other assets, arranges custody, matters of support, etc.

Separate maintenance: Money paid to a wife living apart from the husband, generally while awaiting a divorce or while legally separated.

Service: Notice.

Service by construction: *See* Constructive service.

Service by publication: Notification via publication in a newspaper.

Settlement agreement: *See* Separation agreement.

Shepardization: The process of "bringing a case down to date," legal research directed toward the discovery of how all subsequent cases have dealt with a particular precedent.

Show cause: A requirement that one prove his innocence so as to avoid punishment. Frequently, to show cause why one should not be held in contempt of court for failing to meet the requirements of a court order.

Sole custody: A custodial arrangement between parents in which one parent has custody of the children while the other receives rights to reasonable visitation.

Stare decisis: The legal doctrine that an instant case has the right to be tried according to the same laws and precedents as any other case in the same jurisdiction, where the facts are substantially the same.

Statute: The law as written by the legislature.

Statute of limitations: Generally, a statute which renders wrongful acts unactionable in law because of the passage of time. A bar to divorce on the ground of adultery because of the passage of too much time as set forth by statute.

Summons: A notice that one should present himself to the court for adjudication of an action undertaken against him.

Support: Money paid as alimony, separate maintenance, child care expenses, etc.

Temporary alimony: Alimony awarded pending a final order.

Temporary custody: Custody awarded pending a final order.

Temporary order: A court order which remains in effect until modified or replaced by the order of a final hearing.

Tender-years doctrine: The legal doctrine that young children and girl children of all ages are best awarded to the mother unless she be unfit.

Testimony: Statements made by a witness while being examined under oath during a trial.

Trial: A formal legal hearing to decide the merits of a complaint, and to order relief if necessary.

Unclean hands: A legal doctrine that one who has committed a wrong may not stand before the court to plead for relief on a related matter. Example: In violation of a court order, a father took a child into a different jurisdiction to seek custody; court refused the prayed relief since father had unclean hands.

Visitation schedule: A schedule which sets forth the terms and conditions under which a noncustodial parent may visit with the children.

Voidable marriage: A marriage made under conditions of some technical fault, which might, should the court so decide, be declared void.

Void marriage: A marriage which is no marriage at all, such as one in which the parties were married by someone not entitled to contract marriages.

Waiting period: Interlocutory period.

Witness: One who, because of his personal knowledge and/or observations, gives testimony before the court.

Chapter Notes

CHAPTER 1

1. The names of all presented cases have been changed in order to protect the identities of the parties involved.

CHAPTER 2

1. We believe the best book on domestic law to be: Homer J. Clark, Jr., *The Law of Domestic Relations in the United States,* West Publishing Co., St. Paul, Minn., 1968.

   While the book is somewhat dated, a good familiarity with its contents provides the background necessary to quickly bring oneself up to date on the changes in the law that have been introduced since 1968.

   We believe the best law dictionary to be: Henry Campbell Black, *Black's Law Dictionary,* West Publishing Co., St. Paul, Minn., revised 4th edition, 1968.

   You can order copies of these books directly from the publisher. Alternatively, you can go to nearly any bookstore and order these two books.

CHAPTER 3

1. To some, the language used here may be confusing. We place emphasis on whether a divorce may be considered "complicated," or else "uncomplicated." The corresponding legal terminology is "contested," or else "uncontested." Acting from the viewpoint of legal theory, there is no such thing as an "uncontested" divorce. Despite this fact, one will encounter judges and courtrooms which have been assigned to "uncontested" divorces, while other judges and courtrooms have been assigned to "contested" divorces. This usage of the terms "contested" and "uncontested" refers to whether the legal world expects a protracted period of time to be associated with the divorce—"uncontested" divorces take but little judicial or courtroom time, "contested" divorces take considerably more.

   The reason there is no such thing as an "uncontested" divorce in legal theory is that for the husband and wife to agree that a divorce is necessary is to agree that the marriage should not exist. This agreement, in the eyes of the law, is an undercover agreement made between two of the three parties of the marriage (the state being the third party). It is as if two of three partners got together to scheme up a dissolution of the partnership. Such agreements (between husband and wife) are therefore regarded as "collusive," and are "against public policy," i.e., against the law.

The law faces continuing difficulty in reconciling the feeble logic upon which this viewpoint is based, and has been gradually forced back to the point that a painted sign, "Uncontested cases," can be seen hanging outside many courtrooms. The legal concept of "collusion" in divorce, however, has many different ramifications. These ramifications are detailed in later chapters.

2. The U.S. Supreme Court declared minimum fee schedules illegal on the grounds that they were price-fixing; however, the once-fixed fees have not particularly changed, and the day-to-day contacts among lawyers serve to keep the prices uniform and high.
3. The legal profession prefers the parties to make the agreements themselves, without the assistance or compulsion of the legal system. They feel that this results in a mutually-arrived-at agreement which neither party will be prone to violate in the future. To the knowledge of the authors there has never been a systematic study of whether this contention is correct.
4. This can be quite lucrative, especially in those states where lawyers get a percentage of the property settlement.
5. Thomas L. Shaffer, *The Planning and Drafting of Wills and Trusts,* The Foundation Press, Inc., Mineola, N.Y., 1972, p. 239. Shaffer's other "Principles of the Common Law" are also worth knowing. They are: (2) Creditors always win; (3) Avoid litigation; (4) It's not the principle of the thing, it's the money; and (5) Undertakers are paid first.
6. A recent finding in survey research reinforces this view. In Florida, in the fall of 1975, a representative survey was conducted of both laymen and lawyers to evaluate the way in which laymen viewed lawyers and to assess how well lawyers were able to gauge the public's attitudes of their profession. Only 14.4 percent of the laymen felt that lawyers were honest, and only 16.7 percent of the lawyers felt that the public would perceive lawyers as honest. In a ranking of lawyers and five other professional groups for honesty (ministers, medical doctors, teachers, bankers, and businessmen), the public put lawyers at the bottom of the list. Sixty-five percent of the laymen also indicated that lawyers' fees were more than reasonable. A summary report of this study appears in: Kenneth R. White and R. Thomas Stone, Jr., "Trends in Public Attitudes on the Legal Profession," in *Proceedings of the Social Statistics Section, American Statistical Association,* Part II, 1976, pp. 845–847.
7. *Hearing before the Subcommittee on Representation of Citizen Interests of the Committee on the Judiciary, United States Senate, Ninety-third Congress, Second Session, on the Organized Bar: Self-Serving or Serving the Public?* February 3, 1974, U.S. Government Printing Office, Washington, D.C., 1974, p. 65.
8. Cited in: Michael Wheeler, *No-Fault Divorce,* Beacon Press, Boston, 1974, pp. 74–75.
9. Wheeler, p. 75.
10. Murray Teigh Bloom, *The Trouble With Lawyers,* Pocket Books, Simon and Schuster, Inc., New York, 1970, p. 45.
11. This was the rationale used to introduce pre-trial judicial conferences in the state of New Jersey. A later study found that pre-trial conferences did not, however, improve the processing of cases. Having established

that the pre-trial conferences did not accomplish their objectives, the response of the judiciary was predictable—New Jersey still has pre-trial conferences.

12. Wheeler, p. 36.
13. While these files lie in the public domain (i.e., they are public property), they can, and sometimes are, sealed by order of the court. In some jurisdictions this is routinely done in custody cases where the judge feels it would be harmful for the children to become aware of the mud-slinging that happened during the hearing.

CHAPTER 4

1. This discussion actually oversimplifies the requirements. For a more complete discussion, see: Alexander Lindey, *Separation Agreements and Ante-Nuptial Contracts,* Matthew Bender, New York, 1 (1977):19-9 through 19-56. The book by Homer J. Clark (see Chapter 3 Notes) carries a shorter discussion at pp. 481–487.

CHAPTER 5

1. An excellent book on the topic of no-fault divorce is: Michael Wheeler, *No-Fault Divorce,* Beacon Press, Boston, 1974.

CHAPTER 6

1. The data presented were provided by Mr. Jones in a personal communication and are reproduced with his permission. Data were gathered during the period 1972–76. The interpretations of his data are our own. We are grateful to Mr. Jones and congratulate him on his work.
2. Howard Hague, "Labor Force Activity of Married Women," *Special Labor Force Report 153,* U.S. Department of Labor, Bureau of Labor Statistics, Washington, D.C., 1973. Data are for 1972.
3. Generally, such counternormative behaviors are punished by society. For one example, a husband electrical engineer has a medical doctor wife. During a period when he was unemployed his wife found a good job. They decided that the husband should stay at home, care for the children, and become the househusband. They have been shunned by the housewives in the neighborhood.
4. A series of readings on the topic of father absence is presented in Appendix B. Many of the readings are psychological research reports and can be found at a university library.
5. Differing requirements for jurisdiction in custody in the various states, coupled with inconsistent application of those requirements, mandate that jurisdictional issues be explored in any state where custody may be a problem.
6. Tuter v. Tuter, 120 S.W. 2d 203, at 205.
7. Brashear v. Brashear, 228 P. 2d 243, at 246.
8. Byers v. Byers, 370 S.W. 2d 193, at 195.
9. Dungan v. Dungan, 170 S.W. 2d 22, at 24.
10. Commonwealth ex rel Lucas v. Kreischer, 229 A. 2d 243.
11. Moral unfitness of the mother is nearly a thing of the past except, possibly, for Nebraska. An early case there (Baker v. Baker, 166 Neb. 306,

89 N.W. 2d 35) stated that an adulterous mother was unfit to have custody and numerous later cases relied upon the Baker decision. More recent cases may have overthrown the Baker precedent.

12. Henry Biller and Dennis Meredith, *Father Power,* David McKay Co., New York, 1975, $9.95.

    Fitzhugh Dodson, *How to Father,* New American Library, New York, 1975 (paperback), $1.95.

    Fitzhugh Dodson, *How to Parent,* New American Library, New York, 1971 (paperback), $1.50.

13. Even such steps as these may be inadequate. Even where the father has every legal right to the child, an unscrupulous mother might be able to use the Parent Locator Service to chase down the missing father. A false complaint would have to be sworn, but this has failed to deter some women.

14. If the wife can obtain an order for custody in her own state, never mind how, she may be able to initiate *habeas corpus* against the husband for illegal detention of the child. Unless the father has proof of his own legal right to the children, the court can forcibly remove the child and return it to the mother *without* a hearing regarding custody. The hearing would only go so far as to certify the validity of the wife's writ of *habeas corpus.*

CHAPTER 7

1. In one case, a lawyer, working within his rights of full power of attorney, committed his client, a woman, to an aspect of settlement which was quite against her wishes. "But," he replied, "I've already made the agreement. If you don't stick to it, I'll have to resign." She stuck to it and lost half of her rightful equity in her home. She should have fired the lawyer and gotten a new one.

   She was reluctant to fire the lawyer partially because he hadn't known how she felt about the agreement he made in her name, and had acted, she felt, with her best interests in mind. It is significant, as well, that her lawyer was a personal friend.

   The woman had not realized that the act of firing the lawyer would have been a simple act of necessity in order to preserve her financial rights. Rather than offend a friend, she lost several thousand dollars.

2. In some states, getting rid of an attorney is more difficult because the law requires that a court hearing be held to release the old lawyer and replace him with a new one. In such jurisdictions, frequently the court will not allow the old lawyer to be replaced until his fees have been paid.

CHAPTER 8

1. Lindey, Alexander, *Separation Agreements and Ante-Nuptial Contracts,* Vols. 1 and 2, Matthew Bender, New York, 1977. This is an excellent treatise on separation agreements and we recommend it highly to those who feel a need for in-depth coverage of the topic. However, the two-volume set costs about $100. The book is updated frequently with the issuance of new pieces of text to replace dated material. The cost of keeping the book up to date is about $35 per year. A good law school library will probably have the book on its shelves.

2. Louisiana, and perhaps other states as well, forbid husbands and wives

to enter into contracts with each other. The theory seems to be that husband and wife are legally but one person, and an agreement with one's self is nonsensical; further, no such agreement could be enforceable since it would be nonsense to attempt to sue one's own self. Such legal hogwash aside, in most states the separation agreement is enforceable as soon as it is executed, or signed.

3. If the separation agreement was a consent agreement, after the judge has incorporated it within the court order it becomes known as a *consent order,* an order to which the parties have *consented* prior to the judge making it an order.
4. Actually, the court's order in the divorce may require that the wife not remove the children from the jurisdiction without the prior approval of the court. This is frequently done, but it has little effect. Generally, if she leaves the jurisdiction there is no way to compel her return (or the return of the children). In a Washington State case, the opposite occurred. An ex-wife took the children to California and kept them there with relatives, contrary to the Washington order which required her not to remove the children out of the jurisdiction without prior court approval. It was established that she had no intention of ever returning the children to Washington. The father went to California and "child snatched" his children, returning them to Washington. The ex-wife followed, trying to get the children away from her ex-husband through enforcement of the court order which gave her custody. The court, however, took a dim view of her behavior in taking the kids out of state in order to deny the father access to them, and stripped her of her custodial rights, awarding full custody to the father. Such results, however, are rare.
5. Edward J. Winter, Jr., and Brian R. Hersh, "Child Custody Litigation," in *American Jurisprudence Trials,* 22:347–516. In legal notation, this article is cited as 22 Am Jur Trials 347. For the father involved in custody problems, the article is absolutely *must* reading. It can be found in any good law library. We disagree only with the authors' philosophy that the lawyer will run the show; we prefer that the lawyer serve as legal aide and advisor and that the client make those decisions which affect his own life. Apart from this difference of opinion, the article is one of the most complete and straightforward expositions of the problems and procedures involved in custody litigation that we have uncovered.
6. We take a moral and ethical position on this issue. We feel that it is unconscionable to knowingly and harmfully use the children as a means to acquire money.

CHAPTER 9

1. Appendix A is devoted to the topic of locating legal information.
2. Not only is it your responsibility to discover what the witnesses of either side can say for or against your case, it is also your responsibility to prepare a dossier on each witness which first summarizes very briefly the background and testimony that can be produced by the witness, together with probable strengths and weaknesses which might be used, and second, provides in outline form, the major areas the lawyer may wish to explore with the witness. Parallel to the outline, you should have developed a comprehensive statement of what is to be asked and what should be obtained in testimony as a result. Even during trial, it is your responsi-

bility to compare the responses of witnesses with the testimony you expected—to detect lies, and to check off things the lawyer has covered during the examination of the witness. When the lawyer has completed his examination he will have an opportunity to briefly compare notes with you to pick up any areas he has missed before releasing the witness.

3. Frank J. Cannavale, Jr., and William D. Falcon (ed.), *Improving Witness Cooperation,* August 1976. For sale by the Superintendent of Documents, U.S. Government Printing Office, Washington, D.C. 20402, $1.45.
4. If you are missing copies of your IRS returns, you can obtain photocopies of them by writing the IRS district office. Check the telephone directory for additional information. Toll-free numbers are often available.

CHAPTER 11

1. Transactional Analysis is the development of Dr. Eric Berne. Two of his popular works, and one by Dr. Harris, are cited below:

   Eric Berne, *Games People Play,* Grove Press, Inc., New York, 1967 (paperback), $1.25.

   Eric Berne, *What Do You Say After You Say Hello?,* Bantam Books, New York, 1973 (paperback), $1.95.

   Thomas A. Harris, *I'm O.K.—You're O.K.,* Avon Books, New York, 1973 (paperback), $1.95.
2. Herbert Benson, *The Relaxation Response,* William Morrow & Co., New York, 1975.
3. Royal Canadian Air Force, *Exercise Plans for Physical Fitness,* Essandess Press, New York, 1972.
4. Bernard Gunther, *Sense Relaxation Below Your Mind,* Collier Books, New York, 1970 (paperback), $3.50.
5. Some references on nutrition and cooking, selected with special orientation to the needs of men, are presented in the Appendix.
6. The ability to take good notes quickly is important. Because things tend to move quickly in the courtroom, there is seldom time to take all the notes which should be taken. We strongly encourage anyone engaged in a contested divorce to purchase a book on speedwriting. There are a number of speedwriting methods, most of which are quite adequate for such purposes. Unlike shorthand (which is the tool of the professional secretary), speedwriting is simple and easy to learn. In one or two days, with little practice, one can take notes at twice the former speed. Taking notes from readings in the law library is also facilitated by speedwriting. In the courtroom, the whole matter would be greatly facilitated by tape recording the proceedings, but judges generally will not allow recorders in the courtroom.

Index

Adultery as divorce grounds, 16, 20, 64, 65, 67, 69, 70–72
- connivance of spouses in use of, 65
- and criminal law, 16, 160
- and custody awards, 97, 106, 107
- evidence of, 71–72, 182–183, 184, 186
- *See also* Infidelity

Adversary system and divorce, 17, 32
- effect on costs, 48
- *See also* Fault, concept of; No-fault divorce

Age of spouses and alimony awards, 51

Agreements, pre-divorce,12–13
- *See also* Separation agreements

Alcoholism as grounds for divorce, 82

Alimony
- vs. child support, 47–48
- common law tradition of, 51
- conditions for termination of, 53
- delayed payment of, as tactical measure, 159
- enforcement of court order on, 229
- in *ex parte* divorce, 86
- for husbands, 45–46, 51, 82
- judicial orientation on, 40–41, 53, 55
- lump sum payment of, 47
- model formulas for computation of, 144–145
- as percent of husband's income, 52
- and property settlements, 51
- in separation agreements, 37, 54, 55, 79, 140, 142–143
- tax issues concerning, 47–48
- temporary, 37, 41, 42–47
- waiving of rights to, 53, 55

Alternating custody, 99

American Academy of Matrimonial Lawyers, 29

Anger, feelings of, as reaction to divorce, 220

Annulments, 81

Anxiety feelings as reaction to divorce, 218

Appellate court, 38, 88

Appearance at trial, importance of, 226

Assets
- assembly and organization of documents on, 195, 210
- disposition of, under separation agreement, 37, 147–159
- inventory and valuation of, 148–149, 199
- pre-marriage and jointly acquired holdings, 39–40, 50, 199
- property included as, 50
- strategy for protection of, 11–12
- *See also* Bargaining over division of property

Avoidance of service, 64

Babysitters as witnesses, 10, 194

Bank accounts, handling and disposition of, 12, 151, 164–165, 187

Bank records, uses of, as evidence, 9–10, 127–128, 187, 196, 199, 201

Bar associations, services from, 135

Bargaining over division of property, 147–169

Behavior changes as indication of infidelity, 185
Best interest and welfare test in custody awards, 94–95
Bigamy, 80
"Blackmail" tactics in divorce proceedings, 14, 57–58
Blocking of divorce proceedings
  methods of, 59–69
  strategic value of, 57–58
Bluffing strategies, 13
Boyfriends, reappearance of, as evidence of infidelity, 9
Brashear vs. Brashear, 94
Breach of contract suits, 141
Bugging as source of evidence, 177–178
Business expenses, inflation of, as pre-divorce strategy, 12
Byers vs. Byers, 95

California divorce laws, 17, 70, 78, 95–96
Career prospects as factor in alimony awards, 51
Cash reserves, buildup of, as pre-divorce strategy, 12
Charge accounts
  closure of, 12, 151, 165
  in documentation of expenses, 198
Child abuse and neglect, evidence of, in custody fights, 104, 106
Child custody awards
  ante-nuptial contracts on, 98
  conditions affecting decision on, 3, 46–47, 96–100, 171
  enforcement of, 230
  and default suits, 19, 83
  and disposition of residence, 51
  judicial authority over, 40, 99–100
  pendente lite (temporary), 37, 41, 46–47, 115
  pre-divorce strategy on, 11
  pre-trial equality of spouses' rights, 114
  problems of jurisdiction, 93
  pro-mother bias in, 25–26, 29, 94–97, 113
  self-evaluation of issues involved in, 116–122
  in separation agreements, 54, 55, 79, 141–142
  statistics on, 90
  traditional arrangements, 99
  well-established arrangements as factor in, 98, 116
Child rearing, by father vs. mother, 90–92
Children
  marriage of, 53–54
  tax deductions for, 48
  as witnesses, 181
Child support
  vs. alimony, 47–48
  accounting of expenditures for, 106
  enforcement of court orders for, 229–231
  factors affecting amount of, 53–54
  judicial discretion concerning, 40
  model formulas for computation of, 144–145
  payments by wife, 45–46, 53
  under separation agreement, 37, 54
  tax issues relating to, 47–48
  temporary awards of, 37, 41, 47
  termination of, 53
Claimant, 17, 34, 47
Claim filing in divorce action, 34
Clues to infidelity, 9–10
Collusion
  in divorce testimony, 181–182
  as grounds for blocking divorce, 66–68
Colorado, divorce in, 17
Common law
  fathers' rights dogma, 93–94
  traditions on divorce, 1, 51
Community property laws, 50

Comparative rectitude as grounds for blocking divorce, 69
Condonation as grounds for blocking divorce, 65
Connivance as grounds for blocking divorce, 65
Consent agreements, 140–141
Constructive desertion, 73, 74–75
Constructive service of divorce summons, 34
Consumer price index tied to support payments, 54, 144–145
Contempt of court citations, 37
Contempt power of judge, 56
Contested divorce, 19–20
  division of property in, 157–169
  with mental cruelty grounds, 75–76
  strategic use of, 57–69
Co-respondent, 70
Costs of divorce, 48–50
  of appeals, 88, 233
  of *ex parte* divorce, 85
  inflating factors in, 19, 21, 49, 137
  lawyers' fees, 49, 50, 129–130
  responsibility of husband for, 32
  total annual, 29–30
Counterclaims in divorce suits, 35–36, 64–65, 68–69, 160
  evidence for, 65–66, 183, 205, 209
  tactical delay of, 160
Court of appeals (*see* Appellate court)
Court orders, 37, 55–56, 166, 169
  appealing terms of, 56–57, 166
  on custodial rights, 114–115
  enforcement of, 229
  incorporation of separation agreement terms in, 141
  modification of, 231–232
Courtroom, pre-trial visit to, 225
Credit cards
  closure of accounts for, 12, 151, 165
  in documentation of expenses, 198
  receipts for, as divorce evidence, 9, 187
Criminal conviction as grounds for divorce, 82
Cruelty as grounds for divorce, 66, 68, 69, 75–77, 79, 184
  and custody fights, 106
Custody fights, 101–103
  court-ordered investigations in, 110–112
  delaying tactics, 116
  disappearing act in, 115–116
  generating evidence for, 103–106
  handling of judges in, 112–113
  importance of temporary custody in, 104–105
  psychological tactics in, 106–108
Custody hearings, 60, 99–100, 108
  witnesses for father in, 104, 109–110

Death of spouse
  alimony terminated by, 53
  custodial rights following, 98
Decisiveness, importance of, 12–13
Debts
  in documentation of expenses, 198
  liquidation of, 151, 165
Default judgments of divorce, 19, 83, 85
Defendant, role of, 17, 35, 58
  as counter-claimant, 35–36
  and default judgments, 83–84
  disadvantages of, 88
Delaying tactics, 57–64, 159–160
  in custody fights, 116
Depositions, 49, 159–160
Desertion
  constructive, 73–75
  as divorce grounds, 59, 60, 64, 68, 72–75
  time period for, 73
Discovery process in divorce, 36, 49

Dissolution of marriage, 17
Division of property
  bargaining over, 147–169
  blanket transfers, 167
  in contested divorce, 157–169
  and evidence of marital fault, 171
  legal jurisdiction over, 39–40
  need for signed agreements on, 168
  under separation agreements, 37
  trades and purchases, 149, 155–157
Divorce, strategy for blocking of, 57–58
Divorce *a mensa et thoro,* 79
Divorced men and women, employment rates of, 91–92
Divorce laws, need for change in, 22
Divorce process
  procedures listed, 33–38
  stages of, 5–7
Divorce rate, 1, 29
Domicile, concept of, in divorce actions, 59–60, 87
Drug addiction as grounds for divorce, 82
Dungan vs. Dungan, 95

Economic aspects of divorce, 29–30
Education of children as factor in support payments, 53, 145–146
Education of wife and financial arrangements, 52
Employed wives
  alimony for, 42–45
  loss of job by, 46
  marital duties of, 74
  as percent of married women, 91
  pre-divorce strategy concerning, 11–12
  support payments by, 45–46
Employment as obligation of ex-wife, 147
Enoch Arden statute, 80
Evidence, 170–171, 206
  assembling of, 8–10, 71–72, 177–188
  corroboration of, 172, 174–175, 182, 188–189, 205
  counteracting of, 183, 209
  dates as part of, 185
  documents as form of, 177
  financial, 195–202, 210
  forms of, 172–173, 177, 186–188
  identification of, 173–177
  illegally obtained, 177–178
  manufacture of, 66–67
  organization of, 206–207
  pattern concept of, 184
  refutation of, 65–66
  from witnesses (*see* Witnesses)
Exercise as therapy for divorce, 221–222
Ex parte
  divorce, 60, 83, 85–87
  order for custody, 115
Expenses, documentation of, 195–199
  of wife, 200–212

Fathering
  importance of, 90–93
  self-evaluation of capacity for, 117–122
  as strategy in custody fight, 102–103
Fathers' rights dogma, 93–94
Fault, concept of, in divorce, 17–18, 51, 64–65, 106
Filing of divorce claim, 34, 37
Foreign divorce, 85
Foster, Henry, 27
Freudians' views of custody, pro-mother bias in, 109
Furnishings and equipment
  bargaining for, 153–154
  inventory and appraisal of, 148
Furs, appraisal and disposition of, 148, 155

Grounds for divorce, 33–34
  adultery (*see* Adultery)

alcoholism, 82
criminal conviction, 82
cruelty (*see* Cruelty; Mental Cruelty)
desertion, 60, 64, 68, 72–73
drug-addiction, 82
evidence of (*see* Evidence)
insanity, 82
legal complications to, 18
long imprisonment, 82
Guardians *ad litem* (temporary guardians), 100, 108, 181
Guilt feelings about divorce, 189, 218–220

Harassment (tactical), 49, 68, 107
Health of spouses and alimony awards, 51
Hearings in divorce process, 5, 38
Homemaking skills, learning of, by divorced men, 217–218
Homosexual relations as grounds for divorce, 70, 77
Honesty in lawyer-client relationship, 133–134
House
disposition of, 50–51, 143, 151–153
eviction from, 166
maintaining residence in, 11, 104–105, 169
Husband, legal obligations of, 73, 75, 79

Idaho, custody judgments in, 94
Illinois, custody judgments in, 95
Impotence as grounds for annulment, 81–82
Imprisonment for long period as grounds for divorce, 82
Income
documentation of, 195, 198–199
gross vs. spendable, 167, 198–199
organization of material on, 210
strategy for protection of, 11–12
support payments tied to, 79, 144–146
of wife, 200–201, 210–211
Income tax records, use as financial evidence, 199, 201
Infidelity, 5–6, 9–11
Inventory
of marital faults and good points, 204–205
of property, income and expenses, 148–149, 153, 163–164, 169
Insanity as grounds for divorce, 82
Interrogatories, 36–37, 164

Jewelry, appraisal and disposition of, 50, 148, 153, 155
Joint custody, 99
Jones, P. Clint, 90
Judges
evaluation of lawyers by, 124
orientation of, 27–29, 94, 140, 171–172
at *pendente lite* hearings, 42
power of, 23, 27–29, 38, 39, 56, 171 (*see* Judicial discretion)
recommended handling of, 29, 112–113, 227
Judicial discretion, 28–29, 39–41, 53, 55–56
Judicial errors, 31, 38, 88, 232–233
Judicial reform, need for, 22, 31
Jurisdictional defense against divorce action, 29–60

Kentucky, custody judgments in, 95

Lack of evidence for divorce action, 65–66
Latches, defense of, use in blocking divorce, 61–62
Lawyers
briefing of, 133
changing of, 134–135
Code of Professional Responsibility of, 26
ethical considerations of, 25–27
fees, 22, 49, 50, 129–130
files of, 134

Lawyers (*cont.*)
hiring of, 126–130
influencing wife's selection of, 127
interviewing of, 126–130
knowledge of divorce law of, 25
lawsuit against, 135
orientation of, 22–25, 29–30
personal friend as, 125
power of attorney for, 26–27, 131
pre-trial conference for, 30–31
as representative of both parties, 83
role of, 13, 131–132, 139, 206–207
selection of, 13, 123–130
of wife, 12–13, 132, 226
unsatisfactory, handling of, 134–135, 212
working relationship with, 131–133, 206–207, 211–212
Legal expenses, 45, 46, 49–50
Legal jurisdictions, problems of crossing, 2
Legal research, taking personal initiative in, 205, 206, 210, 211
Legal residence, concept of, in divorce actions, 59
Legal separation, 79
Lindley, Alexander, 138
Loneliness as reaction to divorce, 217
Louisiana, custody judgments in, 95
Lucas vs. Kreischer, 95

Mail, as source of evidence of infidelity, 9, 11
Marital faults, inventory of, 204
Marital problems, criteria for evaluation of, 4
Maternal instinct and child custody, 91
Medical expenses of spouse and children, responsibility for, 82, 145
Memorandum of understanding with lawyer, 133
Men's rights organizations as source of help, 124–125, 189, 195
Mental cruelty as divorce grounds, 2, 16, 19, 39, 68, 75–77
Mental health of spouses as factor in support award, 51, 77, 97
Migratory divorces, 20, 85
Missing spouse, status of marriage to, 80
Missouri, custody judgments in, 94
Monitoring of spouse's activities, 9–10
Moral fitness as influence in custody awards, 97

Nebraska, divorce laws in, 72, 85
Nevada as divorce mill, 20, 85, 87
Newspaper notices of divorce summons, 34, 62
New Jersey, divorce and adultery laws in, 16, 20, 72, 78
New York State, divorce laws in, 20, 74
No-fault divorce, 17, 31, 77, 106
evidence of fault in, 170–171
irreconcilable differences form of, 78–79
separation form of, 77–78
Notification of divorce action, 34–35

Pendente lite hearings and judgment, 37, 41–48, 105
Pennsylvania divorce laws, 38, 52, 86, 95
Personal appearance and conduct, importance of, during divorce suit, 13–14, 172
Personal initiative, importance of, 12–13, 30, 43, 57–58
Personalty items, disposition of, 50, 153–155

Plaintiff, 17, 34, 58, 88, 207–208
Planlessness, as reaction to divorce, 216
Possession of assets, advantage of, 164–165, 168–169
Post office box, use of, 11
Power of attorney, 26–27, 131
Pre-divorce strategy
  collecting evidence against spouse, 9–10, 57
  controlling information, 10–11
  gaining time, 57–58
  protection of assets, 11–12, 164–166
Pre-trial conference of lawyers and judge, 30–31
Pre-trial examination (PTE), 36
Process serving, 34, 62
  avoidance of, 63–64
  in *ex parte* divorces, 85–87
  fees for, 34
  impropriety charged in, 62–63
Property
  division of, *see* Division of property
  inventory and appraisal of, 148–149
  settlements, 37, 39–40, 50, 72
Provocation as grounds for blocking divorce, 68
Psychiatrists, pro-mother bias in custody cases, 109
Psychological pressures, use of, against spouse, 49, 68, 107, 160
Psychological stress during marital breakup, 189–190, 213–225
Psychological tests, use in custody investigations, 111–112
Public disclosure, fear of, 225

Real estate, appraisal and disposition of, 148, 151
  See also House
Reconciliation as grounds for blocking divorce, 66
Record-keeping, importance of, 134–135, 139–140, 148–149, 163–164, 169, 172, 184, 196–198
Recrimination as grounds for blocking divorce, 64–65
Relaxation training, 222
Religion of parents and custody awards, 97
Remanding decision of trial judge, 38
Remarriage of wife, 53
Residence, concept of, in divorce action, 59–60, 87
Retirement of husband and alimony payments, 53, 54
Respondent in divorce cases, 35–37

Schell, Orville H., 27
Separate maintenance, 86–87
Separation agreements, 5–6, 37, 54–55, 136–146
  advantages to husband of, 55, 137
  on alimony, 37, 54, 55, 79, 140, 142–145
  on child support, 143–145
  contents of, 138–139
  on custody, 141–142
  for default divorce judgments, 84
  disposition of property in (*see* Division of property)
  enforceability of, 140–141
  financial arrangements in, 144–146
  husband-wife preparation of, 49, 55, 138–139
  legal specifications for, 55, 142
  long vs. short forms of, 138–139
  signing of, 139–140
  tax considerations in preparation of, 143–144
Sex as legal duty of spouses, 73
Sexual adventurism in post-divorce period, 217
Sexual grounds
  for divorce, 73 (*see* Adultery)

Sexual grounds (*cont.*)
for void and voidable marriage, 81–82
Sexual intercourse as evidence of reconciliation, 66, 67
Shaffer, Thomas L., on common law, 25
Sleep problems, 223
Social life after divorce, 218
Sole custody, 99, 119–120
Splitting the children as custodial arrangement, 99
Standard of living, effect of divorce and support payments on, 52, 54, 144–145, 152–153
Standards of proof, 39, 40, 170
State, as third party in marriage and divorce, 18, 52–53, 70, 142
"Station" in life as factor in alimony, 52
Statute of limitations, use in blocking divorce, 61
Summons and complaint, 34, 61–62
Support, as obligation of husband/wife, 73, 74
See also Alimony; Child support

Tax issues in support payments and settlements, 47, 143
and timing of divorce, 159
Telephone use, as source of evidence of infidelity, 9, 11
Temporary arrangements before divorce trial, 37, 41, 105
See also Pendente lite hearings
Tender-years doctrine on custody, 94–96
Texas, alimony awards in, 86
Timing, importance of, in contested divorces, 159–160
Transactional analysis, 221, 224
Transcendental Meditation (TM), 221
Trial
costs of, 49–50
evidence (*see* Evidence)
fear of, 224–225
lawyer's role, 206–207
procedures of, 37–38
witnesses (*see* Witnesses)
Tuter vs. Tuter, 94

Uncontested divorce, 3, 6, 18–19, 83
role of lawyer in, 131
Uniform Marriage and Divorce Act, 31
Uniform Reciprocal Enforcement of Support Act (URESA), 229

Visitation rights, 54, 79, 107, 113–114, 171, 230–231
Void and voidable marriages, 80

Washington, custody judgments in, 95
Wife, legal obligations of, 74–75, 79
Will, provisions of and divorce settlement, 146
Witnesses, 49, 174–176, 178–180, 189
adverse, dossiers on, 207–208
of character, 179, 192
children as, 181
corroborative, 182, 188–189, 209
court officials as, 181
expert, 179–180, 194
finding and screening of, 189–195
friends and acquaintances as, 181–182, 194
jurisdictional problems with, 176
parties on trial as, 180–181, 182
subpoena of, 175, 178